W9-CAA-016

# Automotive Air Conditioning

CLIFFORD L. SAMUELS
*Ferris State College*

PRENTICE-HALL, INC., *Englewood Cliffs, New Jersey 07632*

*Library of Congress Cataloging in Publication Data*

Samuels, Clifford L. 1926-
    Automotive air conditioning.

    Includes index.
    1. Automobiles—Air conditioning—Maintenance
and repair.  I. Title.
TL271.5.S25    629.2'77    80-26519
ISBN 0-13-054213-X

Editorial/production supervision and interior design: Nancy Moskowitz
Manufacturing buyer: Joyce Levatino
Page layout: Diane Heckler Koromhas
Cover design: Dawn L. Stanley

Printed in the United States of America

10  9  8  7  6  5  4  3  2  1

PRENTICE-HALL INTERNATIONAL, INC., *London*
PRENTICE-HALL OF AUSTRALIA PTY. LIMITED, *Sydney*
PRENTICE-HALL OF CANADA, LTD., *Toronto*
PRENTICE-HALL OF INDIA PRIVATE LIMITED, *New Delhi*
PRENTICE-HALL OF JAPAN, INC., *Tokyo*
PRENTICE-HALL OF SOUTHEAST ASIA PTE. LTD., *Singapore*
WHITEHALL BOOKS LIMITED, *Wellington, New Zealand*

*I would like to dedicate this book to my wife Margaret Samuels*

# Contents

# Preface

At the turn of the century, the only way to keep cool while riding in an automobile was to open the windshield or remove the side curtains. As time moved on the windows could be cranked up or down and vents were placed under the dashboard so that air would circulate throughout the passenger compartment. A rumble seat was a good place to ride to keep cool or the convertible top could be lowered on some automobiles, but in both cases the weather dictated your choice. Odors, dust, and insects were a nuisance but had to be tolerated if you wanted to be cool.

Then in 1940, Packard Motor Car Company offered a complete year-round air-conditioning system. Not only did it cool the air, but it also removed dirt, dust, pollen, and humidity from the passenger's compartment. The air-conditioning unit was very bulky, with its components spread out from the hood to the trunk. The evaporator assembly was located in the trunk of the automobile. The air was passed over cooling coils, pulled through a duct and circulated throughout the car by a blower located behind the rear seat. The cool air followed the contour of the roof toward the front of the car.

To adjust the car for cooling, the right-hand damper lever (located in the trunk) had to be adjusted to its full, up position, where it was locked in place. This would open the damper on the cooling duct. The left-hand lever was adjusted in the down position. This then closed the damper on the heating duct. The hot water line to the heating unit was closed by tightning down the shutoff valves mounted on the engine block.

For heating, the position of the damper levers as described for cooling were reversed. This eliminated the cooling operation and put the heating system into effect. When the heating system was to be used for a long period of time, the compressor belts would be removed so that the compressor did not operate when the engine was running.

Today, the controls for the air-conditioning system are mounted on the dashboard for ease of operation and control. Now a magnetic clutch will connect and disconnect the compressor from the engine. The automatic temperature control system is now a reality; just set the desired temperature and the system will automatically maintain that temperature in the passengers compartment.

Air conditioning has indeed come a long way in meeting the public demand for convenience, comfort, and safety. The growing demand and modern technology have lowered the unit cost, making it possible for nearly every car owner to enjoy the luxury of year-round comfort. In the past, only the most expensive automobiles were equipped with air conditioning, but today it is available in all makes and models. Air conditioning is the control of temperature, humidity, cleanliness, and movement of air. An automotive air conditioner cools the air; removes particles of moisture, dust, and pollen; and provides the automobile with a comfortable, restful compartment in which to ride. This controlled environment contributes to the health, appearance, cleanliness, and safety of the passengers and driver. Since the windows are rolled up at all times when the air conditioner is on, flying insects and traffic noise are kept at a minimum. The air conditioner can keep out odors and exhaust fumes by recirculating the air inside the automobile. A cool driver will arrive at his destination alert, responsive, and calm.

Both large and small garages are now offering air-conditioning service and repair in place of the fewer and fewer tune-ups that once crowded their repair facility. Since air-conditioning units must be serviced and repaired from time to time, the technician in the repair industry must be informed of a simple, systematic approach to repair problems.

This book provides a background of refrigeration and air conditioning, with air flow charts and electrical fundamentals. Troubleshooting the system and minor repairs of the compressor are included. Test questions and lab sheets, where applicable, are found at the end of each chapter. Sixty million air-conditioning units have been sold to date, and this book should be helpful in training technicians to service these units.

I would like to thank Marjorie Samuels and James Whitmer for their assistance with the index. I would also like to thank Gordon Bechelli for his help in preparing some of the artwork.

**Clifford L. Samuels**
*Big Rapids, Michigan*

# Chapter 1

# Cooling and Heating Systems

## COOLING SYSTEM

When fuel is burned in an engine, a great amount of heat will be produced. In fact, temperatures in excess of 4000°F (2204.44°C) can be attained by the burning fuel. A large amount of heat is carried off by the exhaust system, but the rest of the engine will absorb an excessive amount of heat. A cooling system must be incorporated to remove the unwanted heat and also to maintain an efficient temperature under all operating conditions. Most automobiles use a water-cooling system which circulates the water through the engine and the radiator. The water is circulated through the engine and radiator by a water pump. The water pump is driven by the fan belt(s). Water is pumped from the engine to the radiator, where it gives up some heat, and returned back to the engine.

### Radiators

Radiators may be of the down-flow or cross-flow design. In *down-flow designs*, hot coolant from the engine is delivered to the top radiator tank and cool coolant removed from the bottom. In *cross-flow designs*, hot coolant goes to a tank on one side of the radiator and flows across the radiator to the tank on the other side. Neither type is more or less efficient than the other. Design and space dictates the choice (Figs. 1-1 and 1-2). Automatic-transmission-oil cooling is accomplished by a cooler located in the bottom tank of the radiator and cooled by engine coolant (Fig. 1-3).

FIGURE 1-1 Down-flow radiator.

FIGURE 1-2 Cross-flow.

FIGURE 1-3 Transmission oil cooler. (Courtesy of the Chrysler Corporation.)

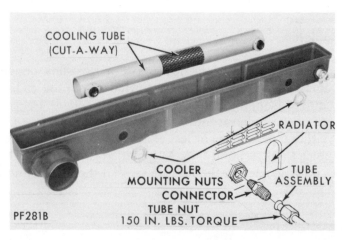

COOLING TUBE
(CUT-A-WAY)

RADIATOR

COOLER
MOUNTING NUTS

TUBE
ASSEMBLY

CONNECTOR

TUBE NUT
150 IN. LBS. TORQUE

PF281B

*ANTIFREEZE*

All vehicles are provided with cooling-system corrosion and antifreeze protection. If it becomes necessary to add or to change the antifreeze in your vehicle, a mixture of 50% ethylene-glycol-type antifreeze and 50% clean water will provide corrosion and freeze protection. Air-conditioned vehicles must be protected with antifreeze year-round to prevent the heater core from freezing.

## Water Pump

The water pump is a centrifugal pump, drawing water in at the impeller center and discharging the water at the impeller tips. The water pump is serviced only as an assembly. When replacing the pump, care should be taken to use the correct pump, since the pump impeller must be compatible with the drive ratio provided by the pulley system, or overheating may result (Fig. 1-4).

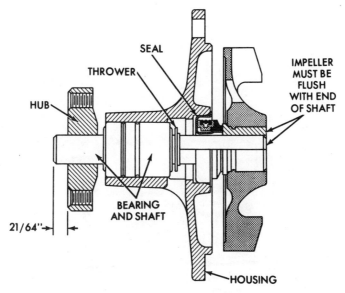

**FIGURE 1-4** Water pump.

The water pump is driven by a fan belt or belts, which are connected to the crankshaft. When replacing a water pump because of a bearing or shaft failure, it is a good idea to replace the fan at the same time.

Water pump problems usually concern worn bearings, leaking seals, and worn or broken impellers.

## Fan Belts

The belt must be in good condition and properly adjusted. Excessive tightness will cause early bearing failure, while looseness will allow the pump and fan to slow down, causing overheating.

**Bug Screen**

Bug screens should not be installed on vehicles equipped with air conditioning. A bug screen installed in front of the condenser will reduce air flow and air-conditioner performance. Under severe heat conditions, a bug screen may cause the engine to overheat.

**Thermostat (Fig. 1-5)**

The engine thermostat is an automatic coolant flow valve designed to open and close at predetermined temperatures. When the engine is cold, the thermostat shuts off the flow of water from the engine to the radiator. As the water is confined to the engine, it heats quickly. When it reaches a predetermined temperature, the thermostat opens and allows the water to flow through the radiator to maintain an efficient temperature under all operating conditions. A malfunctioning thermostat can be a cause of engine overheating or slow warm-up and poor heater performance.

FIGURE 1-5 Pellet type thermostat.

**Fan (Fig. 1-6)**

The fan is used to draw air through the radiator core and is attached to the hub of the water pump shaft. The fan is sometimes shrouded to increase cooling system efficiency. The shroud prevents recirculation of the air and also guides the air into the radiator fins. Many engines use a multibladed fan to help move more air through the radiator fins for better cooling. Multibladed fans require more horsepower to turn, so a fan clutch is used.

# FAN AND FAN CLUTCH INSTALLATION

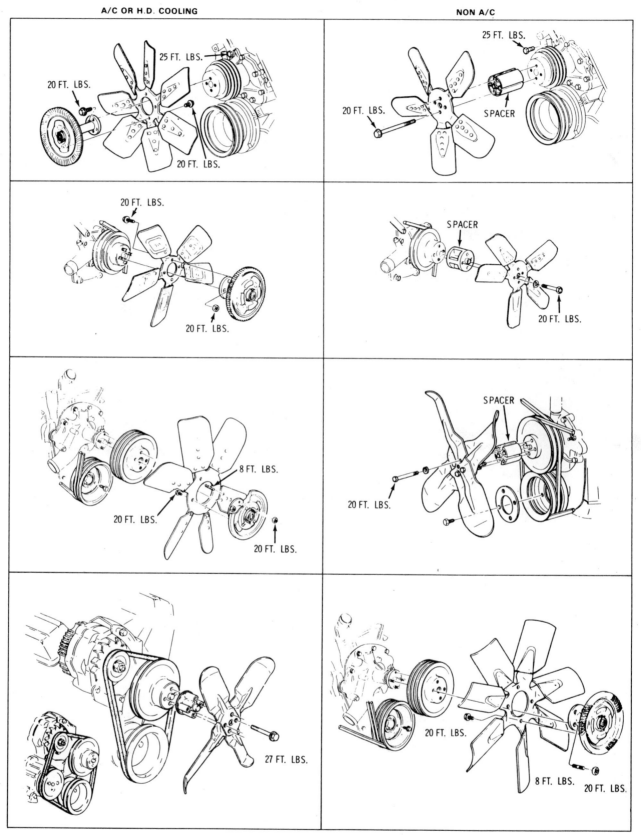

**FIGURE 1-6** Fan and fan clutch installation. (Courtesy of the General Motors Corp.)

**Fan Clutch (Fig. 1-7)**

Fan clutches are used on all cars with air conditioning or heavy-duty cooling systems. Automatic fan clutches are hydraulic devices used to vary the speed of the fan in relation to engine temperature. Automatic fan clutches permit the use of a high-delivery fan to ensure adequate cooling at reduced engine speeds while eliminating overcooling, excessive noise, and power loss at high speeds. The hydraulic fan should be replaced if it leaks fluid, if noise or roughness is detected when turning the unit by hand, or if the unit cannot be turned by hand.

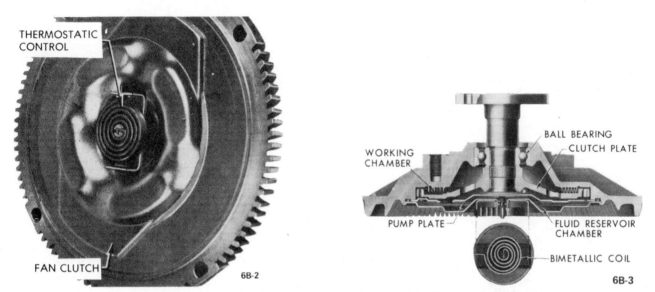

**FIGURE 1-7** Automatic fan clutch components. (Courtesy of the General Motors Corp.)

**Fan Clutch Diagnostic Procedure**

*NOISE*

Fan noise is sometimes evident under the following normal conditions:

1. When the clutch is engaged for maximum cooling.

2. During the first few minutes after startup until the clutch can redistribute the silicone fluid back to its normal disengaged operating condition after overnight settling.

Excessive fan noise will generally occur continuously under all high-engine-speed conditions if the clutch assembly is locked up due to an internal failure.

*LOOSENESS*

Under various temperature conditions, there is a visible lateral movement that can be observed at the tip of the fan blade. This is a normal condition due to the type of bearing used. About ¼ in. maximum lateral movement measured at the fan tip is allowable.

### *SILICONE FLUID LEAK*

The operation of the unit is generally not affected by a small fluid leak around the bearing assembly.

### *ENGINE OVERHEATING*

1.  Start with a cool engine to ensure complete fan clutch disengagement.

2.  If the fan clutch assembly free-wheels with no drag (revolves over five times when spun by hand), the clutch should be replaced.

**NOTE:**

TESTING A FAN CLUTCH BY HOLDING THE SMALL HUB WITH ONE HAND AND ROTATING THE ALUMINUM HOUSING IN A CLOCKWISE/COUNTERCLOCKWISE MOTION WILL CAUSE THE CLUTCH TO FREE-WHEEL, WHICH IS NORMAL WHEN OPERATED IN THIS MANNER. THIS SHOULD NOT BE CONSIDERED A TEST FOR REPLACEMENT.

3.  Use a dial-type thermometer and position it so that the thermometer sensor is centered in the space between the fan blades and the radiator.

**CAUTION:**

CHECK FOR CLEARANCE BETWEEN FAN BLADES AND THERMOMETER.

4.  Cover the radiator to induce a high engine temperature. Start the engine, and turn on the A/C unit (if equipped), and observe the thermometer reading. Increase the engine speed to approximately 2000 rpm.

5.  Observe the thermometer reading when the clutch engages. It will take 5 to 10 minutes for the temperature to become high enough to allow engagement of the clutch. This will be indicated by an increase or roar in fan air noise and by a drop in the thermometer reading. If the clutch did not engage between 150 and 190°F (65.6 to 87.9°C) the unit should be replaced.

**NOTE:**

BE SURE THAT THE FAN CLUTCH WAS DISENGAGED AT THE BEGINNING OF THE TEST. IF THERE WAS NO SHARP INCREASE IN FAN NOISE AND NO TEMPERATURE DROP AND THE FAN NOISE LEVEL REMAINED THE SAME THROUGHOUT THE TEST, THE UNIT SHOULD BE REPLACED.

**CAUTION:**

IF THE THERMOMETER READING REACHES 190°F (87.9°C) DIS-
CONTINUE THE TEST TO PREVENT ENGINE OVERHEATING.

6. As soon as the clutch engages, remove the cover from the radiator and turn
   off the A/C unit to assist in engine cooling.

7. After several minutes the fan clutch should disengage and the fan speed
   roar should decline.

8. Since there is no method available to service the fan clutch, any unit determined to be defective must be replaced.

**WARNING:**

IF A FAN BLADE IS BENT OR DAMAGED IN ANY WAY, NO AT-
TEMPT SHOULD BE MADE TO REPAIR AND REUSE THE DAMAGED
PART. A BENT OR DAMAGED FAN ASSEMBLY SHOULD ALWAYS BE
REPLACED WITH A NEW FAN ASSEMBLY. IT IS ESSENTIAL THAT
FAN ASSEMBLIES REMAIN IN PROPER BALANCE, AND PROPER
BALANCE CANNOT BE ASSURED ONCE A FAN ASSEMBLY HAS BEEN
BENT OR DAMAGED. A FAN ASSEMBLY THAT IS NOT IN PROPER
BALANCE COULD FAIL AND FLY APART DURING USE, CREATING
AN EXTREMELY DANGEROUS CONDITION.

### Radiator Pressure Cap

Radiators are equipped with a pressure cap so that the system can operate at higher
than atmospheric pressure, which raises the coolant boiling point, allowing
increased radiator cooling capacity. With a pressurized system an automobile
engine can run hotter without boiling. The boiling of water under pressure is raised
about 3°F for each pound of pressure.

The radiator pressure cap contains a pressure relief spring that opens at a
predetermined pressure. There is also a vent valve in the center of the cap that
allows a small flow through the cap when below boiling temperature but is closed
by an increase in flow as the boiling point is reached (Fig. 1-8). This valve also
opens when the coolant is cooling and contracting, allowing coolant to return to
the radiator from the coolant reserve tank by vacuum through a connecting hose.

FIGURE 1-8 Swivel type radiator pressure cap—coolant reserve
system (cut-away). (Courtesy of the Chrysler Corporation.)

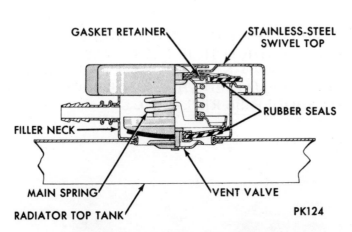

PK124

**WARNING:**

REMOVING A PRESSURE CAP FROM A HOT RADIATOR IS VERY DANGEROUS. TO PREVENT SCALDING OR INJURY, THE RADIATOR CAP SHOULD NOT BE REMOVED WHILE THE SYSTEM IS UNDER PRESSURE. WHEN REMOVING THE PRESSURE CAP, TURN COUNTERCLOCKWISE TO STOP TO PERMIT BUILT-UP PRESSURE TO ESCAPE THROUGH THE OVERFLOW TUBE. TO COMPLETE THE REMOVAL, PUSH DOWN ON THE CAP AND TURN COUNTERCLOCKWISE.

Radiator caps can be tested by using a pressure tester. The cap should retain the pressure within the rating specified by the manufacturer. Clean any deposits on the sealing surface and inspect the radiator filler neck for any irregularities that may prevent the cap from sealing.

### Radiator Hose

A hardened, cracked, swollen, or restricted hose should be replaced. The reinforcement spring inside the lower hose is necessary to prevent collapsing of the hose due to suction at medium or high speeds. If this spring is misplaced in the hose, it should be repositioned. If this spring is deformed, the hose and spring must be replaced.

### Heater Hose (Fig. 1-9)

Heater hoses are made to withstand the high pressure and temperature produced by the automobile engine. Heater hoses should be routed so that they do not come in contact with any sharp objects, the exhaust system, or the radiator fan. They should also be held in place so that vibration will not rub holes in the hose. A hardened, cracked, or swollen hose should be replaced.

**FIGURE 1-9** Heater hose routing. (Courtesy of the Ford Motor Company.)

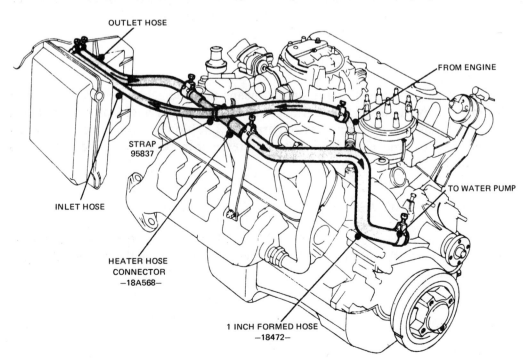

## HEATERS

The heater is designed to provide warm fresh air to the passenger compartment, defrost the windshield, and provide adequate ventilation during adverse weather conditions. The heater assembly contains the heater core and the doors necessary to control mixing and distribution of the air. Air entering the heater assembly is usually divided between two channels. The ratio of the mixture of the heated to unheated air is controlled by the temperature door (Fig. 1-10). Water is circulated from the engine block through the heater core and back to the area of the water pump, to be recirculated again. Some automobiles use a valve to control the amount of water that is permitted through the heater core. Others permit all the water to flow through the heater core and control the amount of air through the heater core.

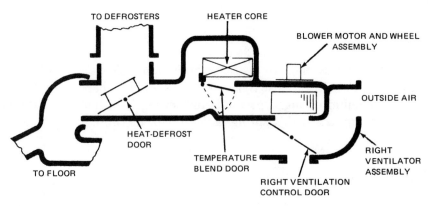

**FIGURE 1-10** Heater air-flow ventilation.

### Blower Motors

In operation, the outside air is drawn in by the blower and pushed into the channel, where the temperature valve, dependent upon its position, distributes all or some of the inlet air through the heater core. There are two types of blower motors used today: a permanent-magnet motor and a wire-wound motor.

#### PERMANENT-MAGNET MOTOR

A permanent-magnet motor simply means that the field poles are permanent magnets. They are made of a hard ceramic material and have no field windings. The motor has a wound armature and brushes. The blower speed can be controlled by the use of external circuit resistors to decrease or increase the applied voltage to the motor.

#### WIRE-WOUND MOTOR

This type of motor uses wire-wound fields. The wire is wrapped around a soft-iron core for added field strength when current flows through the wire windings. A wound armature is used with two brushes. Again, the blower speed can be controlled by the use of external circuit resistors to decrease or increase the applied voltage to the motor. The blower motor is designed to run on 12 volts and a specific amperage for proper maximum speed.

## SAFETY PRECAUTIONS

### Fans and Belts

Turn the engine off and remove the ignition key before working in the engine compartment. Fans and belts can cause serious cuts or even remove fingers.

### Radiator Pressure Cap

NEVER REMOVE A PRESSURE CAP QUICKLY from a hot radiator. Pressure caps should always be removed slowly, always stopping at the detent position long enough to permit steam to escape slowly and safely.

### Adding Coolant

Always allow a hot engine to cool after it has lost coolant. Adding liquid too soon can cause the engine block to crack and ruin the engine. Dangerous amounts of steam may be developed that will blow scalding liquid out the filler neck.

### Cleaning the Radiator

Flush with water. Rust that is suspended in the coolant may be removed by flushing clean water through the radiator as the engine is running at a fast speed. To prepare for flushing, turn the heater temperature lever on the instrument panel to maximum heat position. Open or remove all coolant outlets, and drain all liquid from the cooling system. Temporarily remove the thermostat to permit unrestricted coolant circulation. Insert a water hose in the filler neck, fill, and flush while engine is running until the drain water runs clear. Turn the engine off, stop adding water, drain the system, close the outlets, and replace the thermostat. Refill with coolant.

### Chemical Cleaners

Chemical cleaners will loosen moderate quantities of rust and scale that have formed on the cooling system surface. Follow the directions that are given on the container. After using the cleaner, flush with water and refill with coolant.

> **NOTE:**
>
> USE SPECIAL CAUTION WHEN CLEANING ALUMINUM RADIATORS OR ALUMINUM ENGINE BLOCKS OR PARTS. SOME CHEMICALS MAY DESTROY AN ALUMINUM RADIATOR.

**Pressure Flushing**

Pressure flushing may help to loosen rust when flushing with water or with chemical cleaners. For best results, reverse-pressure-flush the radiator and the engine water jacket (not together, but one at a time), attaching leadaway hose where necessary. The heater core must be flushed in the same direction in which water normally flows.

1. Limit air pressure to 20 pounds. (137.90 kPa).

2. Never use air pressure alone. It must be used together with water.

3. Apply pressure in short blasts.

4. Never reverse-flush a heater.

**Service Tips**

Aluminum radiators and engine blocks should be protected at all times by antifreeze or inhibitor compounds that are specifically recommended for use with aluminum. Aluminum radiators may be destroyed by the caustic solutions found in some cleaners or the chemicals used in some antifreezes and inhibitors. A special aluminum pressure cap and an aluminum drain cock must also be used with these radiators.

**Radiator Surface Plugging**

Plugging of radiator fins or centers will cause overheating. Remove bugs, leaves, and dirt from the front of the radiator by blowing air in from the side with an air hose at reduced pressure.

**Leak Testing (Fig. 1-11)**

If a car overheats and there are no visible leaks, a device can be used to pressure-check the system. Carefully examine the cooling system exterior for any signs of leakage. Pressure loss indicates that there is a leak at some point in the system. If a leak is not visible, the leak is probably internal, such as a faulty or loose head gasket. The pressure applied should not exceed the system relief pressure stamped on the cap.

**NOTES:**

1. Hauling trailers weighing between 2000 lb (8896.00 newtons) and 7000 lb (31,136 newtons) require that the car be equipped with a heavy-duty cooling package.

2. Cars equipped with an add-on air-conditioning system require a heavy-duty air-conditioning radiator.

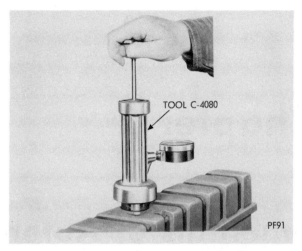

**FIGURE 1-11** Pressure testing cooling system. (Courtesy of the Chrysler Corporation.)

## REVIEW QUESTIONS

1. Ethylene-glycol-type antifreeze must be used year-round in an air-conditioned vehicle for two reasons. What are they?

2. Why is a pressure cap used in the cooling system?

3. Radiators are designed in two different ways. What are they?

4. The water pump is driven by the_____ _____, which is connected to the_____.

5. Name two reasons why a fan clutch is used.

6. A fan blade can be bent and adjusted for alignment. True or false:_____ .

7. There are two types of blower motors. What are they?_____ _____

# Chapter 2

# Fundamentals of Automotive Air Conditioning

We all know what air conditioning does for us, but very few understand how or why it works. An air conditioner is functionally very similar to a refrigerator, so let's take a look at refrigeration. A refrigerator is a simple mechanism which, surprisingly enough, works quite a bit like a teakettle boiling on a stove. That may sound far-fetched, but there is more similarity between the two than most of us would suspect. In fact, a modern refrigerator can make ice cubes and keep food cool and fresh only because a liquid boils inside the freezer.

Of course, everyone knows that a boiling teakettle is "hot" and a refrigerator is "cold." However, that is where most of us are apt to get confused. We usually think of "cold" as a definite, positive condition. Actually, though, there is no such thing as "cold." The only way we can define it is in a rather negative sort of way by saying that "cold" is simply the lack of heat, just as darkness is the lack of light. We cannot make things cold directly. All we can do is remove some of the heat they contain and they will become cold as a result. And that is the main job of any icebox or refrigerator. Both are simply devices for removing heat. All substances contains some heat. Theoretically, the lowest temperature that any substance could obtain is −459° Fahrenheit or −272° Celsius. This may be called "cold," and anything warmer than this contains heat. Since man has never succeeded in getting all the heat out of an object, we must think about the transfer of heat from one object to another when talking about controlling temperatures.

## TRANSFER OF HEAT

The only thing that will attract heat is a colder object. Like water, which always flows downhill, heat always flows down a temperature scale—from a warm level

14

down to a colder one. We hold our hands out toward the fireplace, and heat flows from the hot fire out to our cold hands (Fig. 2-1). When we make a snowball, heat always flows (Fig. 2-2) from our warm hands to the colder snow. In an icebox, the ice always is colder than the stored food, so heat naturally is drawn out of the warm food by the colder ice.

FIGURE 2-1  Heat transfer.

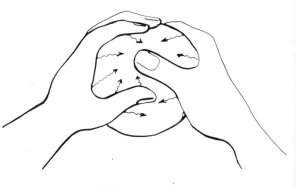

FIGURE 2-2  Heat transfer.

## MEASUREMENT OF HEAT

Everyone things he knows how heat is measured. He or she can tell how hot a substance is, but probably cannot tell us everything about heat. When we apply the flame of the torch on a pan of water (Fig. 2-3), we expect it to get hotter and hotter until it finally boils. All during the process, we can tell exactly how hot the water is by means of a termometer. However, the thermometer will show us that the flame of the torch is just as hot when we first applied it to the pan as it is when the water finally boils. Why doesn't the water boil immediately, then? Also, why does it take

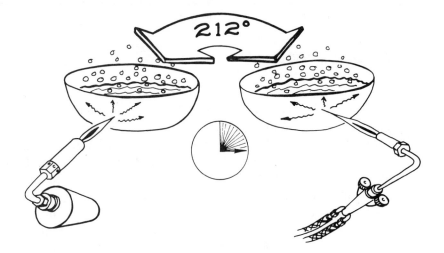

FIGURE 2-3  Applied temperature alone is not the sole measurement of heat.

longer to boil a quart of water than a cupful? (See Fig. 2-4.) Obviously, temperature isn't the only measurement of heat. Even though heat is intangible, it can be measured by quantity as well as intensity. It is recognized that thermometers indicate only the intensity of heat. The unit for measuring quantity of heat is specified as the amount necessary to make 1 pound of water 1 degree (F) warmer. We call this quantity of heat a *British thermal unit* (Btu).

Another unit for measuring the quantity of heat is a *calorie*. The calorie is that quantity of heat which will raise the temperature of 1 gram of water 1 degree Celsius. It may seem a little puzzling to talk about heat in a book on air conditioning, but, when you stop to think about it, we are handling heat exclusively. Although we ordinarily think of an air conditioner as a device, it does not do that directly. It takes heat away from the incoming air and transfers the heat to the outside of the vehicle. (See Tables 2-2 and 2-3 at the end of the chapter.)

**FIGURE 2-4** It takes less time to heat up a small amount than a large amount.

We know now that cold is nothing more than the absence of heat, and that heat always flows from a warm object to a colder one. From everything we've learned about heat so far, it seems to behave in a perfectly normal manner. Yet sometimes heat will disappear without leaving a single clue.

## ICE VERSUS WATER FOR COOLING

Every once in awhile in the old days, the iceman would forget to stop by to refill the icebox. Occasionally, as the last sliver of ice melted away, somebody would come up with a bright idea. He would remember that the water in the drainpan always felt ice-cold when he had emptied it. So he would get the thermometer and check the temperature of the water in the pan. Sure enough, it was usually about as cold as the ice. Why not put the drain pan back in the ice compartment to keep things cold until the iceman returned the next day?

It was a good idea—but it never worked! For some strange reason, the icebox never stayed cold. The drain water soon got warm, and in a few hours the butter in the icebox would begin to melt, the milk would start to sour, and the vegetables would wilt.

Why did this happen? The drain water was just a few degrees warmer than the ice, yet it didn't draw nearly as much heat out of the stored foods. However, the difference between the behavior of cold drain water and ice is the real secret as to how any refrigerator works, and we can easily learn the answer by using an ordinary thermometer.

When we put a drain pan full of cold water into the ice compartment, we expect the heat to flow from the warm foods to the colder water. Remember that heat always flows from a warm object to a colder object, and when we add heat to water, it gets warmer.

If we were to put a thermometer in the cold drain water, we would see the temperature gradually creep upward. That is to be expected, because heat is being absorbed into the cold water, making it warmer. Before long, the water would be as warm as the foods. Then the water could no longer attract heat because heat will not flow from one warm object to another equally warm object. Since we no longer can draw heat out of the foods, we no longer are cooling them.

When an iceberg is in the water, no matter how large it is, it will be 32°F or 0°C (Figs. 2-5 and 2-6). The iceberg will get smaller as it soaks up the heat from the water.

Now let's see what happens when we put ice instead of cold water in the icebox. When we first look at the thermometer, it would read 32°F or 0°C. A couple of hours later, we open the icebox door. The ice chunk is smaller because some of the ice has already melted away, but the temperature is still 32°F or 0°C. Still later, even more of the ice has melted, yet the temperature will still be 32°F or 0°C.

**FIGURE 2-5** The big iceberg is 32°F.

**FIGURE 2-6** The small iceberg is 32°F.

As long as any ice remains, no matter how much of it has melted away, the temperature of the ice stays at 32°F or 0°C. All this time, the ice has been soaking up heat, yet it never gets any warmer, no matter how much heat it draws from the stored food. On the other hand, the cold drain water got progressively warmer as it soaked up heat. Why is it that the addition of heat will make water warmer yet won't raise the temperature of ice above 32°F or 0°C?

If we fill a drinking glass with ice and another with cold water, and put both glasses in the same room where they could absorb equal amounts of heat from the room air, we will find that it takes much longer for the ice to melt and reach room temperature than it did for the water in the other glass to reach the same temperature.

Obviously, most of the heat was being used to melt the ice. But it was the heat that apparently disappeared or went into hiding, because it couldn't be located with a thermometer. To best describe this disappearing heat, scientists turned to Latin for the right word. They chose the word "latent," which means hidden.

### LATENT HEAT

Latent heat is nothing more than hidden heat which can't be found with a thermometer. What happens to the latent heat? Where does it disappear to? At first it was thought it was in the water that melted from the ice. But that wasn't exactly the right answer because, upon checking water temperature as it melts the ice, it will be found that it is only a shade warmer than the ice. It is not nearly warm enough to account for all the heat the ice had absorbed. The only possible answer is that the latent heat had been used up to change the ice from a solid into a liquid.

Many substances can be either a solid, or a gas, or a liquid. It just depends on the temperature. Water can be a solid (ice), or a gas (steam), or a liquid.

All solids soak up huge amounts of heat without getting any warmer when they change into liquids, and the same thing will happen when a substance changes from a liquid into a gas. If we put some hot water in a teakettle, set it over a fire, and watch the thermometer as the water gets hotter and hotter, the mercury will keep rising until the water starts to boil. Then the mercury seems to remain at the 212°F or 100°C mark. If we put more wood on the fire, despite all the increased heat, the mercury will not budge above the 212°F or 100°C mark. As the liquid changes to gas, it absorbs abnormally great amounts of heat without getting any hotter. Here is another instance where heat disappears. Now we have two different kinds of latent heat, which are quite a bit alike. The first one is called latent heat of fusion (melting). The other kind is called latent heat of vaporization (evaporation). We have learned how a simple icebox works. It's because the magic of latent heat of fusion gives ice the ability to soak up quantities of heat without getting any warmer. Since the ice stays cold, it can continue to draw heat away from stored foods and make them cooler. The latent heat of vaporization can be an even better "magnet," because it will soak up even more heat.

Whenever we think of anything boiling, we always think of it as being pretty hot. However, that is not true in every case. Just because water boils at 212°F or 100°C doesn't mean that all other substances will boil at the same temperature.

Some would have to be put in a blast furnace to make them bubble and give off vapor. On the other hand, others will boil violently while sitting on a cake of ice.

Each substance has its own particular boiling-point temperature. Consequently, any liquid that will boil at a temperature below the freezing point of water will make ice cubes and keep vegetables cool in a mechanical refrigerator.

### REFRIGERANT–12

Refrigerant-12 which is used in automotive air conditioning, boils at -21.7° or -29.8°C. That may not mean much until we picture a flask of R-12 sitting on the North Pole boiling away just like a teakettle on a stove. No one would dare pick up the flask with their bare hands because, even though boiling, it would be so cold and it would be drawing heat away from nearby objects so fast that human flesh would freeze in a very short time.

If we put a flask of R-12 inside a refrigerator cabinet, it would boil and draw heat away from everything surrounding it (Fig. 2-7). As long as any refrigerant remained in the flask, it would keep on soaking up heat until the temperature got clear down to -21.7°F, or -29.8°C below zero.

Now we can begin to see the similarity between a boiling pan of water and a refrigerator. Ordinarily, we think of the flame pushing heat into the pan of water. Yet it is just as logical to turn our thinking around and picture the teakettle pulling the heat out of the flame. Both the pan of water and the flask of refrigerant do the same thing—they both draw heat to boil, although they do so at different temperature levels. There is another similarity between the icebox and the mechanical refrigerator. In the icebox, water from melting ice literally carried heat out of the cabinet. In our simple refrigerator, rising vapors do the same job.

Water is so cheap that we could afford to throw it away. But R-12, or any other refrigerant, is too expensive just to let it float away into the atmosphere. If there was some way to remove the heat from the vapor and change it back into a liquid, it could be returned to the flask and used again (Fig. 2-8).

**FIGURE 2-7** Simple R-12 refrigerator.

**FIGURE 2-8** Reusing refrigerant.

There is a way, and that is where we find the biggest difference between the old icebox and the modern refrigerator. We put in the new ice to replace the ice that had melted. Now we use the same refrigerant over and over again.

We know that any substance will condense at the same temperature at which it boiled. This temperature point is a clear-cut division, like a fence. On one side, a substance is a liquid. Immediately on the other side it is a vapor. Whichever way a substance would go, from hot to cold or cold to hot, it will change its character the moment it crosses over the fence.

But pressure moves the fence! Water will boil at 212°F or 100°C under normal conditions. Naturally, we expect steam to condense at the same temperature. But whenever we apply pressure, it doesn't! It will condense at some temperature higher than 212°F or 100°C. The greater the pressure, the higher the boiling point and the temperature at which a vapor will condense. This is the reason why pressure cookers cook food faster, since the pressure on the water permits it to boil at a higher temperature.

All pressure, regardless of how it is produced, is measured in pounds per square inch (psi) or kilopascals (kPa). Atmospheric pressure is pressure exerted in every direction by the weight of the atmosphere. At higher altitudes air is rarified and has less weight. At sea level, atmospheric pressure is 14.7 psi or 101.35 kPa.

Any pressure less than atmospheric is known as a partial vacuum or vacuum. A perfect vacuum has never been mechanically produced.

## BASIC REFRIGERATOR OPERATION

Remember these main points:

1. All liquids soak up lots of heat without getting any warmer when they boil into a vapor.

2. We can use pressure to make the vapor condense back into a liquid so that it can be used over again.

Now here is how we can build a refrigerator. We can place a flask of refrigerant in an icebox. We know that it will boil at a very cold temperature and will draw heat away from everything inside the cabinet. We can pipe the rising vapors outside the cabinet and thus provide a way for carrying the heat out. Once we get the heat-laden vapor outside, we can compress it with a pump. With enough pressure, we can squeeze the heat out of "cold" vapor even in a warm room. An ordinary radiator will help us get rid of heat (Fig. 2-9).

By removing the heat and making the refrigerant into a liquid, it becomes the same as it was before. So we can run another pipe back into the cabinet and return the refrigerant to the flask to be used over again. That is the way most mechanical refrigerators work today. Now, let's look at an air-conditioning unit to see how closely it resembles the refrigerator we have just described.

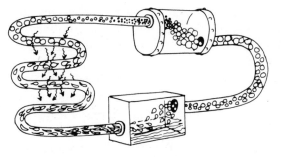

**FIGURE 2-9** Basic refrigerant circuit.

## BASIC AIR CONDITIONER

When we look at an air-conditioning unit, we will always find a set of coils or a finned radiator core through which the air to be cooled passes. This is known as the evaporator. It does the same job as the flask of refrigerant we spoke about before. The refrigerant boils in the evaporator. In boiling, of course, the refrigerant absorbs heat and changes into a vapor. By piping this vapor outside the car, we can bodily carry out the heat that caused its creation.

Once we get the vapor out of the evaporator, all we have to do is remove the heat it contains. Since this is the only thing that expanded the refrigerant from a liquid to a vapor in the first place, removal of that heat will let the vapor condense into a liquid again. Then we can rerun the liquid refrigerant to the evaporator to be used again. Actually, the vapor coming out of the evaporator is very cold. We know that the liquid refrigerant boils at temperatures below freezing and that the vapors arising from it are only a shade warmer. Consequently, we cannot expect to remove heat from subfreezing vapors by cooling them in air temperatures that usually range between 60°F or 15.6°C and 100°F or 37.9°C. Heat refuses to flow from a cold object toward a warmer object. But with a pump, we can squeeze the heat-laden vapor into a smaller space. And when we compress the vapor, we also concentrate the heat it contains. In this way, we can make the vapor hotter without adding any heat. Then we can cool it in comparatively warm air. That is the only responsibility of a compressor in an air-conditioning system.

It is not intended to be a pump just for circulating the refrigerant. Rather, it is to exert pressure, for two reasons. Pressure makes the vapor hot enough to cool off in warm air. At the same time, the compressor raises the refrigerant pressure above the condensing point at the temperature of the surrounding air so that it will condense. As the refrigerant leaves the compressor, it is still a vapor and it is now quite hot and ready to give up the heat that it absorbed in the evaporator. One of the easiest ways to help refrigerant vapor discharge its heat is to send it through a radiator-like contrivance known as a condenser.

The condenser is a simple device having no moving parts. It does exactly the same thing as the familiar radiator in a home steam-heating system. There the steam is nothing more than water vapor. In passing through the radiator, the steam gives up its heat and condenses back into water. The same action takes place in an air-conditioning condenser. The refrigerant vapor gives up its heat, which is quickly radiated into the surrounding air through the large finned surfaces of the condenser.

In giving up its heat, the refrigerant vapor condenses back into a liquid, which collects in a pool at the bottom of the condenser. As we said before, when the refrigerant condenses into a liquid, it is again ready for boiling in the evaporator. So we can run a pipe from the condenser back to the evaporator.

These three units, then—the evaporator, the compressor, and the condenser—are the main working parts in any typical air-conditioning system. We have the evaporator, where the refrigerant boils and changes into a vapor, absorbing heat. We have the pump or compressor, to put pressure on the refrigerant so that it can get rid of its heat. And we have a condenser outside the car body, to help discharge the heat into the surrounding air.

## Pressure and Flow

There is one more unit that cooperates with these three. It acts as sort of a traffic officer in controlling the flow of refrigerant through the system. To get a better idea of what it does, let's first do a little experimenting with an ordinary tire pump.

When we use an ordinary tire pump to inflate an automobile tire, we are creating pressure only because we are pushing against the air already entrapped inside the tire. If you question this, try pumping up a tire that has a puncture in it. You could pump all day and still not be able to build up any pressure. As fast as you would pump the air in, it would leak out. About all you would be doing would be circulating nice fresh air through the tire. Unless you have something to push against, to block the flow of air, you cannot create more than a mere semblance of pressure.

The same situation holds true in an air-conditioning system. The compressor can pump refrigerant vapor through the system, but unless it has something to push against, it cannot build up pressure. All the compressor would be doing would be to circulate the vapor without increasing its pressure. Yet we cannot block the flow through the system entirely. All we want to do is put pressure on the refrigerant vapor so that it will condense at normal temperatures. What's more, this must be done sometime after the vapor leaves the evaporator and before it returns again as a liquid. We cannot have high pressure in the evaporator because that would slow down the boiling of the refrigerant and penalize the refrigerating effect.

### CONTROLLING PRESSURE AND FLOW

Pressure and flow can be controlled with a float valve or with a pressure-regulating valve. They do the same job but in a different way.

Since the float-type valve will give us a better idea of pressure and flow control, let's look at it first. It consists of a float that rides on the surface of the liquid refrigerant. As the refrigerant liquid boils and passes off as a vapor, naturally the liquid level drops lower and lower. Because the float rides on the surface of the refrigerant, it also drops lower and lower as the liquid goes down. This downward movement of the float opens a valve to let the refrigerant in. The incoming liquid raises the fluid level and, of course, the float rides up along with it. When the correct level is reached, the valve will stop the flow of refrigerant liquid. We have described the float and valve action as being wide open or tight shut. Actually, the liquid level falls rather slowly as the refrigerant boils away. The float goes down gradually and opens the valve just a crack. New refrigerant liquid barely seeps in through the cracked valve. At such a low rate of flow, it raises the liquid level in the evaporator very slowly. It is now possible for a stabilized condition to exist. By that, we mean that the valve would be barely open enough to allow just the right amount of refrigerant liquid to enter the freezer to take the place of that leaving as a vapor.

### Pressure–Temperature Relationship of R-12

A definite pressure and temperature relationship exists in the case of liquid refrigerants and their saturated vapors. Increasing the temperature of a substance causes it to expand. When the substance is confined in a closed container, the increase in temperature will be accompanied by an increase in pressure, even though no mechanical device was used. For every temperature, there will be a corresponding pressure within the container or refrigerant. Table 2-1 is a table of the temperature–pressure relationship of R-12. If a gauge is attached to a container of R-12 and the room temperature is 70°F (21.1°C), the gauge will register 70.1 psi (483.33 kPa). The efficient operation of the air-conditioning refrigeration system is dependent on the pressure–temperature relationship of pure refrigerant. As long as the system contains only pure refrigerant (plus a certain amount of compressor oil), it is considered to be chemically stable. When foreign materials, such as dirt, air, or moisture, are allowed to get into the system, they will affect chemical stability, resulting in the formation of acids or sludge which could cause the expansion valve to freeze up and change the pressure–temperature relationship of the refrigerant. Thus, the system will no longer operate at the proper pressures and temperatures and the efficiency will decrease and parts will deteriorate.

### MORE ABOUT REFRIGERANTS

Generally speaking, a refrigerant is any body or substance that acts as a cooling agent by absorbing heat from another body or substance. It should be noted that no one refrigerant is universally suitable for all applications. The safe properties of the refrigerant are the prime consideration in the selection of a refrigerant. To be suitable for use as a refrigerant, a fluid should be chemically inert to the extent that it is nonexplosive, nonflammable, and nontoxic both in the pure state and when

**TABLE 2-1** Pressure–temperature relationship of R-12.

| °F | °C | Pounds/In.² (psi) | Kilopascals (kPa) |
|---|---|---|---|
| −15 | −26.1 | 2.44 | 16.54 |
| −10 | −23.3 | 4.5 | 31.02 |
| −5 | −20.6 | 6.8 | 46.88 |
| 0 | −17.7 | 9.2 | 63.43 |
| 5 | −15.0 | 11.8 | 81.36 |
| 10 | −12.2 | 14.7 | 101.35 |
| 15 | − 9.4 | 17.7 | 122.04 |
| 25 | − 3.9 | 24.6 | 169.61 |
| 30 | − 1.1 | 28.5 | 196.50 |
| 32 | 0 | 30.1 | 207.53 |
| 35 | 1.7 | 32.6 | 224.77 |
| 40 | 4.4 | 37.0 | 255.11 |
| 45 | 7.2 | 41.7 | 287.52 |
| 50 | 10.0 | 46.7 | 321.99 |
| 55 | 12.8 | 52.0 | 358.54 |
| 60 | 15.6 | 57.7 | 397.84 |
| 65 | 18.3 | 63.7 | 439.21 |
| 70 | 21.1 | 70.1 | 483.33 |
| 75 | 23.9 | 76.9 | 530.22 |
| 80 | 26.7 | 84.1 | 579.86 |
| 85 | 29.4 | 91.7 | 632.27 |
| 90 | 32.2 | 99.6 | 686.74 |
| 95 | 35.0 | 108.1 | 745.34 |
| 100 | 37.8 | 116.9 | 806.02 |
| 105 | 40.5 | 126.2 | 870.14 |
| 110 | 43.4 | 136.0 | 937.72 |
| 115 | 46.1 | 146.5 | 1010.11 |
| 120 | 49.0 | 157.1 | 1083.20 |
| 125 | 51.7 | 167.5 | 1154.91 |
| 130 | 54.5 | 179.0 | 1234.20 |
| 140 | 60.0 | 204.5 | 1410.02 |
| 150 | 65.6 | 232.0 | 1599.64 |

mixed with air. The fluid should not react unfavorably with the oil or the material used in the construction of refrigerating equipment. Most of the refrigerants in use are nonflammable and nonexplosive.

Moisture will combine in varying degrees with most refrigerants, causing the formation of acid, which will react with the oil and other materials in the system. This chemical action often results in pitting and other damage to the valves, seals, bearings, cylinder walls, and other smooth surfaces. It also may cause deterioration of the oil and the formation of metallic and other sludges which tend to clog valves and oil passages. Moisture in the refrigerating system may exist and the formation of ice in a controlled orifice will prevent the flow of refrigerant through that part and render the system inoperative until such time that the ice melts and the flow is restored. The refrigeration will be intermittent as the moisture freezes and melts. Oil required for lubrication of the compressor is contained in the crankcase of the compressor, where it is subjected with the refrigerant. The refrigerant must be chemically and physically stable in the presence of oil.

Leaks in the refrigerating system may be inward or outward, depending on whether the pressure in the system is above or below atmospheric pressure. When the pressure in the system is above atmospheric pressure, the refrigerant will leak from the system to the outside. On the other hand, when the pressure in the system is below atmospheric, air and moisture will be drawn into the system. In either case, the system will be inoperative in a short time.

### Precautions in Handling Refrigerants

1. Do not leave the drum uncapped if the drum is so equipped. The metal cap furnished with the drum when it is shipped is to protect the valve in case the drum is accidentally knocked over. This eliminates the possibility of the drum flying through the shop and causing serious damage to people and property. A safety plug is provided on the valve in case the temperature exceeds the safe limits of the drum. The cap is designed so that if the safety plug at the valve should blow, the refrigerant will escape without causing the drum to move.

2. Do not overfill the drum. A safety plug is provided in case the temperature of the refrigerant exceeds the safe limits of the drum. However, if the drum is overfilled, the pressure created could cause the drum to explode before the temperature rises to the point where the safety plug would burst and allow the refrigerant to escape.

3. Do not carry the drum in the passenger compartment of a car. Always place the drum in the luggage compartment of the car. If the drum is carried in an open truck, shield it for protection from the sun's rays. This heat could increase the pressure enough to cause the safety plug to burst.

4. Do not subject the drum to high temperatures when charging the system. Use water no warmer than 125°F (52°C) to heat the drum. Never place the drum on a steam radiator or stove or use torches for heating during charging.

5. Do not discharge refrigerant into areas where there is an exposed flame or where it could be drawn into the engine air intake when the engine is operating. Concentrations of this gas in contact with a flame may produce a poisonous gas (phosgene).

6. Always wear goggles when doing work that involves opening the refrigerant lines. An accident can easily cause liquid refrigerant to strike the eyes. If the refrigerant should strike the eyes, the eyes should be rinsed with a great amount of cool, clean, water. The person should then be taken to a qualified physician.

**TABLE 2-2**    SI metric table.

| Multiply: | By: | To Get Equivalent Number of: |
|---|---|---|
| *Torque* | | |
| Pound-inch | 0.112 98 | newton-metres (N • m) |
| Pound-foot | 1.355 8 | newton-metres |
| *Horse Power* | | |
| Horsepower | 0.746 | kilowatts (kW) |
| *Pressure or Stress* | | |
| Inches of water | 0.249 1 | kilopascals (kPa) |
| Pounds/square inch | 6.895 | kilopascals |
| *Energy of Work* | | |
| Btu | 1.055... | joules (J) |
| Foot-pound | 1.355 8 | joules |
| Kilowatt-hour | 3 600 000 | joules |
| *Velocity* | | |
| Miles/hour | 1.609 3 | kilometres/hour (km/h) |
| *Fuel Economy* | | |
| Miles/gallon | 0.425 1 | kilometres/litre (Km/*l*) |
| *Volume* | | |
| Quart | 0.946 4 | litres (*l*) |
| Gallon | 3.785 4 | litres |
| *Force* | | |
| Kilogram | 9.807 | newtons (N) |
| Ounce | 0.278 0 | newtons |
| Pound | 4.448 | newtons |

**TABLE 2-3**  Temperature conversion.

| °F | °C | °F | °C | °F | °C | °F | °C |
|---|---|---|---|---|---|---|---|
| −15 | −26.1 | 21 | −6.1 | 57 | 13.9 | 93 | 33.9 |
| −14 | −25.6 | 22 | −5.6 | 58 | 14.4 | 94 | 34.5 |
| −13 | −25.0 | 23 | −5.0 | 59 | 15.0 | 95 | 35.0 |
| −12 | −24.4 | 24 | −4.4 | 60 | 15.6 | 96 | 35.6 |
| −11 | −23.9 | 25 | −3.9 | 61 | 16.1 | 97 | 36.2 |
| −10 | −23.3 | 26 | −3.3 | 62 | 16.7 | 98 | 36.7 |
| −9 | −22.8 | 27 | −2.8 | 63 | 17.2 | 99 | 37.2 |
| −8 | −22.2 | 28 | −2.2 | 64 | 17.8 | 100 | 37.8 |
| −7 | −21.7 | 29 | −1.7 | 65 | 18.3 | 101 | 38.4 |
| −6 | −21.1 | 30 | −1.1 | 66 | 18.9 | 102 | 38.9 |
| −5 | −20.6 | 31 | −0.6 | 67 | 19.4 | 103 | 39.5 |
| −4 | −20.0 | 32 | 0 | 68 | 20.0 | 104 | 40.0 |
| −3 | −19.4 | 33 | 0.6 | 69 | 20.6 | 105 | 40.5 |
| −2 | −18.9 | 34 | 1.1 | 70 | 21.1 | 106 | 41.1 |
| −1 | −18.3 | 35 | 1.7 | 71 | 21.7 | 107 | 41.7 |
| 0 | −17.7 | 36 | 2.2 | 72 | 22.2 | 108 | 42.3 |
| 1 | −17.2 | 37 | 2.8 | 73 | 22.8 | 109 | 42.8 |
| 2 | −16.7 | 38 | 3.3 | 74 | 23.4 | 110 | 43.4 |
| 3 | −16.1 | 39 | 3.9 | 75 | 23.9 | 111 | 43.9 |
| 4 | −15.6 | 40 | 4.4 | 76 | 24.4 | 112 | 44.5 |
| 5 | −15.0 | 41 | 5.0 | 77 | 25.0 | 113 | 45.0 |
| 6 | −14.4 | 42 | 5.6 | 78 | 25.6 | 114 | 45.6 |
| 7 | −13.9 | 43 | 6.1 | 79 | 26.1 | 115 | 46.1 |
| 8 | −13.3 | 44 | 6.7 | 80 | 26.7 | 116 | 46.7 |
| 9 | −12.8 | 45 | 7.2 | 81 | 27.2 | 117 | 47.3 |
| 10 | −12.2 | 46 | 7.8 | 82 | 27.8 | 118 | 47.8 |
| 11 | −11.7 | 47 | 8.3 | 83 | 28.4 | 119 | 48.4 |
| 12 | −11.1 | 48 | 8.9 | 84 | 28.9 | 120 | 49.0 |
| 13 | −10.6 | 49 | 9.4 | 85 | 29.4 | 121 | 49.5 |
| 14 | −10.0 | 50 | 10.0 | 86 | 30.0 | 122 | 50.0 |
| 15 | −9.4 | 51 | 10.6 | 87 | 30.6 | 123 | 50.6 |
| 16 | −8.9 | 52 | 11.1 | 88 | 31.1 | 124 | 51.2 |
| 17 | −8.3 | 53 | 11.7 | 89 | 31.7 | 125 | 51.7 |
| 18 | −7.8 | 54 | 12.2 | 90 | 32.2 | 126 | 52.3 |
| 19 | −7.2 | 55 | 12.8 | 91 | 32.8 | 127 | 52.8 |
| 20 | −6.7 | 56 | 13.3 | 92 | 33.4 | 128 | 53.4 |

**TABLE 2-3** (continued)

| °F | °C | °F | °C | °F | °C |
|---|---|---|---|---|---|
| 129 | 54.0 | 160 | 71.2 | 191 | 88.4 |
| 130 | 54.5 | 161 | 71.7 | 192 | 89.0 |
| 131 | 55.0 | 162 | 72.3 | 193 | 89.5 |
| 132 | 55.6 | 163 | 72.8 | 194 | 90.0 |
| 133 | 56.2 | 164 | 73.4 | 195 | 90.6 |
| 134 | 56.7 | 165 | 74.0 | 196 | 91.1 |
| 135 | 57.3 | 166 | 74.5 | 197 | 91.7 |
| 136 | 57.8 | 167 | 75.0 | 198 | 92.3 |
| 137 | 58.4 | 168 | 75.6 | 199 | 92.9 |
| 138 | 59.0 | 169 | 76.2 | 200 | 93.4 |
| 139 | 59.5 | 170 | 76.7 | 201 | 94.0 |
| 140 | 60.0 | 171 | 77.3 | 202 | 94.5 |
| 141 | 60.6 | 172 | 77.9 | 203 | 95.1 |
| 142 | 61.2 | 173 | 78.4 | 204 | 95.6 |
| 143 | 61.7 | 174 | 79.0 | 205 | 96.2 |
| 144 | 62.3 | 175 | 79.5 | 206 | 96.8 |
| 145 | 62.9 | 176 | 80.0 | 207 | 97.3 |
| 146 | 63.4 | 177 | 80.6 | 208 | 97.9 |
| 147 | 64.0 | 178 | 81.1 | 209 | 98.5 |
| 148 | 64.5 | 179 | 81.7 | 210 | 99.0 |
| 149 | 65.0 | 180 | 82.3 | 211 | 99.5 |
| 150 | 65.6 | 181 | 82.9 | 212 | 100.0 |
| 151 | 66.2 | 182 | 83.5 | 213 | 100.5 |
| 152 | 66.7 | 183 | 84.0 | 214 | 101.1 |
| 153 | 67.3 | 184 | 84.5 | 215 | 101.7 |
| 154 | 67.8 | 185 | 85.0 | 216 | 102.2 |
| 155 | 68.4 | 186 | 85.6 | 217 | 102.8 |
| 156 | 69.0 | 187 | 86.1 | 218 | 103.4 |
| 157 | 69.5 | 188 | 86.7 | 219 | 104.4 |
| 158 | 70.0 | 189 | 87.3 | 220 | 104.5 |
| 159 | 70.6 | 190 | 87.9 | 221 | 105.0 |

**REVIEW QUESTIONS**

1.  15 psi is equal to_____kPa.

2.  One pound of pressure will increase the boiling point of water_____degrees.

3.  The only thing that will attract heat is_____.

4.  What is a Btu?

5.  What is a calorie?

6.  Temperature can change many substances into three stages. What are the three stages?

7.  Atmospheric pressure at sea level is_____psi or_____kPa.

8.  Pressure can make vapor condense back into a liquid. True or false?

9.  A compressor is needed in an air-conditioning system for two reasons. What are they?

10. What are the three main parts of a typical air-conditioning system?

11. Two methods are used to control the temperature in an air-conditioning system. What are they?

12. If a can of R-12 is in a room with a temperature of 32.2°C, what is the pressure inside the can of R-12?

13. 20 psi equals_____kPa.

# Chapter 3

# Description and Operation
# of Basic Components

Let's review the basic refrigeration cycle. Keep this basic cycle in mind because knowledge of the cycle, knowledge of the particular system you are working on, and proper use of the gauges will permit quick, accurate diagnosis of problems as they arise.

Refrigerant gas under low pressure is drawn into the compressor, where it is compressed to a high pressure. During compression, the refrigerant gas is heated. When sufficient pressure is built up, the hot gas passes into the condenser.

The compressor is not intended to be a pump just for circulating the refrigerant. Rather, it is to exert pressure for two reasons:

1. Pressure makes the vapor hot enough to cool off in warm air.

2. The compressor raises the refrigerant pressure above the condensing point at the temperature of the surrounding air so that it will condense.

The hot gas passes into the condenser, where it cools by giving off heat to the air passing over the condenser surfaces. As the refrigerant gas cools, it condenses into a liquid at high pressure.

The high-pressure liquid passes on to the receiver-dehydrator. The purpose of the receiver-dehydrator is to store refrigerant and to remove small traces of moisture that may be in the system.

The high-pressure liquid will leave the receiver dehydrator and will continue on to the thermostatic expansion valve. When the thermostatic expansion valve opens, the pressure on the liquid will drop and low-pressure liquid will enter the evaporator. The low-pressure liquid, in the evaporator, will boil (turn to vapor) and remove the heat from the evaporator. The purpose of the thermostatic expan-

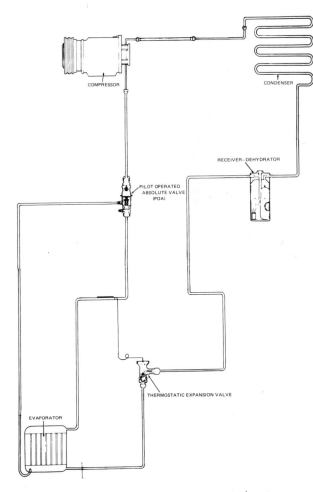

FIGURE 3-1 Evaporator pressure control system.

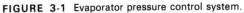

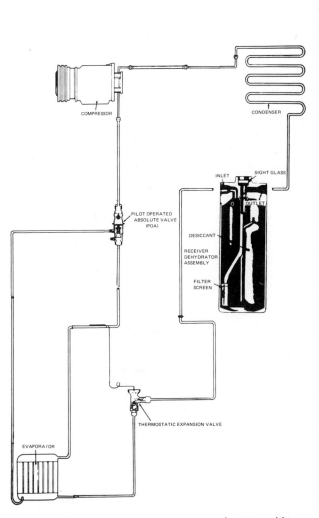

FIGURE 3-2 Evaporator pressure control system with enlarged receiver-dehydrator.

sion valve is to separate the high side of the system from the low side and to restrict or control the refrigerant flow.

The purpose of the evaporator is to cool, dry, and clean the air that enters the passenger compartment. As the heat is transferred through the walls of the evaporator from the warm air passing over it, moisture in the air condenses on its surface and is drained off, removing dust and pollen. However, the temperature in the evaporator must be controlled so that the water collecting on the core will not freeze.

Some automotive air-conditioning systems use a pilot-operated absolute valve (POA), a suction throttling valve (STV), or an evaporator pressure regulator (EPR). In either case, the function is to control evaporator temperature by controlling the pressure within the evaporator.

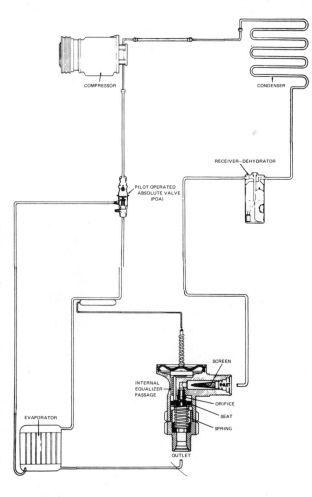

**FIGURE 3-3** Evaporator pressure control system with enlarged TXV.

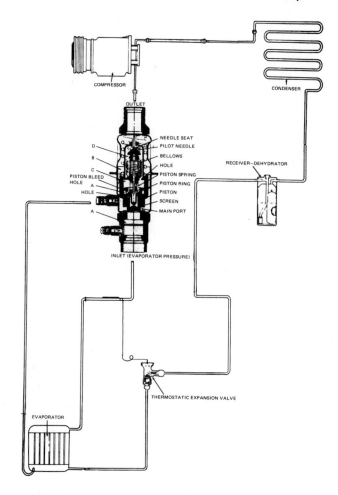

**FIGURE 3-4** Evaporator pressure control system with enlarged POA.

## COMPRESSOR DESIGNS

There are four compressors commonly used on American-made vehicles:

1. Frigidaire.
2. Air Temp.
3. York.
4. Tecumseh.

All are slightly different in size, weight, and so on. However, all are the basic reciprocating-piston type, and all use reed valves to control the piston intake and discharge. We also describe the GM four-cylinder compressor.

**Frigidaire (Fig. 3-5)**

The Frigidaire compressor is quite different from the other three. It has three sets of double-acting pistons. A swash plate, mounted on the compressor shaft, causes the pistons to move back and forth in the cylinders as the shaft rotates. Each cylinder is provided with reed valves at each end of the compressor. Also, there are two internal crossover passages. One connects the suction chambers of the front and rear heads so that there is one common suction port; the other connects the discharge chambers of the front and rear heads so that there is one common discharge port. A gear-type oil pump at the rear of the compressor provides for lubrication.

**FIGURE 3-5** GM 6 cylinder compressor. (Courtesy of AC-Delco.)

**Air Temp (Fig. 3-6)**

The Air Temp compressor is a two-cylinder V-shaped unit. There are separate heads for each cylinder. The system connections and service valves are located at the front and back of the block, between the cylinders. A service port into the cylinder intake is located on one of the heads. Lubrication to the compressor is supplied by a rotor-type oil pump positioned under the rear cover plate.

**FIGURE 3-6** Chrysler compressor. (Courtesy of the Chrysler Corporation.)

**York (Fig. 3-7)**

The York compressor is a two-cylinder in-line unit. However, in appearance, it gives the impression of having only one cylinder. The head and block are constructed of aluminum. Inlet and discharge fittings and service valves are located on the compressor head. The compressors have a positive pressure system for lubrication. This design utilizes the pressure differential between the piston intake stroke and the crankcase and the centrifugal force created by the turning crankshaft.

**FIGURE 3-7** Tecumseh or York compressor. (Courtesy of AC-Delco.)

**Tecumseh**

The Tecumseh compressor is a two-cylinder in-line unit similar to the York in appearance, design, and operation. It also uses a positive-pressure-type system for lubrication. The Tecumseh compressor differs from the York in that its block-and-head construction is of cast iron. Both the Tecumseh and York compressors can be mounted vertically, horizontally, or at any angle between these positions.

**GM Four-Cylinder (Fig. 3-8)**

The basic compressor mechanism is a modified scotch yoke with four cylinders located radially in the same plane. Opposed pistons are pressed into a yoke which rides upon a slider block located on the shaft eccentric. Rotation of the shaft provides reciprocating-piston motion with no "connecting rods." The mechanism is completely balanced with counterweights. Needle bearings are used for the shaft journals and the shaft eccentric. Pistons and yokes, together with the main cylinder housing and front cover, are made from aluminum to provide light weight. Teflon

**FIGURE 3-8** GM 4 cylinder compressor.
(Courtesy of AC-Delco.)

piston rings are used to provide both a gas compression seal and a piston-to-bore bearing surface. The compressor outer shell is a simple steel band that encloses a large annular discharge muffler space. Two O-rings provide a seal between the compressor shell and the compressor cylinder. A rubber seal ring seals the front head to the cylinder assembly, and the shaft seal assembly provides a front head-to-shaft seal.

Refrigerant flows into the crankcase from the connector block at the rear, is drawn through the reeds attached to the piston top during the suction stroke, and is discharged outward through the discharge valve plate, which is held in place at the top of the cylinder by a snap ring. Discharge gas flows out the compressor muffler cavity throuth the connector block at the rear.

The compressor is belt-driven by the engine crankshaft through a clutch pulley. Operation of the pistons draws refrigerant vapor into the suction cavity on the intake strokes. On the compression strokes, the vapor is compressed into the discharge cavity and flows out into the discharge line.

## MAGNETIC CLUTCH (FIG. 3-9)

The compressor is equipped with an electromagnetic clutch that is built in the drive-pulley assembly. It is designed to engage the pulley to the compressor shaft when the clutch coil is energized. The purpose of the clutch is to transmit power from the engine to the compressor and to provide a means of engaging and disengaging the refrigeration system from the engine operation. When the clutch is engaged, power is transmitted from the pulley to the compressor shaft. When the clutch is not engaged, the compressor shaft does not rotate and the pulley freewheels. The clutch is engaged by a magnetic field and disengaged by springs when the magnetic field is broken.

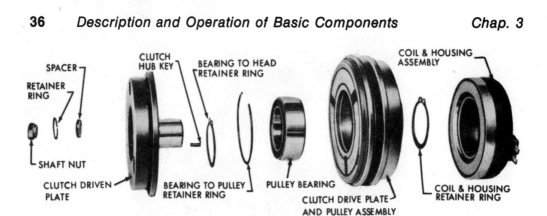

FIGURE 3-9 4t13GM 6 cylinder compressor. (Courtesy of AC-Delco.)

## SERVICE VALVES

### Schrader-Type (Fig. 3-10)

A Schrader-type valve is similar to a regular tire valve and is used on most late-model automobiles. Most test hoses incorporate a valve core depressor that will unseat the valve core when connected. If not, a separate adapter fitting must be installed before connecting test hoses.

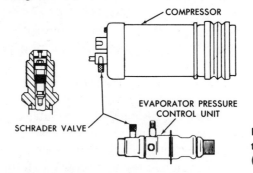

FIGURE 3-10 Schrader type service valve. (Courtesy of AC-Delco.)

### Stem-Type: York Compressor (Fig. 3-11)

This valve has a valve stem located under a cap opposite the hose connections. The valve has three positions.

#### BACK-SEATED POSITION

This is the normal operating position with the valve stem rotated counterclockwise to seat the rear valve face and seal off the service gauge ports.

#### MID-POSITION

This is the test position with the valve stem turned clockwise 1 ½ to 2 turns to connect the service gauge port into the system so that the gauge reading may be

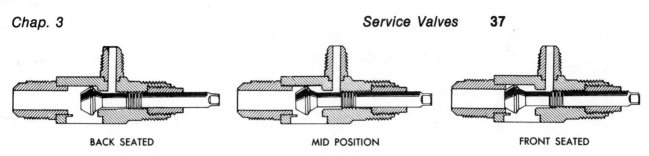

BACK SEATED                    MID POSITION                    FRONT SEATED

**FIGURE 3-11** Service valve positions. (Courtesy of AC-Delco.)

taken with the system operating. (The service gauge hose must be connected with the valve completely back-seated.)

### FRONT-SEATED POSITION

The valve stem has been rotated clockwise to seat the front valve and to isolate the compressor from the system.

## CONDENSER (FIG. 3-12)

The condenser consists of a refrigerant coil tube mounted in a series of thin cooling fins to provide a maximum of heat transfer in a minimum amount of space. Mounted directly in front of the radiator, it receives the full flow of warm air from the movement of the car and from the engine fan.

The purpose of the condenser is to condense the high-pressure hot vapor coming from the compressor. To do so, it must give up heat. The condenser receives very hot, high-pressure, refrigerant vapor from the compressor through its discharge hose. The refrigerant vapor enters the inlet at the top of the condenser, and as the hot vapor passes down through the condenser coils, heat moves from the hot refrigerant into the cooler air as it flows across the condenser coils and fins. This process causes a large quantity of heat to be transferred to the outside air and the refrigerant to change from a high-pressure hot vapor to a high-pressure warm liquid. This liquid flows from the bottom of the condenser to the receiver dehydrator.

**FIGURE 3-12** Condenser. (Courtesy of AC-Delco.)

### RECEIVER-DEHYDRATOR (FIG. 3-13)

The purpose of the receiver-dehydrator is to store refrigerant and to remove small traces of moisture that may be left in the system after purging and evacuating. The body of the receiver-dehydrator is made of heavy-gauge steel or aluminum and contains a reservoir, filter, tube, sack of desiccant (to absorb moisture), and a sight glass. The receiver-dehydrator is usually connected to the condenser, where liquid refrigerant enters the reservoir of the receiver-dehydrator. The liquid will drop to the bottom of the receiver-dehydrator, where it will pass through a screen and enter the outer tube.

A sight glass is usually built into the top of the receiver-dehydrator at the outlet side. At temperatures higher than 70° F or 21° C, the sight glass may indicate whether the refrigerant charge is sufficient. A shortage of refrigerant is indicated after about 5 minutes of compressor operation by the appearance of slow-moving bubbles or a broken column of refrigerant under the glass. Continuous bubbles may appear in a properly charged system on a cool day. This is a normal situation. If the sight glass is generally clear and performance is satisfactory, occasional bubbles do not indicate refrigerant shortage.

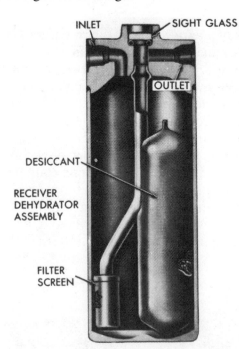

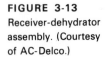

FIGURE 3-13
Receiver-dehydrator
assembly. (Courtesy
of AC-Delco.)

### THERMOSTATIC EXPANSION VALVE (FIG. 3-14)

The expansion valve separates the high side of the system from the low side, and since there is a pressure drop across the valve, the flow of refrigerant is restricted. The state of refrigerant entering the valve is high-pressure liquid. The state of refrigerant leaving the valve is low-pressure liquid. A drop in pressure takes place without causing a change of state.

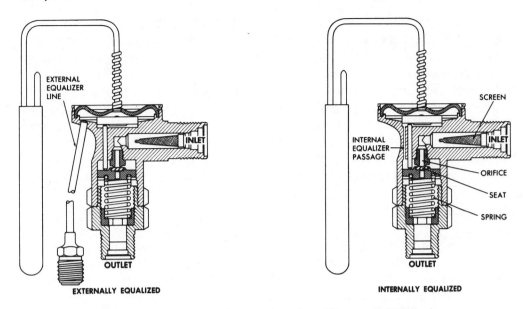

**FIGURE 3-14** Thermostatic expansion valves. (Courtesy of AC-Delco.)

## Operation

The thermostatic expansion valve has been developed for application in air-conditioning systems to control refrigerant flow to the evaporator. Regardless of any change in heat-load conditions at either the condenser or evaporator, the entire evaporator surface will be fully active throughout the cycle. By utilizing the entire evaporator surface, maximum system efficiency will be achieved.

The conventional thermostatic expansion valve does permit a small portion of the evaporator to remain less than fully active at the outlet end. This portion, which contributes very little refrigeration, is utilized to superheat in the final portion of the evaporator, which causes the expansion valve to operate.

Three forces govern operation of the thermostatic expansion valve:

1. Pressure exerted on the top of the diaphragm by the charge in the bulb.

2. Evaporator pressure under the diaphragm.

3. Superheat spring force under the diaphragm.

An orifice in the thermal expansion valve meters flow into the evaporator. To meet variable demand, the flow rate is modulated by varying the orifice opening. This is accomplished through a needle-type plunger-and-seat arrangement.

When the valve is modulating, the bulb pressure is balanced by evaporator pressure and spring force. In applications where the same refrigerant is used in both the thermostatic element and refrigeration system, each will exert the same pressure should their temperatures be identical. After the liquid refrigerant in the evaporator evaporates, suction gas is superheated and temperature increases; however, evaporator pressure, neglecting pressure drop, is unchanged. This superheated vapor, flowing through the suction line, causes the bulb temperature to rise. Since the bulb contains both vapor and liquid refrigerant, not superheated vapor alone as in the suction line, its temperature and pressure increase. This higher bulb pressure acts on the top of the diaphragm and is greater than the opposing evaporator pressure and spring force, causing the valve needle to open. The valve opens to the point where the spring force, combined with the evaporator pressure, is equal to the bulb pressure. The conventional valve uses a small orifice sized to the exact load of the system, and to minimize the high-pressure liquid inlet force a combination of large diaphragm diameter and strong superheat spring is required. The basic disadvantage of the conventional valve is that it will, because of its small orifice, operate satisfactorily only over a very narrow load range.

### Superheated Vapor

Refrigerant vapor operates at a temperature that is higher than its boiling point for a given pressure. The liquid refrigerant in the evaporator will usually completely vaporize before reaching the evaporator outlet. The cold vapors flowing through the remainder of the evaporator continue to absorb heat, becoming superheated. All expansion valves are adjusted at the factory to operate under superheat conditions present in the particular type of unit for which they are designed.

The valves used in some systems have an external equalizer line. Valves in other systems are internally equalized. The only difference between the two valves is that the former uses an equalizer line connected to the STV or POA valve as a means of sensing evaporator outlet pressure. The latter senses evaporator inlet pressure through an internal equalizer passage. Both valves have a capillary tube to sense evaporator outlet temperature.

### Location of the Thermostatic Expansion Valve Bulb (Fig. 3-15)

Since the evaporator performance depends largely upon thermostatic expansion valve control, and good valve control depends upon response to temperature change of the refrigerant gas leaving the evaporator, considerable care must be given to bulb location. It should be clamped to the suction line near the evaporator outlet. The bulb should be protected from the effect of an air stream after it is clamped to the line. Use material that will not absorb water, to prevent ice at the bulb location.

### EVAPORATOR (FIG. 3-16)

The purpose of the evaporator is to cool, dry, and clean the air that will enter the passenger compartment. The evaporator is constructed of aluminum air fins and tubes. Inlet and outlet pipes are welded to the core. The refrigerant enters the evaporator as a low-pressure mixture of liquid and vapor. The liquid boils (vaporizes) at this low pressure, absorbing large quantities of heat. The heat comes from air that passes through the evaporator fins, and will cool the air that will be directed into the passenger compartment. As heat is transferred through the walls

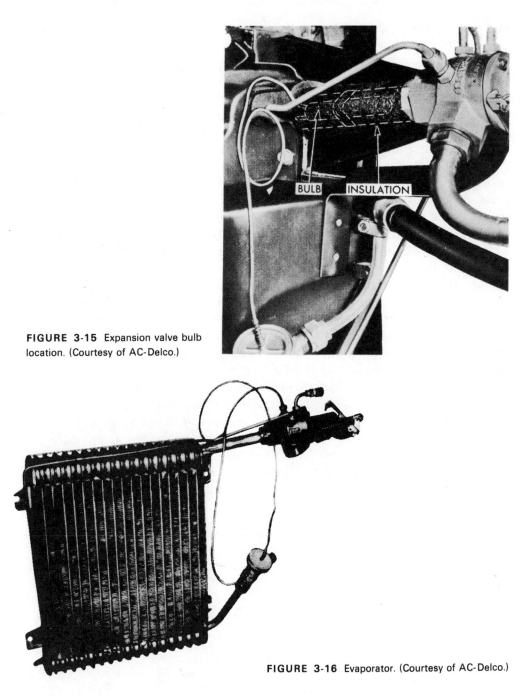

FIGURE 3-15 Expansion valve bulb location. (Courtesy of AC-Delco.)

FIGURE 3-16 Evaporator. (Courtesy of AC-Delco.)

of the evaporator from the warm air passing over it, moisture in the air condenses on its surface and is drained off, removing dust and pollen. The temperature of the evaporator must be controlled so that the water collecting on the core surface will not freeze and block off the air.

In some automotive air-conditioning systems, the evaporator is equipped with a suction throttling valve (STV), a pilot-operated absolute valve (POA) or an evaporator pressure regulator valve (EPR). In all cases the function is to control evaporator temperature.

**41**

## SUCTION THROTTLING VALVE (STV)

The suction throttling valve determines the temperature of the evaporator core by limiting the minimum evaporator pressure. The valve, in this manner, also protects the core against freeze-up, which would result in a partial or complete loss of cooling capacity. While the system is in operation, the evaporator will be held to minimum pressure of 28 psi or 193.06 kPa and will provide maximum cooling at all times. The evaporator pressure will hold at this level as long as maximum cooling is desired. The valve (Fig. 3-17), located in the evaporator outlet line, operates on a spring pressure vs. evaporator pressure principle. In operation, the flow of low-pressure vapor from the evaporator to the compressor is determined and controlled by the position of the piston in the valve body, which is, in turn, determined by the balance of the forces that are applied to the diaphragm. Refrigerant vapors flow through the valve inlet, through three openings in the lower skirt of the piston, and from there through the valve outlet and the suction hose to the compressor. A very small portion of the vapor flow is diverted to the interior of the piston through drilled holes in the piston wall. This pressure, transmitted to the inner side of the diaphragm, permits it to sense the actual pressure in the evaporator. Evaporator vapor pressure thus applied on the inner side of the diaphragm and piston assembly is balanced and opposed by spring load plus atmospheric pressure applied to the outer surface of the diaphragm. An increase of temperature (and thus pressure also) in the evaporator will cause the piston to move against the opposing spring pressure, thus opening the valve and allowing an increasing amount of vapor flow through the valve to the compressor. This, in turn, lowers the evaporator pressure and allows the piston to close as required. Evaporator pressure is thus controlled to a predetermined setting by the action of the valve in "throttling" or choking off the suction line when evaporator pressure drops below the established setting. With the line restricted, the evaporator pressure will rise. As the pressure rises above the valve setting, the valve will be forced open as required to bring the pressure down to the proper level.

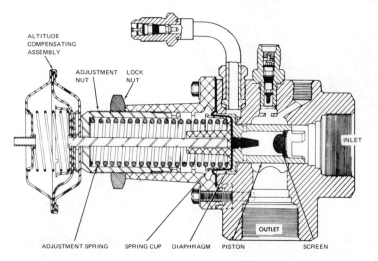

**FIGURE 3-17** Suction throttling valve—sectional view. (Courtesy of AC-Delco.)

The temperature lever on the dash control may be moved to mix heated air with the maximum-cooled air and thus temper the outlet air to a desired temperature. This action, indicating that maximum cooling is no longer needed, acts through the control cable and linkage to close a vacuum valve to which 4 to ½ in. of vacuum has been applied to the vacuum head on the STV. Loss of this vacuum increases the internal spring pressure exerted upon the STV piston and effectively increases the minimum evaporator pressure approximately 3 lbs. to 31 psi. This results in less evaporator cooling capacity.

## NOTE:

THE PRIMARY REASON FOR THIS FEATURE IS TO GUARD AGAINST EVAPORATOR FREEZE-UP WHEN OPERATING AT HIGHER ELEVATIONS. WHEN OPERATING THE SYSTEM AT ELEVATIONS IN EXCESS OF 4000 FEET, THE TEMPERATURE LEVER SHOULD BE MOVED ABOUT ½ IN.

STV valves have two ports with Schrader valves. One port is capped and utilized to obtain "low" system pressure with a manifold gauge set. The other port connects to the oil bypass line from the bottom of the evaporator. The small threaded opening near the oil-pass fitting connects to the equalizer line of the thermostatic expansion valve.

## PILOT-OPERATED ABSOLUTE VALVE (POA) (FIG. 3-18)

The function of the POA valve is to control evaporator pressure. This is accomplished in the same manner as the previously described STV valve, that is, by throttling or restricting the evaporator outlet so that the pressure within the evaporator is maintained at a predetermined point. Although the end result of using this valve in the system is the same as with the STV, there is no similarity in the operation of the two valves. As its name implies, the POA valve contains a pilot valve. This valve has a bronze evacuated bellows. The POA is referenced to the nearly perfect vacuum in this bellows rather than to atmospheric pressure as in the case of the STV. The POA, therefore, requires no external altitude-compensating device.

With the system in operation, evaporator pressure (A) is applied to the inlet fitting of the valve. This pressure passes through the piston screen and drills holes in the piston to apply itself to the area beneath the piston ring. As the evaporator pressure becomes higher, the force of the piston spring will be overcome and the piston will begin to move, gradually opening the main port to refrigerant flow (B). This action is possible because the pressure in the area (C) above the piston is less than evaporator pressure. However, as the valve is being forced open, evaporator pressure is slowly flowing through the piston bleed hole into the area (C) above the piston. As the pressure in area (C) approaches evaporator pressure (A), the spring will begin to force the piston toward its closed position. When the pressure is equal on both sides of the piston, the main port would normally be closed and any valve

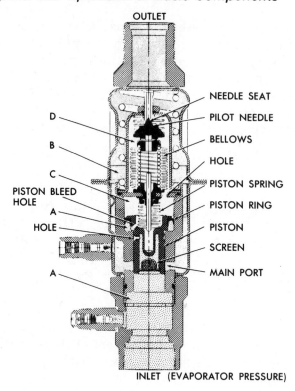

**FIGURE 3-18** Pilot operated absolute valve (POA).
(Courtesy of AC-Delco.)

would be inoperative. Here is where bellows and pilot valve come into the picture. The area (D) surrounding the bellows and needle valve is connected by a hole in the area (C) above the piston. Therefore, the pressures in area (C) and area (D) will be equal. As pressure builds up in area (C), allowing the piston spring to move the piston toward its closed position, it also builds up in area (D) surrounding the evacuated bellows. The higher pressure will begin to collapse the bellows, thus pulling the pilot needle from the needle seat. The pressure in area (D) will be reduced through the resulting orifice to the point where the bellows will expand to close the pilot needle. When the pressure is reduced in area (D), it will also be reduced in area (C), allowing evaporator pressure to overcome the force of the piston spring and move the piston to open the main port. Of course, in operation this cycle operates in such a way that the operation of the various valve components balance out to hold the piston in the proper position to maintain the predetermined control pressure and thus the desired evaporator temperature. The POA valve is preset at the factory and is not repairable. If malfunctioning, it should be replaced as a unit.

Aside from the inlet and outlet, the valve has three external connections. As with the STV valve, the POA valve has two ports with Schrader valves. One connects to the oil bypass line from the evaporator. The other is for connecting a manifold gauge set to the low-pressure side of the system. The small threaded opening connects to the equalizer line of the thermostatic expansion valve.

## EVAPORATOR EQUALIZED VALVE–IN–RECEIVER (EEVIR)

The evaporator equalized valve-in-receiver (EEVIR) assembly (Fig. 3-19) combines the expansion valve with a moisture-indicator sleeve, POA valve, receiver dehydrator, and sight glass into one unit mounted on the evaporator case. The power element or diaphragm end of the expansion valve is exposed directly to the refrigerant vapor entering the EEVIR inlet connector shell from the evaporator and controls operation of the expansion valve. The liquid sight glass is located in the valve housing as shown and provides the best advantage for checking the moisture indicator and liquid refrigerant at the inlet of the expansion valve. The drier desiccant bag is replaceable by removing the receiver shell. The expansion valve and POA capsules can be replaced by removing the inlet connector shell assembly at the top of the valve housing. The system must be completely discharged before removing the shell assembly. The EEVIR is identified by a gold-colored housing and a gold-colored expansion valve.

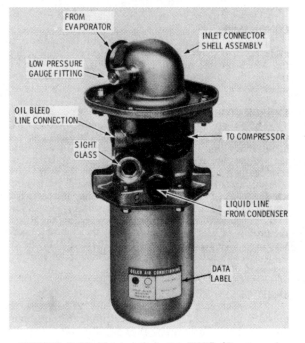

**FIGURE 3-19** Moisture indicator EEVIR. (Courtesy of Oldsmobile Division of General Motors Corp.)

### Operation (Fig. 3-20)

Liquid refrigerant from the condenser flows into the liquid intake port of the valve housing to the receiver, where it comes in contact with the drier desiccant. Liquid refrigerant flows directly from the receiver through the filter screen at the bottom of the liquid pickup tube, through the pickup tube, to the lower portion of the expansion valve cavity. The expansion valve meters the liquid refrigerant to the evaporator.

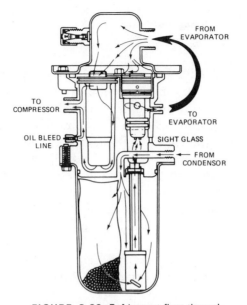

**FIGURE 3-20** Refrigerant flow through EEVIR. (Courtesy of Oldsmobile Division of General Motors Corp.)

Refrigerant vapor from the evaporator returns through the inlet connector shell assembly at the top of the EEVIR assembly, and the POA valve regulates the rate of refrigerant flow back to the compressor. The evaporator gauge fitting is also located in the inlet connector shell assembly. The liquid bleed fitting is located in the valve housing and vents directly into the suction outlet of the POA valve. The liquid bleed valve opens to bypass oil mixed with liquid refrigerant when the pressure differential between the evaporator pressure and suction pressure is greater than 10 to 20 psi. This ensures the return of oil to the compressor under low refrigerant charge or low evaporator load conditions. The valve is closed below 10 psi pressure differiential to prevent loss of capacity.

**Thermostatic Expansion Valve**

The expansion valve is located in the EEVIR unit (Fig. 3-21). This valve controls the flow of refrigerant to the evaporator by sensing the temperature and pressure of the refrigerant gas as it passes through the VIR unit on the return to the compressor.

The pressure within the power diaphragm of the expansion valve is affected by the temperature of the return of refrigerant passing through the EEVIR inlet connector shell assembly to the inlet of the POA valve.

With the EEVIR assembly, the equalizer function is accomplished by permitting pressure within the inlet connector shell assembly to be transmitted to the expansion valve equalizer port.

The diaphragm is assembled into the valve body, crimped in place, and charged with a specific amount of R-13 refrigerant. The opening is then sealed with a steel ball plug.

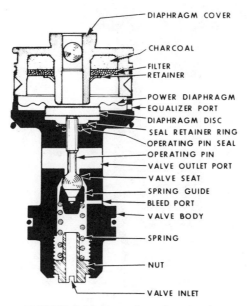

**FIGURE 3-21** Expansion valve capsule. (Courtesy of Oldsmobile Division of General Motors Corp.)

The operating pin, spring guide, adjusting spring, and adjusting nut are assembled into the valve body and the valve adjusted to a predetermined operating range.

The expansion valve meters the flow of refrigerant to the evaporator in response to the pressure–temperature changes to maintain a flooded evaporator for maximum cooling efficiency. The valve operation is basically the same as that described for previous expansion valves, with external sensing bulb and equalizer connections. The valve is factory-set and is not adjustable. When it is determined that the valve is malfunctioning, it must be replaced.

**Pilot-Operated Absolute Valve**

*DESCRIPTION (FIG. 3-22)*

The POA valve is located in the EEVIR unit next to the expansion valve. This valve controls the flow of refrigerant from the evaporator to maintain a constant evaporator pressure of 29.5 psi. At this pressure the evaporator temperature is maintained at approximately 32°F. Should the evaporator pressure drop much lower than 29.5 psi, it is possible that ice would form in the finned area of the evaporator and block the air flow through the coil.

The capability of the valve to maintain 29.5 psi is dependent on compressor capacity. At low compressor speed and high evaporator load, the pressure may be well above 29.5 psi and the valve could be wide open. At high compressor speed and low evaporator load, the valve closes and restricts the flow of the refrigerant from the evaporator to maintain evaporator pressure to no lower pressure than 29.5 psi. The POA valve is factory-set and is not adjustable. When it is determined that the valve is malfunctioning, the complete POA valve must be replaced.

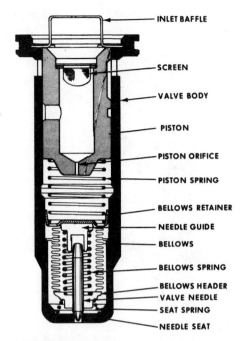

INLET BAFFLE

SCREEN

VALVE BODY

PISTON

PISTON ORIFICE

PISTON SPRING

BELLOWS RETAINER

NEEDLE GUIDE

BELLOWS

BELLOWS SPRING

BELLOWS HEADER
VALVE NEEDLE
SEAT SPRING
NEEDLE SEAT

**FIGURE 3-22** POA valve operation. (Courtesy of Oldsmobile Division of General Motors Corp.)

## OPERATION

Freon from the evaporator enters at the top of the POA valve at the baffle, goes through the screen, and to the piston. Freon then goes through the piston orifice to the chamber below the piston. From here Freon goes through the bellows retainer to surround the bellows. The bellows is evacuated and controls needle valve movement. The spring inside the bellows references it to 29.5 psi. The bellows controls Freon pressure below the piston, thereby setting piston position. When evaporator pressure is under the piston, the piston moves down to open the evaporator to compressor suction. When evaporator pressure drops below 29.5 psi, the bellows expands and seats the needle. This increases Freon pressure below the piston, which, with the piston spring, moves the piston up, closing the evaporator from compressor suction.

### Moisture-Indicator Sleeve

A moisture indicator has been added to the evaporator equalized valve-in-receiver (EEVIR) assembly to provide a visual moisture check of the internal air-conditioning system. The moisture indicator consists of a sleeve with a moisture-sensitive coating assembled to the lower end of the expansion valve capsule (Fig. 3-23). The sleeve is visible through the EEVIR assembly sight glass and changes in color from blue (dry system) to pink (wet system) or white (very wet). A dry-wet condition color guide has been added to the EEVIR data label as a visual guide for color comparison. The purpose of the moisture indicator is to assist in the proper diagnosis of an air-conditioning system's malfunction resulting from moisture in the system.

EXPANSION VALVE

MOISTURE INDICATOR
SLEEVE

**FIGURE 3-23** Moisture indicator sleeve. (Courtesy of Oldsmobile Division of General Motors Corp.)

The moisture-indicator sleeve will change from pink to blue when the system is operated after the desiccant has been replaced and the system evacuated and charged with refrigerant if the system is dry. The moisture-indicator sleeve must be replaced whenever the desiccant is replaced. If the system still shows wet, the car should be placed back into service (normal driving) for 1 or 2 days (assuming that the refrigerant system performs normally) to recheck the moisture-indicator color. If the system still shows wet, again replace the desiccant. To check the moisture indicator, proceed as follows:

**NOTE:**

DO NOT CHECK THE MOISTURE-INDICATOR COLOR BEFORE OPERATING AND CHECKING THE SYSTEM ACCORDING TO THE FOLLOWING PROCEDURE. IF THE SYSTEM IS NOT AT NORMAL OPERATING TEMPERATURE, A DRY SYSTEM WITH A SMALL AMOUNT OF MOISTURE COULD BE INDICATED AS WET.

1. Jump thermal limiter connector B to C and set the A/C controls on MAX.

2. Operate the engine on high idle until the A/C system is stabilized. Check for the following conditions:

   a. Repeated blown thermal limiter fuse.

   b. Warmer-than-normal A/C outlet temperature.

   c. Reduced air volume from A/C outlets.

3. Feel the liquid line at a point close to the inlet of the EEVIR assembly. The line must be warm to the touch before observing the color of the moisture indicator (approximately 120°F or 49°C or greater).

4. Observe the color of the moisture indicator through the sight glass. If the color is other than blue or a blue tint, discharge the system according to procedures.

**VIR and EEVIR Assemblies**

There are two basic designs of the VIR, with a third variation. The original design (black label) has the equalizer port between the POA capsule cavity and the TXV capsule diaphragm of the valve body. The latest design, designated EEVIR (red label), does not have an equalizer port between the valve cavities, but the top O-ring is left off the TXV to permit evaporator pressure to pass through to the diaphragm area. The EEVIR will replace the VIR as an assembly *only*.

> **NOTE:**
>
> THERE ARE TWO SPECIFIC COMPONENTS OF THE EEVIR THAT MUST *NOT* BE INTERCHANGED WITH THE EARLY DESIGN:
>
> 1.   The valve housing.
>
> 2.   The expansion valve capsule.

Also, on the original VIR, the expansion valve has an O-ring in the upper groove which must *not* be used in the EEVIR.

**EVAPORATOR PRESSURE REGULATOR (EPR) and EVAPORATOR TEMPERATURE REGULATOR (ETR) VALVES**

The evaporator pressure regulator (EPR) valve (Fig. 3-24) or the evaporator temperature regulator (ETR) valve (Fig. 3-25) is installed in the Chrysler compressor suction passage. It is accessible after the compressor inlet or suction fitting is removed.

The EPR valve was the original design. In the early 1970s, the ETR valve was used with automatic-temperature-control systems. Currently, all Chrysler systems with evaporator pressure control use a modified EPR valve. It is fully interchangeable with early EPR and ETR valves.

Evaporator pressure is regulated by a modulating valve located in the suction or inlet side of the compressor EPR valve. It is pressure-sensitive and its operation is entirely automatic. As the temperature of the evaporator approaches the frosting point, the refrigerant pressure gets lower. A pressure-sensitive bellows in the valve reacts to this reduced pressure and the EPR valve begins to close. The valve never closes completely, just enough to modulate the refrigerant flow. Restricting the flow of refrigerant gas slows down the cooling process so that moisture on the evaporator will not freeze. As long as the evaporator pressure is above 26 psi or 179 kPa, this pressure acting on the diaphragm will compress the spring and hold the valve open to permit free passage of refrigerant through the valve. As the refrigerant pressure drops below 26 psi or 179 kPa, the valve will tend to close, and this restriction of refrigerant flow will increase evaporator outlet pressure and evaporator core temperature. The valve will maintain an evaporator outlet pressure between 22 psi (152 kPa) and 26 psi (179 kPa). The main function of the EPR valve is the same as the POA or suction throttling valve.

(a)                  (b)

**FIGURE 3-24** (a) Early model evaporator pressure regulator valve (EPR); (b) late model evaporator pressure regulator valve (EPR). (Courtesy of the Chrysler Corporation.)

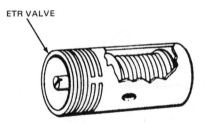

**FIGURE 3-25** ETR valve. (Courtesy of AC-Delco.)

## FORD EXPANSION AND SUCTION THROTTLING VALVE

A combination valve (Fig. 3-26) is installed on some Ford systems, combining the TXV and STV in a single assembly. The combination valve is mounted at the evaporator. However, the system has a separate receiver-dehydrator at the condenser and no sight glass. Otherwise, it functions the same as the EEVIR. Original designs of the combination valve had an equalizer port between the TXV and STV. Later designs have eliminated this equalizer by notching the valve seat. A calibrated Schrader valve (liquid bleed valve) is part of the combination valve assembly, as well as a pressure gauge port with a noncalibrated Schrader valve.

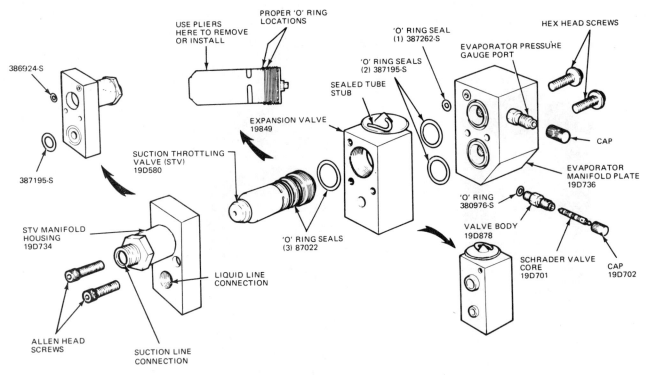

**FIGURE 3-26** Combination valve (TXV & STV) Ford. (Courtesy of AC-Delco.)

## THERMOSTATIC SWITCH SCHEMATIC (FIG. 3-27)

In a cycling air-conditioning system, the clutch is intermittently energized and deenergized through the use of a thermostatic switch in the electrical control circuit. The thermostatic switch senses evaporator temperature and is in series with the compressor clutch electrical circuit. The opening and closing of the switch contacts will cycle the compressor. When the temperature of the evaporator approaches the freezing point, the thermostatic switch opens the circuit and disengages the compressor clutch. The compressor remains inoperative until the evaporator temperature rises to the present temperature, at which time the switch closes and compressor operation resumes. If the thermostatic switch fails in the open position, there will be no electrical circuit to the compressor clutch and the compressor will not operate. If the switch fails in the closed position, the clutch will be engaged and the compressor will run continuously, which may result in the evaporator freezing up. Operationally, the thermostatic switch incorporates a capillary tube that senses evaporator discharge air temperature. With a high temperature the thermostatic switch is closed and the compressor clutch is energized. As the evaporator discharge air temperature drops to a preset level, the thermostatic switch opens the circuit to the compressor clutch and the compressor ceases to operate until such time as the evaporator temperature rises above the switch setting. In effect, the thermostatic switch is calibrated to allow the lowest possible evaporator discharge air temperature that will prevent the freezing of condensation that might form on the evaporator. The temperature control depends on intermittent operation of the compressor. During some A/C operating conditions, slight increase and decrease of engine speed may be noticed. This should be considered normal, as the system is designed to cycle the compressor.

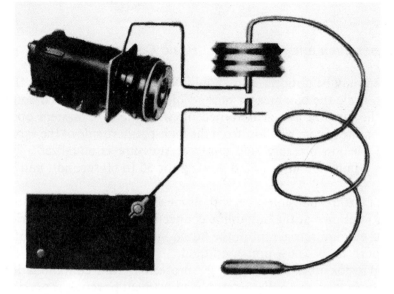

FIGURE 3-27 Thermostatic switch schematic. (Courtesy of AC-Delco.)

There are two types of thermostats; capillary tube, which are used on factory-installed air-conditioning units, and bimetal thermostats, which are used on after-market air-conditioning units.

### Cycling Clutch Expansion Tube (CCOT) Fig. 3-28

The CCOT refrigerant control system operates on the basic principle that a temperature-sensing switch turns the compressor on and off to prevent evaporator freeze-up. As the A/C compressor pumps refrigerant through the system, it will run only as long as necessary to maintain in-car comfort.

During some A/C operating conditions, slight increases and decreases of

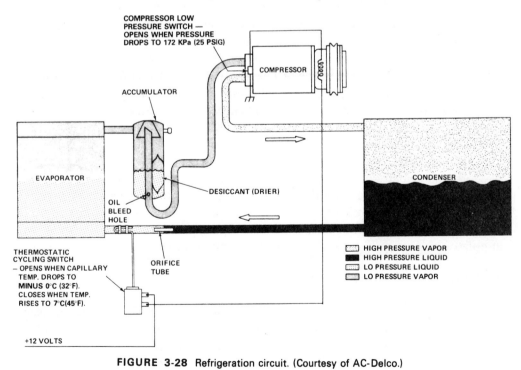

FIGURE 3-28 Refrigeration circuit. (Courtesy of AC-Delco.)

engine speed may be noticed. This should be considered normal, as the system is designed to cycle the compressor on and off to maintain desired cooling.

When the ignition switch is turned off with the A/C system operating, the refrigerant in the system will flow from the high-pressure side of the expansion tube (orifice) to the low-pressure side until the pressure is equalized. This may be detected as a faint sound of liquid flowing for 30 to 60 seconds, and is a normal condition.

The plastic expansion tube, with its mesh screen and orifice, is located in the evaporator inlet pipe at the liquid-line connection. It provides a restriction to the high-pressure liquid refrigerant in the liquid line, metering the flow of refrigerant to the evaporator as a low-pressure liquid.

The expansion tube and orifice are protected from contamination by filter screens on both inlet and outlet sides. No adjustment or repair is possible, and it is serviced as an assembly (Fig. 3-29).

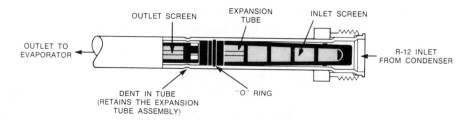

**FIGURE 3-29** Expansion tube.

### OPERATION OF CCOT

The radial four (R-4) or the axial six (A-6) compressor discharges high-temperature, high-pressure vapor into the condenser, where it releases heat to the air stream and changes to a medium-temperature high-pressure liquid. This liquid flows through the liquid line to the orifice where it undergoes rapid expansion and changes from a medium-temperature, high-pressure liquid to a low-temperature, low-pressure liquid and vapor mixture. This mixture enters the evaporator core at the bottom and flows upward through the core. Heat from the warm air stream passing through the core is transferred to the refrigerant, vaporizing the liquid and cooling the air.

Under high-load conditions, all the liquid is vaporized in the evaporator and only vapors flow to the accumulator and through the suction line to the compressor, and the cycle is repeated.

Under light-load conditions, the liquid and vapor are separated in the accumulator so that only vapor is drawn into the compressor.

### Compressor Cutoff Switch

If the CCOT system loses its refrigerant charge, the compressor (low-pressure) cutoff switch will sense the reduction in head pressure and open the electrical circuit to the compressor clutch, turning off the compressor to prevent internal damage.

Some units use a cutoff switch mounted in the compressor head which senses compressor high-side pressure. The switch is a single-contact type that completes the compressor coil ground circuit when ambient air temperature causes sufficient rise in refrigerant pressure to close the contacts about $25 \pm 5$ psi ($170 \pm$ kPa) (Fig. 3-30).

**FIGURE 3-30** Cut-off switch location R-4 compressor. (Courtesy of AC-Delco.)

**Thermostatic Switch (Fig. 3-31)**

The thermostatic switch is operated by a small bellows, which in turn is connected to a metallic tube which is charged with R-22. The tube is positioned on the evaporator inlet pipe and secured by two clamps. As the temperature of the evaporator decreases, the charge inside the tube contracts, reducing the pressure on the switch bellows.

The switch contacts open, and the compressor clutch disengages. With the compressor off, the temperature at the evaporator rises, causing the charge inside the tube to expand and exert pressure on the bellows. The expansion of the bellows closes the switch contacts, causing the compressor to engage. In this way, the compressor cycles off and on to maintain the proper temperature at the evaporator.

**FIGURE 3-31** Thermostatic swtich. (Courtesy of AC-Delco.)

**Accumulator (Fig. 3-32)**

Connected to the evaporator outlet pipe, the sealed accumulator assembly acts as a refrigerant storing container, receiving vapors and some liquid and refrigerant oil from the evaporator. At the bottom of the accumulator is the desiccant, which acts as a drying agent for moisture that may have entered the system. An oil bleed hole is also located near the bottom of the accumulator outlet pipe to provide an oil-return path to the compressor.

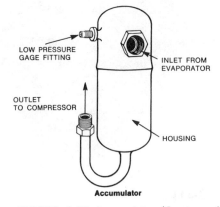

FIGURE 3-32 Accumulator. (Courtesy of AC-Delco.)

**CCOT Quick Check**

This hand-feel procedure can be used to determine whether the system has the proper charge of refrigerant. The ambient temperature must be above 70°F (21°C) and the engine must be warm and at normal idle.

1. Hood and doors must be open.

2. Temperature lever in the normal position.

3. Selector lever in the normal position.

4. Fan blower on high.

With the compressor engaged, feel the evaporator inlet pipe near the thermostatic switch capillary tube connection and the accumulator surface.

1. If they are both the same temperature and somewhat cooler than ambient temperature, the refrigerant charge is O.K.

2. If the inlet pipe is cooler than the accumulator, the system has a low refrigerant charge. Add a small amount of refrigerant until both feel the same temperature. Allow the system to stabilize and add one can (14 oz) of refrigerant.

3. If the inlet pipe has frost and the accumulator is warm, repeat step 2.

## SAFETY CONTROLS

### General Motors

*AMBIENT SWITCH (FIG. 3-33)*

The ambient switch senses the outside air temperature and is designed to prevent compressor clutch engagement when air conditioning is not required or when compressor operation might cause internal damage to seals and other parts. The switch is in series with the compressor clutch electrical circuit and closes about 32°F (0°C). At all lower temperatures, the switch is open to prevent clutch engagement. The ambient switch is located in the air inlet ducts to the air-conditioning system, which are regulated by evaporator pressure controls. This switch is found only on the POA, VIR, and the EEVIR systems.

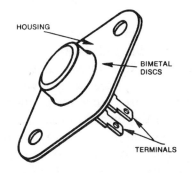

**FIGURE 3-33** Ambient compressor switch. (Courtesy of AC-Delco.)

*THERMAL LIMITER AND SUPERHEAT SWITCH (FIG. 3-34)*

A thermal limiter (fuse) and superheat switch, designed to protect the air-conditioning compressor against damage when the refrigerant is totally or partially lost, is incorporated in late-model GM cars. The thermal fuse may be located in various underhood locations and the superheat switch is located in the rear head of the compressor. The fuse and switch are connected in series. A wiring diagram of the fuse and switch electrical system is shown in Fig. 3-35.

**FIGURE 3-34** Superheat switch and thermal limiter. (Courtesy of AC-Delco.)

**SUPERHEAT SWITCH**                  **THERMAL FUSE**

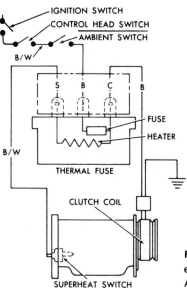

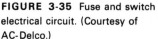

IGNITION SWITCH
CONTROL HEAD SWITCH
AMBIENT SWITCH
B/W
S  B  C  B
FUSE
HEATER
B/W
THERMAL FUSE
CLUTCH COIL
SUPERHEAT SWITCH

FIGURE 3-35 Fuse and switch electrical circuit. (Courtesy of AC-Delco.)

When the air-conditioning system is operating, current flows through the control head switch, ambient switch, and the thermal fuse to the clutch coil to energize the compressor clutch. If a total or partial loss of refrigerant occurs, the contacts in the superheat switch close, because the switch senses low system pressure and high suction gas temperature. When the contacts close, current flows to energize a resistor-type heater in the thermal fuse.

The heat will melt the fuse link and the circuit to the compressor clutch coil will open. The compressor will cease to operate and damage to the system will be prevented. Before the thermal fuse is replaced, the cause of the refrigerant loss must be corrected. The thermal limiter will also blow under a high-temperature, low-pressure gas condition entering the compressor, such as a stuck TXV in the closed position or a POA stuck closed.

### PRESSURE RELIEF VALVE (IN COMPRESSOR)

If the compressor discharge pressure becomes too high, a pressure relief valve opens at 440 lb (3033 kPa) to release excessive pressure. It closes again when the pressure is reduced. Opening of the relief valve may cause a loud popping noise and perhaps some loss of oil with the refrigerant. Any condition that causes this valve to open should be corrected immediately.

## Chrysler

### LOW-PRESSURE CUTOFF SWITCH (FIG. 3-36)

The lowpressure cutoff switch, which is located on the filter-drier (receiver-dehydrator), is connected in series with the compressor clutch. If the refrigerant pressure drops below the control point of the switch, the switch will open and cut off the electrical supply to the compressor clutch. The switch is a sealed unit and no attempt should be made to adjust or repair it. Whenever the system is shut down by the low-pressure cutoff switch due to the loss of refrigerant,

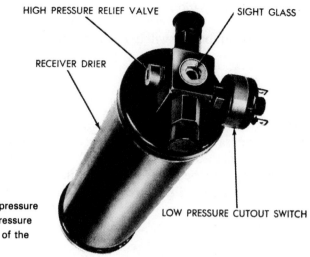

HIGH PRESSURE RELIEF VALVE    SIGHT GLASS

RECEIVER DRIER

LOW PRESSURE CUTOUT SWITCH

**FIGURE 3-36** Low pressure
cutout switch. High pressure
relief valve. (Courtesy of the
Chrysler Corporation.)

oil in the compressor may also have been lost. Therefore, to prevent damage to the compressor, the leak must be repaired and the compressor oil level checked. The low-pressure cutoff switch also acts as an ambient switch by shutting off the compressor during low temperatures. Chrysler installs this switch on the receiver-dehydrator. GM uses this switch on the discharge part of the system.

### HIGH-PRESSURE RELIEF VALVE (FIG. 3-36)

The high-pressure relief valve is located on the receiver-dehydrator opposite the low-pressure cutoff switch. Its function is to prevent damage to the air-conditioning system in the event that excessive pressure develops due to condenser air flow being restricted. The high-pressure relief valve allows only a small amount of refrigerant to escape, and then it will reseat itself when the excessive pressure has been reduced. The valve is calibrated to vent at a pressure of 450 to 550 psi (3102 to 3792 kPa).

## American Motors

### AIR-CONDITIONING THERMOSTAT

The air-conditioning thermostat "cycles" the compressor on and off to prevent evaporator freeze up.

The fan switch must be on to operate the air conditioner.

### OVERRIDE SWITCH

The override switch (ambient switch) is located on the right side in front of the radiator. It will prevent compressor operation when the outside temperature is below 50°F (10°C).

## Ford

### AMBIENT-TEMPERATURE SWITCH

At about 55°F (12.7°C) ambient temperature, the ambient switch located in front of the condenser will close to complete the circuit to the compressor clutch.

Below 40°F (4.4°C) the ambient switch is open and the compressor cannot operate.

### THERMOSTATIC (DE-ICING) SWITCH

The thermostatic (de-icing) switch is connected in series with the magnetic clutch and controls the operation of the compressor. The temperature-sensing tube of the de-icing switch is placed in contact with the evaporator fins. When the temperature of the evaporator becomes too cold, the de-icing switch opens the magnetic clutch electrical circuit, disconnecting the compressor from the engine.

### HIGH-PRESSURE RELIEF VALVE

Under extreme conditions, the valve will open, allowing refrigerant vapor to escape to prevent damage to the compressor.

### REVIEW QUESTIONS

1. What position is the normal operating position of the stem-type service valve?

2. Which position would the stem-type service valve be in to isolate the compressor?

3. What is the purpose of a magnetic clutch?

4. The condenser changes high-pressure _____ to high-pressure _____.

5. What is the purpose of the receiver-dehydrator?

6. What does the thermal expansion valve do?

7. The thermal expansion valve bulb should be connected to the _____.

8. What is the purpose of the evaporator?

9. What does VIR mean?

10. What does EEVIR mean?

11. What is the main difference between the VIR and the EEVIR?

12. What does EPR mean?

13. What does the EPR do?

14. What does CCOT mean?

15. What does the accumulator do in the system?

# Chapter 4

# Air-Conditioning Service

One of the most important things, in air-conditioning diagnosis, is that the air-conditioning system be checked out thoroughly. An understanding of the proper operating characteristics of the components is helpful in system diagnosis.

The complaint of a new owner may be due to his not fully understanding how to operate the controls. The serviceman and the owner should understand the functions of these controls, which change from car to car and year to year.

A visual check should be made to see if the compressor is running or if the fan belts are tight. After 5 minutes of compressor operation, check the sight glass to see if it is clear and no bubbles are present. On a cool day some bubbles may appear in a properly charged system.

Air-conditioner malfunctions may be traced to the air flow system, or the electrical system, or the refrigeration system. Insufficient cooling may be traced to air flow through the heater, improper engine idle speed, or warm-air leaks from the engine compartment through the firewall. Air leaks around the doors and the windows can cause insufficient cooling.

## VISUAL TESTS

Some visual tests that can be made if the compressor is not operating:

1. Fan belts.

2. Clutch coil terminal connector.

3. Compressor frozen.

4. Fuse blown.

5.  Ambient-temperature switch.

6.  Superheat switch.

7.  Low-pressure switch.

8.  Bad ground.

9.  Control switch.

Blower motor not operating:

1.  Fuse.

2.  Frozen blower motor.

3.  Control switch.

Check the operation of the doors that direct the air flow into the passenger compartment.

To determine if the air-conditioning system is operating properly and efficiently, it must be performance-tested. Discharge air and refrigerant pressures must be to specifications. Test conditions also vary. You may have to refer back to a particular shop manual for the correct operating conditions for the performance test.

After a visual check of the system has been made, and nothing was found defective, a pressure test should be made. To make a pressure test, a manifold gauge set should be used.

## PRESSURE TESTS

### Manifold Gauge Set

The gauge set shown in Fig. 4-1 is one of the most valuable of the air-conditioning tools. It is used when discharging, charging, evacuating, and for diagnosing trouble in the system.

The gauge at the left is the low-pressure gauge. The dial is graduated into pounds of pressure from 0 to 100 lb (0 to 689.50 kPa) and, in the opposite direction, in inches of vacuum from 0 to 30 in. This is the gauge that should always be used in checking pressure on the low side of the system.

The gauge at the right is graduated from 0 to 300 lb (0 to 2058.50 kPa). This is the high-pressure on the high-pressure side of the system.

The center manifold fitting is common to both the low and high sides and is for evacuating or adding refrigerant to the system. When this fitting is not being used, it should be capped. A hose connected to the fitting directly under the low-side gauge is used to connect the low side of the test manifold to the low side of the system, and a similar connection is found on the high side. The gauge manifold is designed to control refrigerant flow. When the manifold test set is connected into the system, pressure is registered on both gauges at all times. During the tests, both the low and high-side hand valves are in closed position.

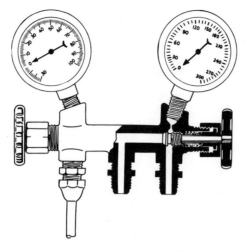

**FIGURE 4-1** Manifold gauge set. (Courtesy of
AC-Delco.)

Refrigerant will flow around the valve stem to the respective gauges and register the system low-side pressure on the low-side gauge and the high-side pressure on the high-side gauge. The hand valves isolate the low- and high-side pressures from the central portion of the manifold. When gauges are connected to the gauge fittings with the system charged, the gauge lines should always be purged. Purging is done by "cracking" each valve on the gauge set to allow the pressure of the refrigerant to force the air to escape through the center line. Failure to purge lines may result in air or other contaminants entering the system.

**CAUTION:**

ALWAYS WEAR GOGGLES TO PROTECT THE EYES WHEN WORKING WITH REFRIGERANT CONTAINERS AND OPENING REFRIGERANT CONNECTIONS IN THE AIR-CONDITIONING SYSTEM.

### Schrader-Type Service Valve (Fig. 4-2)

A Schrader-type valve is similar to a regular tire valve and is used on GM and other late-model automobiles. Most test hoses incorporate a valve core depressor that

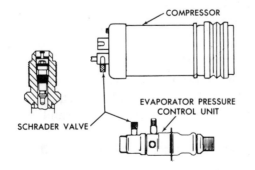

**FIGURE 4-2** Schrader-type service valve.
(Courtesy of AC-Delco.)

will unseat the valve core when connected. If not, a separate adapter fitting must be installed before connecting the test hose.

*CONNECTING MANIFOLD GAUGE SET*

**CAUTION:**

**WEAR SAFETY GOGGLES.**

1. With engine stopped, remove the protector caps from the service test fittings.

2. Be certain that all valves on the manifold gauge set are closed.

3. Leave the center hose connection on the manifold capped or connect the hose to a refrigerant storage container.

4. Connect the high-pressure hose to the test fitting on the high side of the system.

5. Purge the test hoses by opening the high-pressure manifold valve one turn. Crack open the low-pressure manifold valve and allow refrigerant vapor to hiss from the low-pressure hose for three seconds. Close both valves and then connect the low-pressure hose to the test fitting on the low side of the system. Also purge the center manifold connection by opening either valve slightly and cracking the manifold cap for three seconds. If the center manifold is connected to a hose to a refrigerant supply, purge the supply hose as well.

6. Before accurate pressure tests can be made, the system must be stabilized.

**Stabilizing Procedure**

1. Start the engine and adjust to 1500 to 2000 rpm.

2. Turn the air conditioner and set for maximum cooling (fresh air) with the blower fan on high speed.

3. Close car doors and windows.

4. Operate the air conditioner for five minutes to stabilize the system.

5. Check the refrigerant charge by noting the sight glass indication.

6. Check for normal high and low system pressure (refer to performance, Tables 4-1, 4-2 and 4-3). An insufficient charge will be indicated by the high-side gauge registering lower than normal pressure.

If a low refrigerant charge is indicated is indicated by the gauge or sight-glass reading, the system should be leak-tested and charged before accurate tests can be performed.

**TABLE 4-1**  Performance Table.

| IN FRONT OF CONDENSER | | | | | Discharge Air Temperature | | High Pressure | |
|---|---|---|---|---|---|---|---|---|
| Relative Humidity (%) | Air Temp. °F | °C | Evaporator Pressure | Engine Speed (rpm) | °F | °C | psi | kPa |
| 20 | 70 | 21 | 29.5 | 2000 | 40 | 4 | 150 | 1034.25 |
| | 80 | 27 | 29.5 | | 44 | 7 | 190 | 1310.05 |
| | 90 | 32 | 30.0 | | 48 | 9 | 245 | 1689.27 |
| | 100 | 38 | 31.0 | | 57 | 14 | 305 | 2102.97 |
| 30 | 70 | 21 | 29.5 | 2000 | 42 | 6 | 150 | 1034.25 |
| | 80 | 27 | 30.0 | | 47 | 8 | 205 | 1413.47 |
| | 90 | 32 | 31.0 | | 51 | 11 | 265 | 1827.17 |
| | 100 | 38 | 32.0 | | 61 | 16 | 325 | 2240.87 |
| 40 | 70 | 21 | 29.5 | 2000 | 45 | 7 | 165 | 1137.67 |
| | 80 | 27 | 30.0 | | 49 | 9 | 215 | 1482.42 |
| | 90 | 32 | 32.0 | | 55 | 13 | 280 | 1930.60 |
| | 100 | 38 | 39.0 | | 65 | 18 | 345 | 2378.77 |
| 50 | 70 | 21 | 30.0 | 2000 | 47 | 8 | 180 | 1241.10 |
| | 80 | 27 | 32.0 | | 53 | 12 | 235 | 1620.32 |
| | 90 | 32 | 34.0 | | 59 | 15 | 295 | 2034.02 |
| | 100 | 38 | 40.0 | | 69 | 21 | 350 | 2413.25 |
| 60 | 70 | 21 | 30.0 | 2000 | 48 | 9 | 180 | 1241.10 |
| | 80 | 27 | 33.0 | | 56 | 13 | 240 | 1654.80 |
| | 90 | 32 | 36.0 | | 63 | 17 | 300 | 2068.50 |
| | 100 | 38 | 43.0 | | 73 | 23 | 360 | 2482.20 |
| 70 | 70 | 21 | 30.0 | 2000 | 50 | 10 | 185 | 1275.57 |
| | 80 | 27 | 34.0 | | 58 | 14 | 245 | 1689.27 |
| | 90 | 32 | 38.0 | | 65 | 18 | 305 | 2102.97 |
| | 100 | 38 | 44.0 | | 75 | 24 | 365 | 2516.67 |
| 80 | 70 | 21 | 30.0 | 2000 | 50 | 10 | 190 | 1310.05 |
| | 80 | 27 | 34.0 | | 59 | 15 | 250 | 1723.75 |
| | 90 | 32 | 39.0 | | 67 | 19 | 310 | 2137.45 |
| 90 | 70 | 21 | 30.0 | 2000 | 50 | 10 | 200 | 1379.00 |
| | 80 | 27 | 36.0 | | 62 | 17 | 265 | 1827.17 |
| | 90 | 32 | 42.0 | | 71 | 22 | 330 | 2275.35 |

**TABLE 4-2** AMC Performance Table.

| Relative Humidity | Air Temp. | | Engine Speed | Discharge Air Temp. | | Suction Pressure | | High Pressure | |
|---|---|---|---|---|---|---|---|---|---|
| (%) | °F | °C | (rpm) | °F | °C | psi | kPa | psi | kPa |
| 20 | 70 | 21 | 1500 | 40 | 4 | 11 | 75.84 | 177 | 1220.41 |
| | 80 | 27 | | 41 | 5 | 15 | 103.42 | 208 | 1434.16 |
| | 90 | 32 | | 42 | 5.6 | 20 | 137.90 | 226 | 1558.27 |
| | 100 | 37 | | 43 | 6.1 | 23 | 158.58 | 255 | 1758.22 |
| 30 | 70 | 21 | 1500 | 40 | 4 | 12 | 82.74 | 181 | 1247.99 |
| | 80 | 27 | | 41 | 5 | 16 | 110.32 | 214 | 1475.53 |
| | 90 | 32 | | 42 | 5.6 | 22 | 151.69 | 234 | 1613.43 |
| | 100 | 37 | | 44 | 6.7 | 26 | 179.27 | 267 | 1840.96 |
| 40 | 70 | 21 | 1500 | 40 | 4 | 13 | 89.63 | 185 | 1275.57 |
| | 80 | 27 | | 42 | 5.6 | 18 | 124.11 | 220 | 1516.90 |
| | 90 | 32 | | 43 | 6.1 | 23 | 158.58 | 243 | 1675.48 |
| | 100 | 37 | | 44 | 6.7 | 26 | 179.27 | 278 | 1916.81 |
| 50 | 70 | 21 | 1500 | 40 | 4 | 14 | 96.53 | 189 | 1303.15 |
| | 80 | 27 | | 42 | 5.6 | 19 | 131.00 | 226 | 1558.27 |
| | 90 | 32 | | 44 | 6.7 | 25 | 172.37 | 251 | 1730.64 |
| | 100 | 37 | | 46 | 7.8 | 27 | 186.16 | 289 | 1992.65 |
| 60 | 70 | 21 | 1500 | 41 | 5 | 15 | 103.42 | 193 | 1330.73 |
| | 80 | 27 | | 43 | 6.1 | 21 | 144.79 | 233 | 1606.53 |
| | 90 | 32 | | 45 | 7.2 | 25 | 172.37 | 259 | 1785.80 |
| | 100 | 37 | | 46 | 7.8 | 28 | 193.06 | 300 | 2068.50 |
| 70 | 70 | 21 | 1500 | 41 | 5 | 16 | 110.32 | 198 | 1365.21 |
| | 80 | 27 | | 43 | 6.1 | 22 | 151.69 | 238 | 1641.01 |
| | 90 | 32 | | 45 | 7.2 | 26 | 179.27 | 267 | 1840.96 |
| | 100 | 37 | | 46 | 7.8 | 29 | 199.95 | 312 | 2151.24 |
| 80 | 70 | 21 | 1500 | 42 | 5.6 | 18 | 124.11 | 202 | 1392.79 |
| | 80 | 27 | | 44 | 6.7 | 23 | 158.58 | 244 | 1682.38 |
| | 90 | 32 | | 47 | 8.3 | 27 | 186.16 | 277 | 1909.91 |
| | 100 | 37 | | — | — | — | — | — | — |
| 90 | 70 | 21 | 1500 | 42 | 5.6 | 19 | 131.00 | 206 | 1420.37 |
| | 80 | 27 | | 47 | 8.3 | 24 | 165.48 | 250 | 1723.75 |
| | 90 | 32 | | 48 | 8.9 | 28 | 193.06 | 284 | 1958.18 |
| | 100 | 37 | | — | — | — | — | — | — |

**TABLE 4-3** Performance Table.

| Ambient Temperature (Outside) | High Pressure[a] | STV POA VIR | Cycling Clutch TXV Rec.—Dehyd. | Cycling Clutch CCOT |
|---|---|---|---|---|
| 60°F | 120–270 | 28–31 | 7–5 | — |
| 70°F | 150–250 | 28–31 | 7–15 | 24–31 |
| 80°F | 180–275 | 28–31 | 7–15 | 24–31 |
| 90°F | 200–310 | 28–31 | 7–15 | 24–31 |
| 100°F | 230–330 | 28–35 | 10–30 | 24–32 |
| 110°F | 270–360 | 28–38 | 10–35 | 24–32 |
| 15.6°C | 827.40–1172.15 | 193.06–213.74 | 48.26–103.42 | |
| 21.1°C | 1034.25–1723.75 | 193.06–213.74 | 48.26–103.42 | 165.48–213.74 |
| 26.7°C | 1241.1–1896.12 | 193.06–213.74 | 48.26–103.42 | 165.48–213.74 |
| 32.2°C | 1379.00–2137.45 | 193.06–213.74 | 48.26–103.42 | 165.48–220.64 |
| 37.8°C | 1585.85–2275.35 | 193.06–241.32 | 68.95–206.85 | 165.48–220.64 |
| 43.4°C | 1861.65–2482.20 | 193.06–262.01 | 68.95–241.32 | 165.48–220.64 |

[a]Pressures may be slightly higher on very humid days or lower on very dry days.

**TABLE 4-4    Performance Table.**

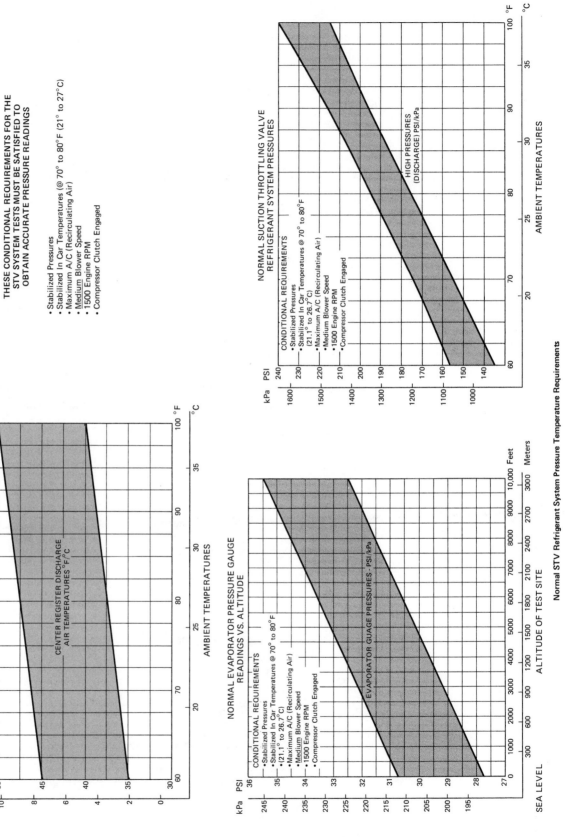

THESE CONDITIONAL REQUIREMENTS FOR THE
STV SYSTEM TESTS MUST BE SATISFIED TO
OBTAIN ACCURATE PRESSURE READINGS

• Stabilized Pressures
• Stabilized In Car Temperatures (@ 70° to 80°F (21° to 27°C)
• Maximum A/C (Recirculating Air)
• Medium Blower Speed
• 1500 Engine RPM
• Compressor Clutch Engaged

NORMAL CENTER REGISTER DISCHARGE TERMERATURES

Note: Conditional Requirements Must Be Maintained For System Being Tested

CENTER REGISTER DISCHARGE AIR TEMPERATURES °F/°C

AMBIENT TEMPERATURES

NORMAL SUCTION THROTTLING VALVE
REFRIGERANT SYSTEM PRESSURES

CONDITIONAL REQUIREMENTS
• Stabilized Pressures
• Stabilized In Car Temperatures @ 70° to 80°F (21.1° to 26.7°C)
• Maximum A/C (Recirculating Air)
• Medium Blower Speed
• 1500 Engine RPM
• Compressor Clutch Engaged

HIGH PRESSURES (DISCHARGE) PSI/kPa

AMBIENT TEMPERATURES

NORMAL EVAPORATOR PRESSURE GUAGE
READINGS VS. ALTITUDE

CONDITIONAL REQUIREMENTS
• Stabilized Pressures
• Stabilized In Car Temperatures @ 70° to 80°F
• (21.1° to 26.7°C)
• Maximum A/C (Recirculating Air)
• Medium Blower Speed
• 1500 Engine RPM
• Compressor Clutch Engaged

EVAPORATOR GUAGE PRESSURES- PSI/kPa

ALTITUDE OF TEST SITE

Normal STV Refrigerant System Pressure Temperature Requirements

**Sight-Glass Diagnosis**

At temperatures higher than 70°F (21.1°C) the sight glass may indicate whether the refrigerant charge is sufficient. A shortage of liquid refrigerant is indicated after five minutes of compressor operation by the appearance of slow-moving bubbles or a broken column of refrigerant under the glass. Continuous bubbles may appear in a properly charged system on a *cool* day. This is a normal condition. If the sight glass is generally clear and the performance is satisfactory, occasional bubbles do not indicate refrigerant shortage. If the sight glass shows foaming or a broken liquid column, partially block the air to the condenser. The high pressure should go up at least 250 psi (1723.75 kPa). If the sight glass is clear, the charge is sufficient.

**Stem-Type Service Valve**

This valve has a valve stem located under a cap opposite the hose connections (Fig. 4-3). The valve has three positions:

1. Back-seated position—the normal operating position with the valve stem rotated counterclockwise to seat the rear valve face and seal off the service gauge port.

2. Mid position—the test position with the valve stem turned clockwise 1 ½ to 2 turns to connect the service gauge port into the system so that gauge readings may be taken with the system operating. (The service gauge hose must be connected with the valve completely back-seated.)

3. Front-seated position—the valve stem has been rotated clockwise to seat the front valve face and to isolate the compressor from the system.

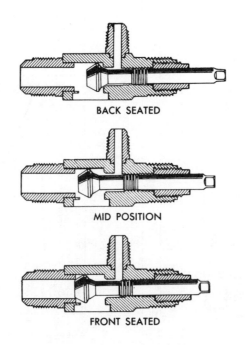

BACK SEATED

MID POSITION

FRONT SEATED

FIGURE 4-3 Service valve positions. (Courtesy of AC-Delco.)

*CONNECTING THE MANIFOLD GAUGE SET*

1. Make sure that both hand valves are closed on the manifold gauge set.

2. Remove protective caps from the low- and high-side service ports.

3. Attach the high-pressure gauge hose to the high-side service port. This service port is usually located on the compressor at the line leading to the condenser.

4. Attach the low-pressure gauge hose to the low-side service port. This service port is usually located on the compressor at the line leading to the evaporator or located at some point on the low-pressure line.

5. Mid-position both high- and low-pressure service valves by using a special ratchet wrench to turn them 1 ½ to 2 turns inward. This will connect the gauge into the system so that gauge readings may be taken with the system operating.

6. Refer to the stabilizing procedure.

If a leak is in the system, most of the refrigerant will have leaked out and pressures on the gauges will be low. To test for leaks, 1 lb. of refrigerant should be added to the system and the leak test performed.

**Ford STV and Bypass Orifice**

On some Ford products, their air-conditioning systems are equipped with a combination valve that includes the suction throttling valve (STV), and a thermal expansion valve (TXV), and a bypass orifice (BPO). To connect a gauge set into the high-pressure side of the system, a special adapter is needed. The Motorcraft part number is YT-367 or YT-373. This adapter is needed because the high-pressure port does not have a threaded stem. The adapter is designed to "snap over" the gauge port.

**Chrysler Gauge Set**

The Chrysler air-conditioning system requires three gauges. The third gauge is required to check the evaporator pressure regulator. Connect the gauges as follows (Fig. 4-4):

1. The low-pressure gauge is connected where the low-pressure line enters the compressor. It will read evaporator outlet pressure *before* the EPR valve.

2. The auxiliary low-pressure gauge is connected to a fitting on the compressor head. It will read compressor inlet pressure *after* the EPR valve.

3. The high-pressure gauge is connected to the high-pressure side and will read compressure outlet pressure.

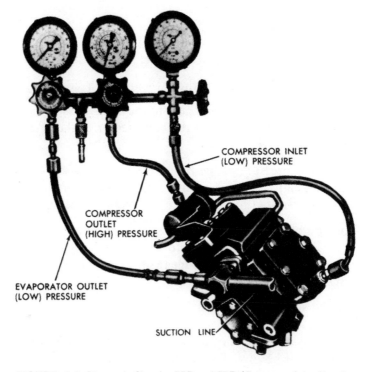

**FIGURE 4-4** Diagnosis Chrysler EPR and ETR. (Courtesy of the Chrysler Corporation.)

## LEAK TESTING

Whenever a refrigerant leak is suspected in the system, it is advisable to test for leaks. There are several leak testing methods in common use.

1. Halide leak detector (Fig. 4-5)
   Used to detect leaks by watching for the change in color of the flame when pickup hose is moved from point to point along the system.

2. Electrical leak detector (Fig. 4-6)
   This instrument will indicate leaks electronically by flashing a light or sounding an alarm signal. Directions for use of this equipment are furnished with the instrument.

### Halide or Propane Leak Detector

The propane leak detector is a gas-burning torch designed to locate a leak in any part of the system. Refrigerant gas drawn into the sampling tube attached to the torch causes the torch flame to change color in proportion to the size of the leak. Propane gas cylinders used with the torch are readily available throughout the country.

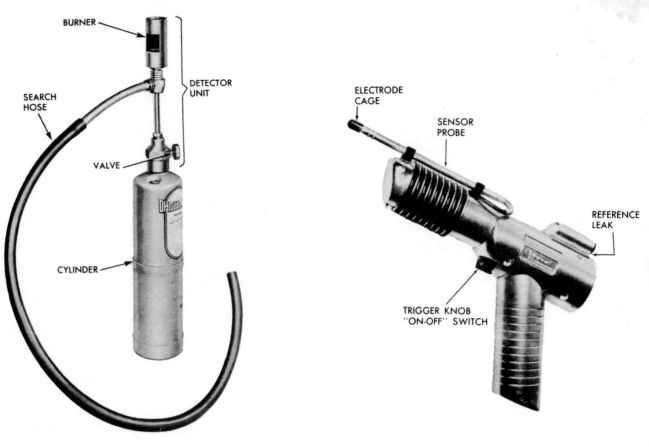

**FIGURE 4-5** Propane leak detector. (Courtesy of AC-Delco.)

**FIGURE 4-6** Electronic leak detector. (Courtesy of AC-Delco.)

## OPERATING THE PROPANE LEAK DETECTOR

1.  Determine if there is sufficient refrigerant in the system for leak testing.

    a.  If the manifold gauges indicate low pressure on the low side and low pressure on the high side, add partial refrigerant charge before leak testing.

2.  Open the control valve until a slight hiss of gas is heard, then light the gas at the opening in the chimney.

3.  Adjust the flame until the desired volume is obtained. A pale blue flame approximately ⅜ in. above the reaction plate is best for detecting leaks. (The reaction plate will be heated to a cherry red.)

4.  If the flame is yellow, insufficient air is being aspirated or the reaction plate is dirty. Insufficient air may be caused by

    a.  An obstructed or partially collapsed suction tube.

    b.  Dirt or a foreign substance in the burner tube.

    c.  A dirty or partially clogged orifice. Blowing air through the suction tube and back through the detector will usually clear dirt or foreign matter.

*CHECKING FOR REFRIGERANT LEAKS*

After the leak detector flame is adjusted, check for refrigerant leaks in an area having a minimum amount of air flow.

**NOTE:**

DO NOT BREATHE THE FUMES AND BLACK SMOKE THAT ARE PRODUCED IF THE LEAK IS A BIG ONE. THEY ARE POISONOUS. (Phosgene Gas).

Any time an open flame is used near a car there is a certain amount of danger. It is recommended that a fire extinguisher be close at hand for any emergency that might arise.

Inspect for leaks by slowly moving the end of leak detector hose around all connections and points of possible leakage. R-12 is heavier than air and will be more apparent at the bottom of the fitting.

The evaporator core can be checked for leaks by removing the resister in the evaporator case and inserting the end of leak detector hose into the evaporator case. Others can be checked by removing the blower motor cooler tube and probing with the leak detector hose in the evaporator. The color of the flame will turn to a yellow-green when a small leak is detected. Large leaks will be indicated by a change in color to brilliant blue or purple. When the suction hose is moved away from the leak, the flame will clear to an almost colorless pale blue again.

To test for leaks on the high-pressure side, operate the system for a few minutes and then turn the system off. The leak will be more apparent with the high pressure in the system.

A leak on the low-pressure side will be more apparent if the system is shut off for a few minutes. They system pressure will equalize and the pressure will be higher than normal operating pressures.

**NOTE:**

WATCH FOR A COLOR CHANGE IN THE FLAME ABOVE THE REACTOR PLATE.

1. Pale blue: no refrigerant loss.

2. Pale yellow: very small leak.

3. Yellow: small leak.

4. Purplish blue: large leak.

5. Violet: very large leak—may extinguish flame.

**WARNING:**

NEVER INHALE THE VAPORS OR FUMES FROM THE HALIDE LEAK DETECTOR. WHEN THE REFRIGERANT COMES IN

CONTACT WITH AN OPEN FLAME, PHOSGENE GAS IS FORMED
AND MAY BE POISONOUS.

### Electronic Leak Detector

Various electronic leak detectors are available and they are generally more sensitive for detecting small leaks. A typical air-conditioning system will leak approximately ¼ oz. of refrigerant per year. Some units are so sensitive that they can detect this normal refrigerant leak. The tester should be set to detect abnormal leaks of greater than ¼ oz. of refrigerant per year. It is extremely important that the manufacturer's instructions for setting a sensitivity adjustment be followed to the letter.

A typical electronic leak detector was shown in Fig. 4-6. It is powered by batteries and uses a combination on-off sensitivity adjustment control knob. Operation is as follows:

1. Turn the control knob on.

2. Place the probe over the calibrated sample. (This sample on most units represents ¼ oz. of leakage per year.) Noise will sound or a lamp will start flashing.

3. Turn sensitivity knob until a point is found where rotating the knob slightly one way turns the sound or light off and rotating back turns the sound or light on. At this point the tester is ready for use. The sound will be louder and the light will flash faster for large leaks. Be sure to follow recommended procedures in setting the unit up so that time will not be wasted working on nondefective items.

After the leak has been found, the system *must* be discharged completely and the leak repaired. The system can be discharged in the following manner.

### DISCHARGING THE SYSTEM (FIG. 4-7)

With the engine turned off, proceed as follows:

1. Place the free end of the manifold gauge set center hose in a shop towel.

2. Slowly open either the high- or low-side manifold hand valve and adjust the valve until a moderate flow of refrigerant is blowing out. Do not open the valve too wide and check the shop towel to make certain that no oil is being discharged with the refrigerant.

**CAUTION:**

IF REFRIGERANT IS ALLOWED TO ESCAPE TOO FAST, COMPRESSOR OIL WILL BE CARRIED OUT WITH THE REFRIGERANT AND WILL BE LOST FROM THE COMPRESSOR.

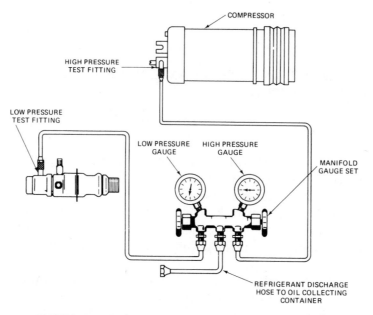

COMPRESSOR

HIGH PRESSURE
TEST FITTING

LOW PRESSURE
TEST FITTING

LOW PRESSURE
GAUGE

HIGH PRESSURE
GAUGE

MANIFOLD
GAUGE SET

REFRIGERANT DISCHARGE
HOSE TO OIL COLLECTING
CONTAINER

**FIGURE 4-7** Discharging the system. (Courtesy of AC-Delco.)

3. Slowly open the other manifold hand valve so that the refrigerant is discharged from both the high and low sides of the system and adjust the valve for refrigerant flow from the center hose. Do not open the valve too wide. Again check the shop towel to make certain that no oil is being discharged with the refrigerant.

4. As system pressure drops on the gauge reading, slowly increase the opening of both manifold valves until the gauge indicates 0 psi.

5. Measure any quantity of oil that might have been discharged from the system so that it can be replaced with an equal amount of new refrigerant oil when recharging.

While the system is discharged, it is a good idea to check the compressor oil, since it is impossible to tell how much oil leaked out with the refrigerant. The compressor oil can be checked in the following manner.

## COMPRESSOR–OIL–LEVEL CHECKS

### General Motors Compressors

It is not recommended that the oil be checked as a matter of course. Generally, the compressor oil level should be checked only where there is evidence of a major loss of system oil, such as might be caused by

1. A broken refrigerant hose.

2. A severe hose fitting leak.

3. A very badly leaking compressor seal.

4. Collision damage to the system components.

*OIL CHARGE FOLLOWING EXCESSIVE LEAKAGE OR UNIT
REPLACEMENT*

A six-cylinder GM compressor requires 11 oz of 525 viscosity refrigerant oil in the system. A four-cylinder compressor system requires 6 oz. It is important that only the specified type and quantity of oil be used in the compressor. If there is a surplus of oil in the system, too much oil will circulate with the refrigerant, causing the cooling capacity of the system to be reduced. Too little oil will result in poor lubrication of the compressor.

When there has been excessive leakage or it is necessary to replace a component of the refrigeration system, certain procedures must be followed to assure that the total oil charge in the system is correct after leak repair or the new part is on the car. When the compressor is operated, oil gradually leaves the compressor and is circulated through the system with the refrigerant. Eventually, a balanced condition is reached in which a certain amount of oil is retained in the compressor and a certain amount is continually circulated. If a component of the system is replaced after the system has been operated, some oil will go with it. To maintain the original total oil charge, it is necessary to compensate for this by adding oil to the new replacement part.

As a quick check on compressor oil charge, operate the engine at 2000 rpm on maximum cold for 10 minutes, turn off the engine, and momentarily crack open the oil drain plug on the bottom of the compressor, letting a slight amount of drain out. Retighten the plug. Again slightly crack open the drain plug. If oil comes out, the compressor has the required amount of oil. (Note: The oil may appear foamy. This is normal.)

*TO ADD OIL*

1. Connect the gauge set into the system and proceed with leak checking, repairing, and evacuating.

2. After the proper vacuum has been obtained, shut off the vacuum pump and close the high- and low-side valves of the gauge set.

3. Disconnect the low-side charging hose from the gauge set and the car compressor and connect an A-10576 oil injector (Robinair) to the low side of the gauge set. Connect the charging hose (removed from the low side of the gauge set) to the control valve of the oil injector.

4. Connect the other end of the charging hose to the low-pressure side of the car compressor.

5. Disconnect the center hose from the vacuum pump and connect to the refrigerant source.

6. Make certain that the control valve of the oil injector is closed, remove the ⅛-in. pipe plug, from the oil injector, and fill with 525 viscosity refrigeration oil to 2 oz.

7. Replace the ⅛-in. pipe plug, open the injector control valve, open the low-side valve of the gauge set, and allow the refrigerant to carry the oil into the low side of the compressor.

8. Allow approximately 1 lb of refrigerant to enter the car system and close the low-side valve of the gauge set.

9. Start the engine and adjust the air-conditioning controls for full cold.

10. Operate the engine at 2000 rpm for 10 minutes.

11. Turn off the engine.

12. Open the oil drain plug on the compressor and allow oil to escape onto a shop rag.

    a. If oil escapes in a heavy flow, the oil level is O.K.

    b. If oil escapes in a fine mist, oil must be added.

13. If the oil level is still low, repeat steps 6 through 8.

14. When oil is at the proper level, proceed to charge the balance of refrigerant required into the system.

To further check the compressor oil charge, it is necessary to remove the compressor from the vehicle, drain, and measure the oil.

### TO DRAIN

1. Run the system for 5 minutes at 1000 rpm with the controls set for maximum cooling and high blower speed.

2. Turn off the engine, discharge the system, remove the compressor from the vehicle, and place it in a horizontal position with the drain plug downward. Remove the drain plug and, tipping the compressor back and forth and rotating the compressor shaft, drain the oil into a clean container. Measure and discard the oil. Refer to Table 4-5.

**TABLE 4-5**

| Compressor | Amount of Oil Drained (oz) | Amount of Oil to Install |
|---|---|---|
| 6-cylinder (A-6) | More than 4 | Refill with same amount as drained. |
| 6-cylinder (A-6) | Less than 4 | Install new oil in the compressor—6 oz. |
| 4-cylinder (R-4) | More than ½ | Refill with same amount as drained. |
| 4-cylinder (R-4) | Less than ½ | Install new oil in the compressor—3 oz. |

*OIL CHARGE CORRECTION*

## COMPONENT RUPTURE—FAST DISCHARGE

1. Correct the leak and flush the system.

2. Drain the compressor and add 5.5 oz of 525 viscosity oil to the compressor crankcase through the suction ports of the compressor.

3. Install the compressor and evacuate the system.

4. Charge the system and check for leaks.

5. Performance-check the system.

## SLOW LEAK

1. When a loss of refrigerant has occurred over an extended period of time, add 3 oz of 525 viscosity oil to the system.

2. Recharge as required.

**NOTE:**

WHEN SYSTEM PERFORMANCE, EFFICIENCY, AND PROPER OIL CHARGE ARE IN DOUBT AND MUST BE EVALUATED ACCURATELY, IT IS RECOMMENDED THAT THE SYSTEM BE FLUSHED AND THE EXACT OIL CHARGE BE ADDED TO THE COMPRESSOR PRIOR TO ANY FURTHER CHECKS OF THE SYSTEM.

*FLUSHING THE SYSTEM*

1. Install a charging line to the compressor discharge valve and to a drum of refrigerant R-12.

2. Disconnect the liquid line from the receiver-dehydrator assembly on the inlet side and immediately cap the receiver-dehydrator.

3. Open the refrigerant drum valve and turn the drum upside down to allow liquid refrigerant to flush through the condenser and out the line. Use approximately 2 lb of refrigerant for this operation.

4. Close the drum valve and connect the dehydrator-receiver assembly.

5. Remove the charging line from the compressor, install the gauge set, and evacuate the entire system.

6. Recharge the system.

### Chrysler Compressor

When a new compressor is installed at the factory, the compressor contains 10 to 11 oz of a special wax-free refrigerant oil. While the air-conditioning system is in operation, the oil is carried through the entire system by the refrigerant. Some of this oil will be trapped and retained in various parts of the system. Consequently, once the system has been in operation, the amount of oil left in the compressor will always be less than the original charge. The compressor oil level should be checked as a matter of routine whenever the refrigerant has been released from the system.

1.  Operate the system for 15 minutes at 1000 engine rpm.

2.  Open the car windows and keep the engine hood raised.

3.  Press the A/C button and turn blower switch to high. On completion of the above operation, shut the air conditioning off, without changing any of these settings.

    After the system has bled down, wait 10 minutes for the refrigerant to boil off and then measure the oil in the compressor by inserting a dipstick through the crankcase oil filler hole. The oil level on the dipstick should measure between 1 5/8 to 2 3/8″ with the compressor in the vertical position. 1 5/8″ equals 6 ounces of oil in the compressor. 2 3/8″ equals 8 ounces of oil in the compressor. It may be necessary to compensate for dipstick indications if compressor is mounted on an angle. If sump contains less than 6 ounces of oil, add fresh clean refrigerant oil to bring the oil level to 2 3/8″. Remove any oil in excess of 8 ounces.

### FLUSHING THE CHRYSLER SYSTEM

If moisture or foreign material is observed in the oil drained from the A/C system, it is recommended that the system be flushed.

### Tecumseh or York Compressor

Check the compressor oil level only if a portion of the refrigerant system is being replaced, or if there was a leak in the system and the refrigerant is being replaced. Check the oil after the system has been charged and has been operating at an engine speed of 1500 rpm for 15 minutes in 70°F. (21.1°C.) surrounding air temperature or above. Turn off engine, and isolate the compressor. (Front seated position). Remove the oil filler plug from the compressor: insert a flatten 1/8″ diameter rod in the oil filler hole until it bottoms. The rod should show at least the minimum amount of oil as shown in Table 4-6. It may be necessary to rotate the compressor crankshaft slightly by hand so that the dipstick will clear the crankshaft.

**TABLE 4-6**

| *YORK* | *Min.* | *Max.* |
|---|---|---|
| Vertical Mounted | 7/8″ | 1 1/8″ |
| Horizontal Mounted | 13/16″ | 1/13/16″ |
| *TECUMSEH* | | |
| Vertical Mounted | 7/8″ | 1 3/8″ |
| Horizontal Mounted | 7/8″ | 1 5/8″ |

### WITH SENSING-TUBE EXPANSION VALVE

1. Discharge the system.

2. Remove the filter-drier lines and install a bypass system (Fig. 4-8).

3. Disconnect the suction line from the compressor suction fitting and put the open end over a fender into a collection can.

4. Remove the discharge line muffler valve core with tool C-4089 (Fig. 4-9).

5. Connect the bulk refrigerant container to tool C-4089 on the discharge line muffler service port with a charging hose.

6. Insert an expansion valve-sensing tube into a container of 125 to 150°F (51.7 to 65.6°C) (Fig. 4-10).

7. Open the bulk refrigerant container valve slowly, sending 5 lb (minimum) through the system and out the open end of the suction line.

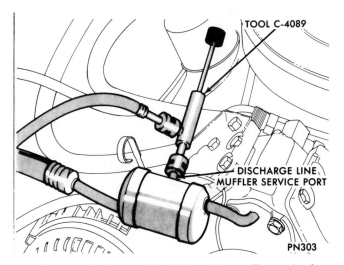

**FIGURE 4-8** Filter drier by-pass hose. (Courtesy of the Chrysler Corporation.)

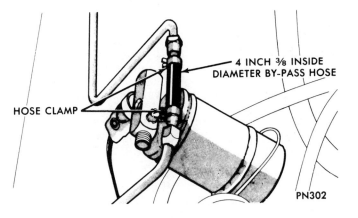

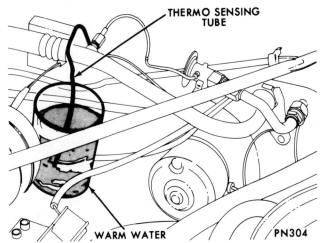

**FIGURE 4-9** Special tool for discharge line muffler service fort. (Courtesy of the Chrysler Corporation.)

**FIGURE 4-10** Immerse expansion valve thermo bulb in warm water. (Courtesy of the Chrysler Corporation.)

8. After the system is completely flushed, change the oil in the compressor sump, replacing it with 10 to 12 oz of new refrigerant oil.

9. Reconnect the suction line using a new O-ring.

10. Replace the discharge line muffler service valve core.

11. Remove the filter-drier bypass and install a new filter-drier using new O-rings.

12. Recharge the system with the proper amount of refrigerant.

### WITH "H"-TYPE EXPANSION VALVE

1. Fabricate the equipment needed for flushing as shown in Figs. 4-8 and 4-11.

2. Discharge the system.

3. Remove the "H" valve and install a bypass system.

4. Remove the filter-drier lines and install a bypass system (Fig. 4-8).

5. Disconnect the suction line from the compressor suction fitting and put the open end over a fender into a collector can.

6. Remove the discharge line muffler valve core with tool C-4089 (Fig. 4-9).

7. Connect the bulk refrigerant container to tool C-4089 on the discharge line muffler service port with a charging hose.

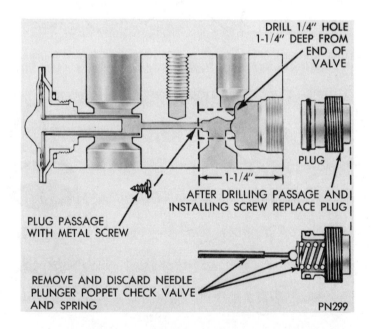

**FIGURE 4-11** Rework discarded "H" valve for flushing system. (Courtesy of the Chrysler Corporation.)

8. Open the bulk refrigerant container valve slowly, sending 5 lb (minimum) through the system and out the open end of the suction line.

9. After the system is completely flushed, change the oil in the compressor sump, replacing it with 10 to 12 ounces of new refrigerant oil.

10. Reconnect suction line using new O-ring.

11. Remove expansion valve by-pass and install "H" valve using new O-rings.

12. Replace discharge line muffler service valve core.

13. Remove filter-drier by-pass and install new filter-drier using new O-rings.

14. Recharge system with the proper amount of refrigerant.

## REFRIGERANT-LINE REPAIR

All major components of an air-conditioning system have inlet and outlet connections that use either "flare" or O-ring fittings. The refrigerant lines that connect between these units are made up of the correct length of hose with flare or O-ring fittings at each end as required. In either case, the hose end of the fittings is constructed with sealing bond to accommodate a hose-clamp connection. Typical flare and O-ring fittings are shown in Fig. 4-12.

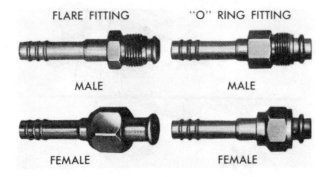

**FIGURE 4-12**    Flare & O-ring fittings. (Courtesy of AC-Delco.)

### Repairing Leaks at O-Ring Connections

1. Check the torque on the fitting and, if too loose, tighten to the proper torque. Always use a backing wrench to prevent twisting and damage to the O-ring. *Do not overtighten.* Again leak-test the joint.

2. If the leak is still present, discharge the system.

3. Inspect and replace fitting if damaged in any way. Discard the old O-ring and install a new O-ring after coating it with clean refrigerant oil.

4.  Retorque the fitting, using a backing wrench. Refer to Table 4-7.

5.  Evacuate and charge the system.

**TABLE 4-7**    Correct Torque Specifications.

| Metal Tube O.D. (in.) | Thread and Fitting Size | Steel Tubing Torque (foot-pounds | Aluminum Tubing Torque foot-pounds |
|---|---|---|---|
| 1/4 | 7/16 | 13 | 6 |
| 3/8 | 5/8 | 33 | 12 |
| 1/2 | 3/4 | 33 | 12 |
| 5/8 | 7/8 | 33 | 20 |
| 3/4 | 1 1/16 | 33 | 25 |

### Repairing Leaks at Hose-Clamp Connections

1.  Check the tightness of the clamp itself and tighten if necessary. Recheck for leaks.

2.  If the leak has not been corrected, discharge the system, loosen the clamp and remove the hose by making an angular cut as shown in Fig. 4-13. This should loosen the hose so that it can be worked off the fitting.

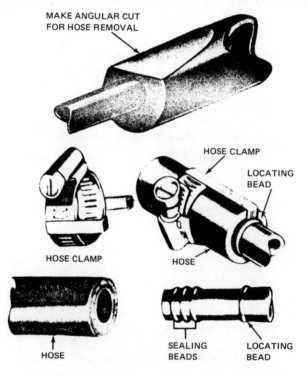

**FIGURE 4-13** Hose clamp connections. (Courtesy of AC-Delco.)

**CAUTION:**

USE EXTREME CARE NOT TO NICK OR SCORE THE SEALING BEADS WHEN CUTTING OFF THE HOSE. CUTTING THE HOSE LENGTHWISE MAY RESULT IN THIS PROBLEM.

3. If reusing old hose, make a clean square cut just beyond the angular cut used for removing hose.

4. Inspect the fitting and replace if sealing beads are nicked or scored.

5. Dip the end of the hose in clean refrigerant oil and carefully reinstall over the connector. Never push the end of the hose beyond the locating bead.

6. Install the clamps on the hose, hooking the locating arms over the cut on the hose.

7. Tighten the hose clamps to 35 to 42 in.-lb torque.

8. Evacuate and charge the system.

### Repairing Leaks in Crimped Hose Assemblies

Some factory installations use crimped hose assemblies in which the hose is permanently affixed to the connector fitting. Depending on where the leak might occur, repairs can be made to these assemblies by using a hose-clamp type of splicer or hose-clamp type of replacement connector fitting. In some cases it might be desirable to use a combination of both repairs if there is not enough length of original hose remaining. (Fig. 4-13.) A splicer repair should only be made when there is a leak in the middle of the hose. If there is a leak at the crimped connection and enough of the hose is still available, a new hose-clamp type of connector can be used. When there is not enough of the hose remaining, the combination splicer-connector repair can be made. After the system has been discharged and the leaks repaired, the system must be evacuated.

## EVACUATING THE SYSTEM

*Evacuating* is the process of removing all air from a refrigeration system, thereby creating a vacuum. A system should be evacuated before it is charged with refrigerant. A system should not be evacuated, however, if it has a leak, as this would draw air and moisture into the refrigerant lines. Therefore, always test for leaks before discharging a system. When refrigerant is removed and a system is opened for service, some air will enter the lines regardless of how quickly the openings are capped. To remove this air and the moisture it contains, the complete system must be evacuated. A discharged system may be evacuated as follows:

1. Remove the suction and discharge caps from the compressor fittings.

2. With both valves on the gauge set closed (fully clockwise), attach the gauge

set to the compressor fittings. Schrader valve adaptors may be required at the fittings.

3.  Attach one end of the hose to the center fitting of the gauge set and the other end to the pump.

4.  Slowly open the high-pressure gauge by turning it counterclockwise, letting any pressure buildup escape. Then close this valve.

5.  Start the vacuum pump and slowly open the low- and high-pressure valves. This must be done slowly so that refrigerant oil will not be forced out of the system. Pump operation forms a vacuum on both sides of the system.

6.  Observe the low-pressure gauge. In a leak-free system, the pump should operate until the gauge shows 26 to 28 in. of vacuum. Then operate the pump for 10 additional minutes.

7.  With the vacuum operating, close the low- and high-pressure valves (fully clockwise) and then stop the pump. If vacuum cannot be pulled to or held at the required 26 to 28 in. for about 10 minutes, there may be a leak either in the system or in the gauge connections, or the vacuum pump may be defective. To find the leak a small amount of refrigerant (1 lb maximum) must be added to give positive internal gas pressure for leak detection.

8.  If the system holds the vacuum for 10 minutes, the system can be charged.

## CHARGING THE SYSTEM (FIG. 4-14)

The system should be charged with refrigerant only after it has been leak-tested and evacuated. It is important to add only the specified quantity. Even if bubbles appear in the sight glass, no more than this amount should be added. The refrigerant supply or source may be a drum cylinder, can, or other type of

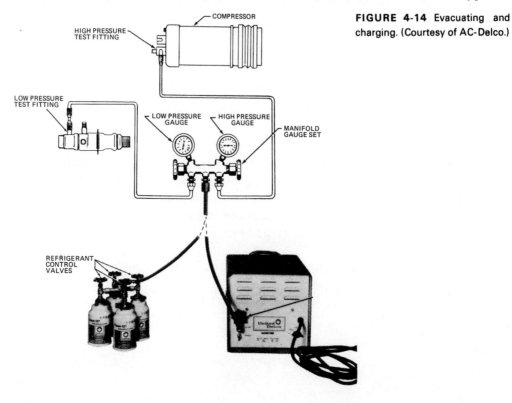

**FIGURE 4-14** Evacuating and charging. (Courtesy of AC-Delco.)

container. The charge must be measured with a scale that is accurate to within 2 oz, or a calibrated liquid column, or a charging board. A container of known quantity is also acceptable. Only refrigerant vapor should be charged into the suction side of the system when the compressor is running. A vapor charge should be taken from the top of the refrigerant container.

**WARNING:**

DO NOT CONNECT AN R-12 CONTAINER TO THE HIGH-PRESSURE SIDE OF THE SYSTEM OR ANY SYSTEM OF HIGHER PRESSURE. THIS MAY CAUSE EXCESSIVE PRESSURE AND RESULT IN VIOLENT BURSTING OF THE CONTAINER.

### Can Method

1. Obtain the required quantity of refrigerant.
2. If using 1-lb (15-oz) containers, mount four containers in a multicontainer. Some containers are 14 oz in size.

**CAUTION:**

MAKE SURE THAT THE CONTROL VALVE IS CLOSED BEFORE IN-STALLING ON THE REFRIGERANT CONTAINER.

3. Connect the center line of the manifold gauge set to fitting on the container valve.
4. After the R-12 can is attached, open the can valve, and purge air from the center hose by slightly loosening the hose connector at the manifold momentarily allowing all air to escape; then retighten the connector.
5. Open the low-side manifold hand valve and allow refrigerant to flow into the system with the refrigerant can upright in the vapor position. (The refrigerant will be sucked into the system by the existing vacuum.)
6. If the system is charged using 1-lb containers and a single container valve, close the valve and remove the empty container. Install the valve on a new and full container of refrigerant and repeat until the specified quantity of refrigerant has been used to charge the system.

**NOTE:**

IN SOME CASES, NOT ALL OF THE REFRIGERANT WILL BE DRAWN INTO THE SYSTEM.

   a. Close the low-side manifold valve and the can valve.

   b. Start the engine and adjust to normal fast idle.

   c. Turn the air container on to maximum cool with the high-speed blower fan.

d. Open the can valve on refrigerant-12, open the low-side manifold valve, and draw refrigerant-12 through the low side.

e. The refrigerant can may be rocked from side to side to increase the flow of refrigerant into the system.

**CAUTION:**

NEVER OPEN THE HIGH-SIDE VALVE WHEN THE VEHICLE IS RUNNING.

7. Close the valves on the manifold gauge set.

8. Operate the engine at 2000 rpm with the temperature control lever at full cold position and the blower speed on high.

**NOTE:**

IF THE AIR INLET TEMPERATURE AT THE CONDENSER IS BELOW 70°F (21.1°C), BUBBLES MAY APPEAR IN THE SIGHT GLASS EVEN THOUGH THE PROPER AMOUNT OF REFRIGERANT IS IN THE SYSTEM.

9. Check the thermometer at the air vent nearest the evaporator for temperature. The normal reading should be 35° to 45°F (1.7 to 7.2°C) on the lower blower fan speed.

10. When satisfied that the air-conditioning system is operating properly, stop the engine, remove the gauge set, and replace the protective caps on the suction and discharge fittings.

a. Manual service valves—back-seat (fully open) the service valves, remove the hose connections, and reinstall the valve cover caps.

b. Schrader service valves—remove the hose connections and reinstall the valve cover caps.

11. Use the leak detector and check the system for leaks.

### Charging Station Method (Fig. 4-15)

1. Be sure that all the valves on the charging station are closed.

2. Fill the charging cylinder with the required quantity of refrigerant.

**NOTE:**

WHILE FILLING THE CHARGING CYLINDER, PERIODICALLY OPEN AND CLOSE THE AIR BLEED VALVE LOCATED ON TOP OF THE CHARGING CYLINDER. OBSERVE THE REFRIGERANT LEVEL WITH THE VALVE CLOSED.

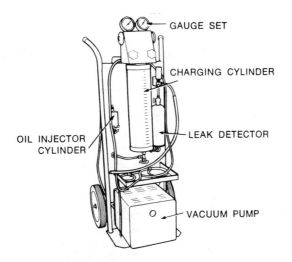

**FIGURE 4-15** Charging. (Courtesy of AC-Delco.)

3. Connect the charging cylinder heater to the 110-volt outlet.

4. Open the charging cylinder outlet valve.

5. Momentarily open the high- and low-side hand valves on the charging station to purge the hoses and the manifold of air.

6. Remove the protective caps from the high- and low-side test fittings and connect the high- and low-side hoses to the fittings.

7. Open the low-side hand valve to allow refrigerant to enter the system.

8. When the charging system is empty, close the low-side hand valve and the charging cylinder outlet valve.

9. Test the performance of the system.

## HUMIDITY AND SYSTEM PERFORMANCE

*Humidity* (the amount of moisture in the air) has an important bearing on the temperature of the air delivered to the vehicle's interior. This is true of all air-conditioning systems. It is important to understand the effect that humidity has on the performance of the system. When the humidity is high, the evaporator has to perform a double duty. It must lower the air temperature and the temperature of the moisture carried in the air. Condensing the moisture in the air transfers a great deal of heat energy into the evaporator fins and tubing. This reduces the amount of heat the evaporator can absorb from the air. In other words, the high humidity greatly reduces the evaporator's ability to lower the temperature of the air delivered to the vehicle interior. The evaporator capacity used to reduce the amount of moisture in the air is not wasted. Removing some of the moisture from the air entering the vehicle adds to the comfort of the passengers. However, an owner may expect too much from the air-conditioning system on humid days. A performance test is the best way to determine whether or not the system is performing up to standard. This test also provides clues to the possible causes of trouble.

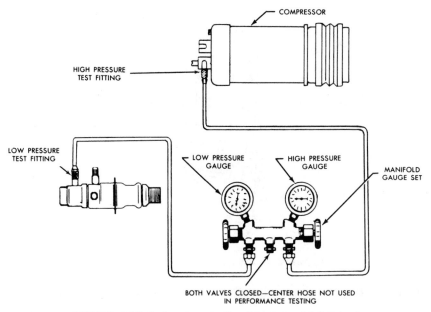

FIGURE 4-16 Performance testing. (Courtesy of AC-Delco.)

## PERFORMANCE TEST

The performance test should be made according to the manufacturer's specifications to see if the conditions of the vehicle are met to make the test. Such as:

1. Are the doors open or closed?
2. Is the hood opened or closed?
3. What is the rpm of the engine?
4. In what position is the A/C control?
5. What is the fan speed?
6. What about the water valve?
7. Where should the thermometer be placed?
8. How long do you run the A/C to stabilize the system?

To perform this test, proceed as follows:

1. Connect the manifold gauge set to the respective high- low-pressure fittings with both valves closed.
2. Position the doors, windows, and hood according to the manufacturer's specification.
3. Adjust the air-conditioning controls to the manufacturer's specification.
4. Adjust the blower speed to the manufacturer's specification.
5. Idle the engine for 10 minutes in neutral or park with the brake on. For best

results, place a high-volume fan in front of the radiator to ensure an adequate supply of air flow across the condenser.

6. Increase the enginee speed to the manufacturer's specification.

7. Measure the temperature at the evaporator outlet.

8. Read the "high" and "low" pressures and compare to the normal range of operating pressures in the performance chart.

If operating pressures are found to be within the normal range, it can be considered that the refrigeration portion of the air-conditioning system is functioning properly. This can be further confirmed with a check of evaporator outlet air temperatures.

Evaporator outlet air temperature will also vary according to outside (ambient) air and humidity conditions. Further variations will be found depending on whether the system is controlled by a cycling clutch compressor or an evaporator pressure control valve. Because of these variations, it is difficult to pinpoint what evaporator outlet air temperature should be on all applications.

Since it is impractical to provide a specific performance chart for all the different types of A/C systems, it is desirable to develop an experience factor for determining the correlation that can be anticipated between operating pressures and outlet air temperatures on the various systems.

## REVIEW QUESTIONS

1. The stem-type service valves have three positions. What are they?

2. Explain each position.

3. What is the difference between the EPR valve and the ETR valve?

4. Name two types of leak detectors.

5. What two dangerous conditions are always present while using the halide leak detector?

6. It is best to check for leaks on the high-pressure side while the engine is _____.

7. It is best to check for leaks on the low-pressure side while the engine is _____.

8. Why should the system be evacuated?

9. The operating pressures will be _____ on humid days.

10. R-12 should never be heated over _____°F (_____°C).

**WORK SHEET 1**

Name_____

Date _____

1. Attach the gauge manifold.

**NOTE:**

IF SERVICE VALVES ARE USED:

    a.   Back-seat both service valves and connect hoses.

    b.   Turn both service valves in 1/4 turn, cracked position.

    c.   Open the low-side manifold valve, purging air from the hose out the center hose fitting. Repeat with the high side of the hose.

    d.   Close both manifold valves.

2. Record the pressures on the gauges before starting the engine.
Low _____High _____

3. If the system has 50 psi (344.75 kPa) on both the low and high sides, start the engine and proceed with the test.

Run the unit at each speed for 10 minutes before taking any readings.

|  |  | FAN SPEED | | |
|---|---|---|---|---|
|  |  | Low | Med. | High |
| a. | Record evaporator temperatures | | | |
|  | Air temperature into evaporator | ___ | ___ | ___ |
|  | Air temperature out of evaporator | ___ | ___ | ___ |
|  | Temperature difference | ___ | ___ | ___ |
| b. | Record gauge pressures | | | |
|  | Discharge pressure (high side) | ___ | ___ | ___ |
|  | Suction pressure (low side) | ___ | ___ | ___ |
| c. | Record condenser air temperature | | | |
|  | Air into condenser | ___ | ___ | ___ |
|  | Air out of condenser | ___ | ___ | ___ |

    d.   Are there any bubbles in the sight glass?   Yes _____ No _____

    e.   Stop the unit and when the pressure on the low side reaches 50 psi, use the leak detector and check the system for leaks.
Did you find any leaks?_____
If so, where?_____

**WORK SHEET 2**

Name _____
Date  _____

1.  Discharge the system.

2.  Evacuate the system.

3.  Charge the system.

|     |                                      | Low | Med | High |
| --- | ------------------------------------ | --- | --- | ---- |
| a.  | Record evaporator temperatures       |     |     |      |
| b.  | Air temperature into the evaporator  | ___ | ___ | ___  |
| c.  | Air temperature out of the evaporator| ___ | ___ | ___  |
| d.  | Temperature difference               | ___ | ___ | ___  |
| e.  | Record gauge pressures               |     |     |      |
| f.  | Discharge pressures                  | ___ | ___ | ___  |
| g.  | Suction pressure                     | ___ | ___ | ___  |
| h.  | Record condenser air temperature     |     |     |      |
| i.  | Air into condenser                   | ___ | ___ | ___  |
| j.  | Air out of condenser                 | ___ | ___ | ___  |

k.  Are there any bubbles in the sight glass?    Yes _____ No _____

# Chapter 5

# Electrical Fundamentals

## CURRENT-FLOW THEORIES

### Conventional Theory

In this theory the direction of current flow was arbitrarily chosen to be from the positive terminal of the voltage source, through the external circuit, and then back to the negative terminal of the source. The conventional theory is used throughout this text.

### Electron Theory

This theory states that current flows from the negative terminal, through the external circuit, and then back to the positive terminal of the source.

In order for electrons to flow, they must have a path to travel in. For simplicity, think of the path as a circle (circuit) from the source (positive battery terminal), around and back to the source (negative battery terminal). Electrons move through some substances more easily than through others. Some substances, such as copper, iron, and aluminum, form good paths through which electrons can move, and are therefore called *conductors*. Other substances, such as rubber or glass, strongly oppose electron movement. These substances are called *nonconductors* or *insulators*.

An insulator is made up of a substance that does not have many free electrons. Without free electrons, a flow of electrons cannot be set up, for the flow depends upon repelling free electrons along the circuit. If an insulator blocks the circuit, free electrons cannot push through. Insulators are used to cover and protect wires and other metal parts of electrical devices. The insulators keep the free electrons (or current) from going off in the wrong direction and taking a short cut to ground. If an insulator fails, the result can be what is called a "short circuit."

## CIRCUITS

The first step in the study of electricity is to become familiar with electric circuits and how they are used. When voltage forces current through a load, work is done. For instance, in starting an engine the starting motor is the load and the turning of the engine is the work done. When a battery is connected to a headlamp, the headlamp is the load and the production of light is the work done.

Many different types of loads can be connected to a battery. However, all loads have one thing in common; they all convert electrical energy from the battery into some usable form of energy. The headlamps change electric energy to light. The starting motor changes electric energy to motion.

One side of the load must be connected to the positive terminal and the other side to the negative terminal of the battery. The connection of a load to a battery can be shown in a drawing by using symbols instead of pictures. A drawing using symbols to represent actual parts is called a *schematic*. Each load is designed to operate with a certain amount of current through it. If the current rating is exceeded for a period of time, the load will be damaged. For example, excessive current through a lamp filament will heat the filament to such an extent that it will burn out. This opens the current path and the lamp cannot light. To avoid this, loads are rated to operate from a source of specified voltage. Automobile headlamps are rated at either 6 or 12 volts. A 6-volt headlamp connected across a 6-volt battery will operate properly with normal light output. If a 6-volt headlamp were connected across a 12-volt battery, the headlamp would burn out from the excessive current. If a 12-volt headlamp were connected across a 6-volt battery, the headlamp would glow dimly because the lower voltage would not force enough current through the headlamp to light it brightly. In some cases a load is designed to work at a lower voltage than that provided by the source. Usually in this case, current through the load must be controlled by using a resistor. Resistors are simply a fixed opposition to current. By putting a resistor in series with a load, the current through the load is decreased.

### Circuit Components

A *circuit* means a circle. Electricity must return to its source. A basic circuit should have a switch to turn it on or off, a protection device such as a fuse, and an electrical load (Fig. 5-1).

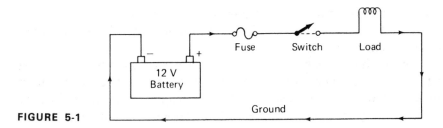

**FIGURE 5-1**

A simple automotive electrical circuit is made up of four parts (Fig. 5-2):

1. Battery (power source).

2. Wires (conductors to carry the electricity).

3. Load (lights, motors, radio, etc.).

4. Ground (return back to the battery).

The *battery* is the heart of the electrical system and must be kept in a fully charged condition for the other electrical components to operate properly.

The *wires* carry the electrical current to the load and back to the battery. The wire going to the load is called the *hot circuit*, and the wire carrying the current back to the battery is called the *ground circuit*.

The *load* can be any electrical device that uses electricity—a motor, radio, cigar lighter, light bulb, and so on. All electrical circuits must have a load to use the electricity.

The *ground* returns the electricity back to the battery, since one pole of the battery is customarily grounded. All electrical circuits must have a ground. The electrical symbol for ground is $/\overline{\overline{\phantom{x}}}$

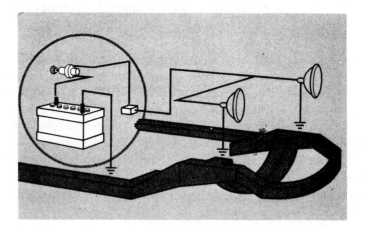

FIGURE 5-2 (Courtesy of Ford Customer Service Division.)

Most of the circuits in this book are single-wire circuits, as shown in Fig. 5-3. The metal part of the car is used as a ground, to carry the electricity back to the battery.

We identify circuits in three ways: series, parallel, and series–parallel.

In a series circuit (Fig. 5-4), current flows in one path only. Any break in a series circuit stops the current (Fig. 5-5).

The load in the circuit may be grounded by a wire from the load to a metal part of the car. The ground wire need not be insulated (Fig. 5-6), since the common ground is not insulated. The load also may be self-grounded. Many bulbs, for instance, are grounded by the contact of the bulb socket with the car sheet metal.

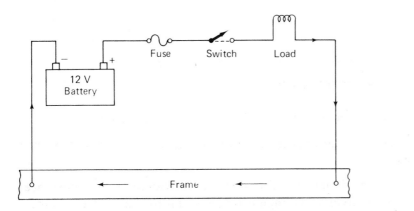

FIGURE 5-3

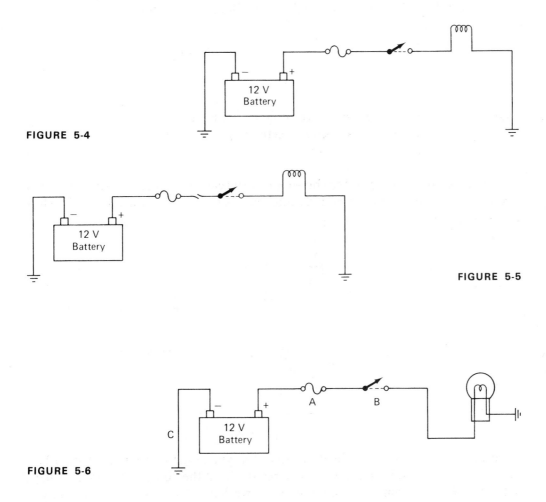

FIGURE 5-4

FIGURE 5-5

FIGURE 5-6

## OHM'S LAW

Ohm's law defines the relationship between current, voltage, and resistance. It is the basic law of electricity, and indicates the amount of current that will flow in a circuit. It is used in designing circuits that will operate efficiently for a maximum amount of time. The service technician must understand Ohm's law (1) to understand the operation of automotive electrical circuits, and (2) to diagnose electrical circuit problems.

## Series Circuit

A *series circuit* has three characteristics:

1. The current flow is the same throughout all parts of the circuit.

2. The total circuit resistance is the sum of the individual circuit resistances added together.

3. The source voltage divides itself among the individual circuit resistances. The sum of the individual voltage drops is equal to the source voltage.

*Ohm's law* states that if 1 volt is applied to 1 ohm of resistance 1 ampere of current will flow. This is determined by the Ohm's law formula:

$$I = \frac{E}{R} \qquad E = I \times R \qquad R = \frac{E}{I}$$

where
$E$ = volts (electromotive force or pressure)
$R$ = ohms or resistance (electrical symbol $\Omega$ )
$I$ = amperes or current

Let's take an example and see how Ohm's law can be applied to a simple 12-volt circuit with a miniature light-bulb design load resistance of 6 ohms (Fig. 5-7). How many amperes will flow?

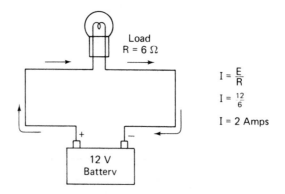

**FIGURE 5-7**

Figure 5-8 shows a simplified version of a typical ignition circuit, with a battery, a resistor, a coil, and points. The resistor and the coil are designed to have 1.5 ohms each to control current flow. If we have two known values, we can always find the unknown value, by using the formula circle adapted to Ohm's law (Fig. 5-9).

If you cover the unknown value, you can write Ohm's law in three ways:

$$I = \frac{E}{R} \qquad E = I \times R \qquad R = \frac{E}{I}$$

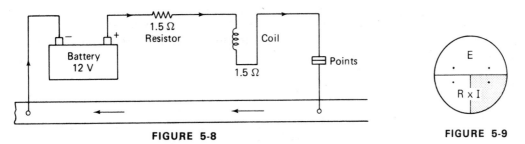

**FIGURE 5-8**

**FIGURE 5-9**

In this case the unknown value is amperes (*I*). When you cover *I*, the formula looks like this:

$$I = \frac{E}{R} = \frac{\text{volts}}{\text{resistance}} = \frac{12 \text{ volts}}{3 \text{ ohms}} = 4 \text{ amperes}$$

Don't forget that in a series circuit the resistances are added together:

$$R_T = 1.5 + 1.5 = 3 \, \Omega$$

## Parallel Circuit

The *parallel circuit* has three characteristics:

1. The applied voltage is the same for all the parallel branches.

2. The main circuit current flow divides itself among the parallel branches according to resistance values. The sum of the separate currents equals the total circuit current.

3. The total effective resistance is always less than the parallel branch offering the smallest resistance.

In a parallel circuit current flows in two or more paths or branch circuits. A parallel circuit always starts with a *common point,* where the hot wire splits or branches to supply power to more than one circuit. It could be a terminal, a splice, or a connector.

In Fig. 5-10, the common point provides current to load A and load B. If load A switch is open and load B switch is closed, load B will operate, and vice versa, so the common point supplies current to more than one circuit. If the fuse blows open, neither A nor B will operate.

**FIGURE 5-10**

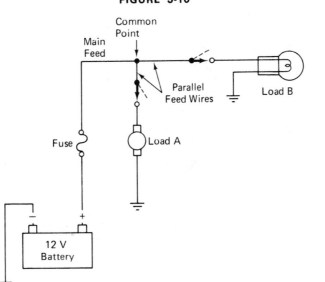

A study of a parallel circuit (Fig. 5-11) shows how Ohm's law relates to the circuit. In a parallel circuit, to find the total current flow in the circuit, we must first find the total effective resistance.

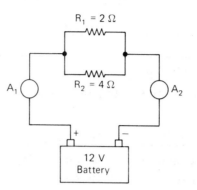

**FIGURE 5-11**

To find total effective resistance, we must use a special formula.

$$\text{total resistance} = \frac{\text{resistance of leg 1} \times \text{resistance of leg 2}}{\text{resistance of leg 1} + \text{resistance of leg 2}}$$

$$R_t = \frac{R_1 \times R_2}{R_1 + R_2}$$

$$= \frac{2 \times 4}{2 + 4} = \frac{8}{6} = \frac{4}{3} = 1.33 \text{ ohms}$$

To find the total current flow reading in ammeter₁ and ammeter₂:

$$I = \frac{E}{R_t} = \frac{12 \text{ volts}}{1.33 \text{ ohms}} = 9 \text{ amperes}$$

Ammeter₁ reads 9 amperes.
Ammeter₂ reads 9 amperes.

The current flow in $R_1$ is

$$I = \frac{E}{R} = \frac{12 \text{ volts}}{2 \text{ ohms}} = 6 \text{ amperes}$$

The current flow in $R_2$ is

$$I = \frac{E}{R} = \frac{12 \text{ volts}}{4 \text{ ohms}} = 3 \text{ amperes}$$

The main circuit current is equal to the current in $R_1$ and $R_2$:

main circuit current = 6 amperes + 3 amperes = 9 amperes

Figure 5-12 will help you to better visualize why the total circuit resistance (equivalent resistance) in a parallel circuit system is even less than the resistance value of the individual parallel circuit with the lowest resistance value.

Let's assume that we have a supply pipe through which water is flowing (Fig. 5-12, view A). In view B, we have taken the original supply pipe and added a reducer and a smaller-diameter pipe. Obviously, the resistance to the flow is now greater because of the smaller pipe. Then in view C, we've taken the original supply pipe again and changed to an even smaller reducer and pipe than those used in view B. The resistance to the flow is now even greater.

In view D we've started over with the original supply pipe and changed the plumbing to allow us to incorporate in *parallel* both of the smaller pipes that were used in views B and C. Therefore, the total resistance (equivalent resistance of the two parallel pipes) in view D is obviously less than the resistance of either of the individual pipes (views B and C), because there is now a greater total cross-sectional area of unrestricted flow. Thus, it can be seen that when circuits are in parallel, they present less total resistance than the resistance value of either of the individual circuits.

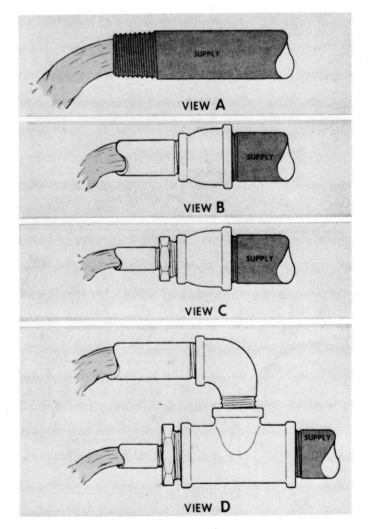

**FIGURE 5-12**
(Courtesy of
General Motors Corp.)

## Series–Parallel Circuit

*Series-parallel* circuit characteristics are a combination of those related to a pure series circuit and a pure parallel circuit. The series-parallel circuit in Fig. 5-13 illustrates how Ohm's law relates to the combined characteristics.

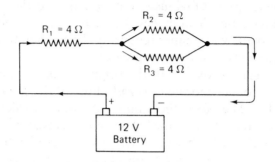

**FIGURE 5-13**

The total effective circuit resistance is

$$R_T = R_1 + \frac{R_2 \times R_3}{R_2 + R_3}$$

$$4 + \frac{4 \times 4}{4 + 4} = 4 + \frac{16}{8} = 4 + 2 = 6 \text{ ohms}$$

The main circuit current flow is:

$$I = \frac{E}{R} = \frac{12 \text{ volts}}{6 \text{ ohms}} = 2 \text{ amperes}$$

The voltage drop across $R_2$ is

$$E = I \times R = 2 \text{ amperes} \times 4 \text{ ohms} = 8 \text{ volts}$$

The applied voltage to parallel branches is equal to the battery voltage *minus* the $R_1$ voltage drop:

$$\text{applied voltage} = 12 \text{ volts} - 8 \text{ volts} = 4 \text{ volts}$$

To determine the current flow through $R_2$ and $R_3$, we can say that since the resistances are equal, the main current splits equally, and 1 ampere flows through each parallel branch; or we can calculate the current in each resistance:

$$\text{current } (I) \text{ in } R_2 = \frac{E}{R_2} = \frac{4 \text{ volts}}{4 \text{ ohms}} = 1 \text{ ampere}$$

$$\text{current } (I) \text{ in } R_3 = \frac{E}{R_3} = \frac{4 \text{ volts}}{4 \text{ ohms}} = 1 \text{ ampere}$$

**TABLE 5-1** Ohm's Law Relationship Table.

| Voltage | Resistance | Amperage |
|---------|------------|----------|
| up | down | up |
| up | same | up |
| up | up | same |
| same | down | up |
| same | same | same |
| same | up | down |
| down | down | same |
| down | up | down |
| down | same | down |

Although the table reflects the typical relationship between voltage, resistance, and amperage, there are a couple of variables to be considered. For example, line three indicates that if voltage is "up," and resistance is also "up," the amperage will stay the same. It is obvious that in this example the voltage would have to be increased proportionately to offset the increased resistance in order for the amperage to remain the same. Similarly, the example on line seven—in order to be exact, as stated—would require the voltage to be decreased proportionately with the decrease of resistance if the amperage were to stay the same.

Examples three and five, then, are shown only as the probable situation that would exist in those instances. One can better see the relationship of these particular two examples if the table is used from right to left. That is, if the amperage is the same, and the resistance or voltage is "up," the third factor (resistance or voltage) must be up. It follows then that if the voltage is the same and the resistance or voltage is "down," the remaining factor must also be down.

The following list of electrical terms are used throughout the book.

## ELECTRICAL TERMS

**Voltage:** Electrical pressure measured in volts. This is the force that causes current to flow in an electrical circuit. The electrical symbol is $E$.

**Current:** Flow of electricity measured in amperes. Current can be compared to the flow of water in a pipe. The rate of flow (amount of current) is measured in amperes (abbreviated as amps). The electrical symbol is $I$.

**Resistance:** Electrical friction (opposition to current flow) measured in ohms (abbreviated as $\Omega$, the Greek letter omega). Everything has some degree of resistance. The resistance in wiring can be compared to the friction in a pipe. Wiring resistance increases as the length increases, and decreases as the cross-sectional size increases. The smaller the size number of the wire, the larger the cross section of the wire. For example, No. 6 wire is larger in cross section than No. 14 wire and has less resistance per foot. The electrical symbol for resistance is $R$.

**Voltage Drop:** The loss of voltage caused by a flow of current through a resistance. It increases as current flow or resistance increases. Voltage drop, sometimes called *voltage loss* or *line loss,* can be measured with a voltmeter connected from one point to the other with current flowing in the circuit. The total voltage drop in a circuit is equal to the voltage of the source.

**Applied Voltage:**    The actual voltage read at a given point in a circuit.

**Available Voltage:**    The voltage delivered by the power supply.

**Circuit:**    A complete path for the flow of electricity. If there is a difference in pressure (voltage) between the ends of the circuit, current will flow. The amount of current that will flow is determined by the voltage applied and the total resistance of the circuit.

**Short Circuit:**    A connection in a circuit that results in lower resistance and usually results in higher-than-normal current flow.

**Grounded Circuit:**    A grounded circuit is similar to a "short circuit" in that the current bypasses part of the normal circuit, in this instance, by going directly to ground. This may be caused by a wire touching ground, or part of the circuit within a unit coming in contact with the frame or housing of the unit.

**Open Circuit:**    A break in a wire or connection that prevents any current flow through that wire or connection.

**Excessive Resistance:**    A bad connection due to corrosion, loose connections, or any other connection that would add unwanted resistance in the circuit.

## REVIEW QUESTIONS

1. Name four parts of a simple circuit.

2. What does the word "load" mean in an electrical circuit?

3. What is a single-wire circuit?

4. Circuits are identified in three ways. Name them.

5. Define the following terms.
    a. Series circuit
    b. Parallel circuit
    c. Voltage
    d. Ampere
    e. Resistance
    f. Open circuit
    g. Voltage drop
    h. Applied voltage
    i. Available voltage
    j. Short circuit

6. How do you determine the total circuit resistance in a series circuit?

7. In a 12-volt series circuit with a 2-ohm resistor and a 2-ohm coil, how many amperes will flow?

8. In a parallel circuit the applied voltage to each branch is _____.

9. What is the total circuit resistance in a parallel circuit if each branch has a 2-ohm resistor? The circuit has only two branches.

10. What is the total circuit resistance in a parallel circuit if one branch has a 3-ohm resistor and the other branch has a 6-ohm resistor?

11. How many amperes will flow in a series circuit with a 12-volt battery and an 8-ohm resistor?

12. How many amperes will flow in a 6-volt circuit with a 1.5-ohm coil?

## Ohm's law problems

What's your Ohm's law IQ? Test yourself on the following problems, and make a drawing for each problem.

13. In a series circuit consisting of a 6-ohm resistor, a 4-ohm resistor, and a 12-volt battery, what is the voltage drop across each resistor?

14. In a parallel circuit consisting of a 4-ohm resistor, a 6-ohm resistor, and a 12-volt battery, what is the total circuit current supplied by the battery?

15. In a series–parallel circuit consisting of a 6-ohm resistor in series, a 10-ohm resistor in parallel, a 15-ohm resistor in parallel, and a 12-volt battery, how much current (amperes) flows through the 10-ohm and the 15-ohm resistor?

## ELECTRICAL DIAGRAMS AND QUESTIONS

A. Blower Motor

B. Blower Switch

C. Battery

D. Switch

E. Fuse

F. Resistor Block

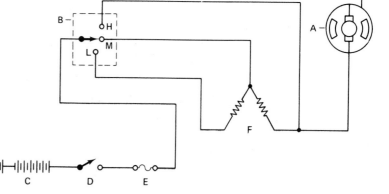

**FIGURE 5-14**

1.  The wiring diagram, of the blower motor circuit, has three speeds. Trace the circuits to understand how the blower speed is controlled.

   A.  Compressor Clutch Coil

   B.  Switch

   C.  Fuse

   D.  Battery

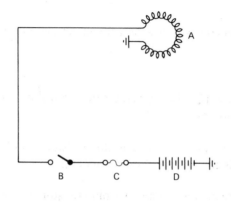

B          C          D                    **FIGURE 5-15**

2.  The wiring diagram, of the compressor clutch coil, has a 4-ohm resistance in the coil. How many amperes will flow?

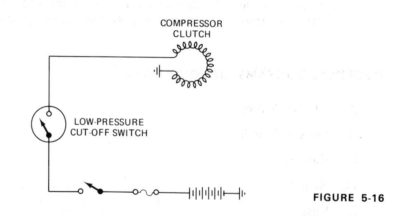

**FIGURE 5-16**

3.  The low-pressure cutoff switch is wired in series with the compressor magnetic clutch. It cuts off the electrical power supply to the clutch when refrigerant pressure drops below the control point of the switch.

   A.  Compressor Clutch Coil

   B.  Switch

   C.  Fuse

D. Battery

E. Thermal Limiter

F. Super Heat Switch

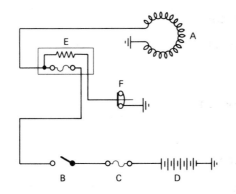

**FIGURE 5-17**

4. The thermal limiter and superheat switch are designed to protect the air-conditioning compressor against damage when the refrigerant is totally or partially lost. The fuse and switch are connected in series.

A. Compressor Clutch Coil

B. Switch

C. Fuse

D. Battery

E. Thermal Limiter

F. Super Heat Switch

G. Ambient Switch

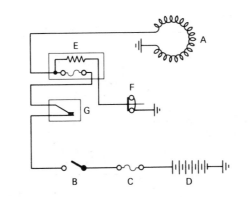

**FIGURE 5-18**

5. The ambient switch senses outside air temperature and is designed to prevent compressor clutch engagment below 32°F or 0°C.

   A. Blower Switch

   B. Blower Motor

   C. Resistor Block

   D. Battery

   E. Ignition Switch

   F. Fuse

   G. A.C. Switch

   H. A.C. Fuse

   I. Compressor Clutch Coil

   J. Thermal Limiter

   K. Superheat Switch

   L. Ambient Switch

6. Trace the circuit for the blower motor and the compressor clutch.

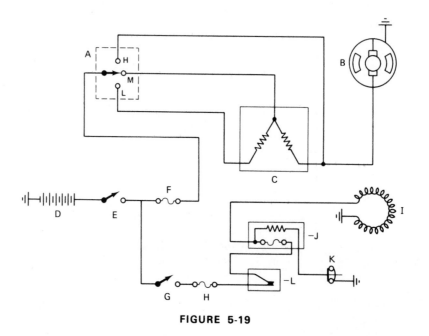

**FIGURE 5-19**

7.  In Fig. 5-20:

    a.  With the blower speed switch in the low position:

        (1)  How many amperes will flow?

        (2)  What will the voltage be at the blower motor?

    b.  With the blower speed switch in the medium position:

        (1)  How many amperes will flow?

        (2)  What will the voltage be at the blower motor?

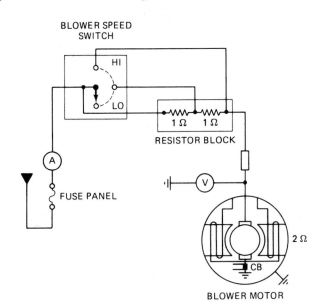

**FIGURE 5-20**

8.  Fig. 5-21:

    a.  Connect the battery, ignition switch, and fuse.

    b.  Wire the blower motor to operate at medium speed.

    c.  Install an ammeter to read the total current flow.

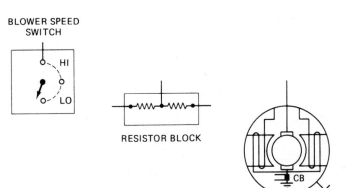

**FIGURE 5-21**

## SELECTOR LEVER—OFF POSITION

With the engine running and the selector lever in the OFF position, current is directed from the ignition switch to the heater - A/C fuse in the fuse block. From the fuse block current is directed to the coil in the Delay Relay.

The Delay Relay coil circuit is completed through the closed engine thermo switch. The engine thermo switch closes when engine coolant reaches approximately 120 degrees F.

Current is then directed through the closed points to the resistor block, through all of the resistors, through the normally closed Hi Blower Relay points to the blower motor. The blower motor is operating at Lo speed.

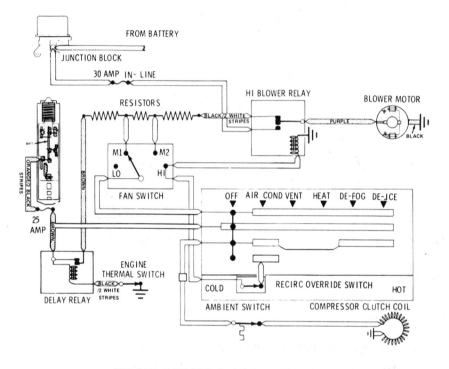

FIGURE 5-22 Electrical circuit—off position.

## SELECTOR LEVER—AIR CONDITIONING POSITION

Current is directed from the ignition switch to the fuse block then to the control. With the selector lever in the AIR CONDITIONING position, current is then directed through the contacts in the switch to the other three contact bars.

From the upper contact bar current is directed to the fan switch. With the fan switch in the M2 position, as shown, current is directed through the resistor on the right through the normally closed HI blower relay points to the blower motor. The blower motor is operating at medium two speed. Medium one (M1) is obtained by adding another resistor in series with the blower motor.

With fan speed switch in the LO position, the feed circuit from the control is

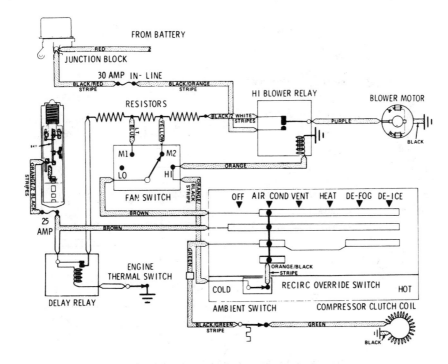

**FIGURE 5-23** Electrical circuit—air conditioning position.

opened at the switch. Low speed is then obtained in the same manner as when the selector lever is in the OFF position.

With the fan speed switch in the HI position, current from the control is directed through the fan speed switch to the HI blower relay, energizing the coil. With the coil energized the lower set of points in the relay close and current from the junction block is directed through a 30 AMP in-line fuse to the lower points in the HI blower relay. Current is then directed through the closed relay points to operate the blower motor at high speed.

From the control, current is directed to the ambient switch. If ambient temperature is above approximately 32°F. the ambient switch is closed and the compressor clutch coil is energized.

Also from the control, current is directed to the Recirc override switch. With the temperature lever in the MAXIMUM COLD position, the Recirc override switch is closed and current is directed to the HI terminal at the fan speed switch. Current is then directed to the HI blower relay coil and the blower motor will operate at high speed.

## SELECTOR LEVER—VENT POSITION

Current is directed from the ignition switch to the fuse block then to the control. With the selector lever in the VENT position the only electrical connection through the control is to the fan switch to operate the blower motor.

Current is directed through the control to the fan switch.

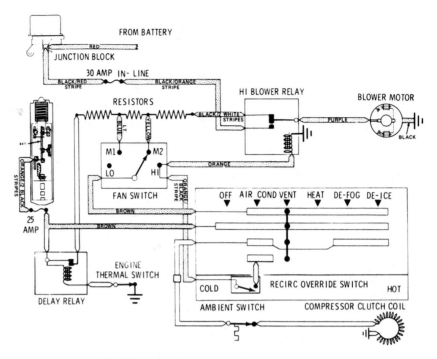

**FIGURE 5-24** Electrical circuit—vent position.

LO blower speed is obtained the same as low speed with the selector lever in the OFF position. Engine coolant temperature must be at least 120 degrees F. to close the engine thermo switch in order to energize the Delay Relay coil.

M1 and M2 blower speeds are obtained in the same manner as shown with the selector lever in the AIR CONDITIONING position.

HI blower speed is obtained by energizing the Hi Blower Relay which directs current from the Junction block, through the closed set of points and directly to the blower motor.

## SELECTOR LEVER—HEAT POSITION

Current is directed from the ignition switch to the fuse block then to the control. With the selector lever in the HEAT position the only electrical connection through the control is to the fan switch to operate the blower motor.

Current is directed through the control to the fan switch.

LO blower speed is obtained the same as low speed with the selector lever in the OFF position. Engine coolant temperature must be at least 120°F. to close the engine thermo switch in order to energize the delay relay coil.

M1 and M2 blower speeds are obtained in the same manner as shown with the selector lever in the air condition position.

HI blower speed is obtained by energizing the HI blower relay which directs current from the junction block, through the closed set of points and directly to the blower motor.

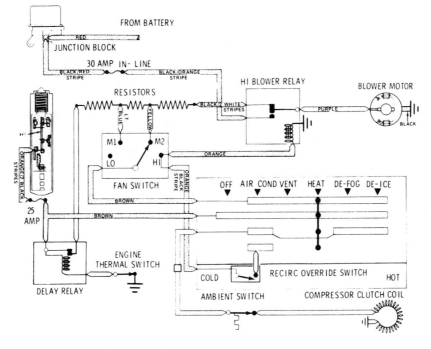

**FIGURE 5-25** Electrical circuit—heat position.

## SELECTOR LEVER—DE-FOG POSITION

Current is directed from the ignition switch to the fuse block then to the control. With the selector lever in the DE-FOG position, electrical connection is made through the control to the fan switch to operate the blower motor and to the air conditioning compressor clutch coil circuit.

The blower motor will operate at the speed selected by the fan switch.

The compressor will operate in the DE-FOG position if the ambient temperature is above approximately 32°F. to close the ambient switch.

**FIGURE 5-26** Electrical circuit—de-fog position.

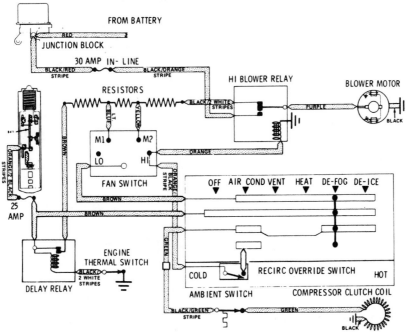

## SELECTOR LEVER—DE–ICE POSITION

Current is directed from the ignition switch to the fuse block then to the control. With the selector lever in the DE-ICE position, electrical connection is made through the control to the fan switch to operate the blower motor and to the air conditioning compressor clutch coil circuit.

The blower motor will operate at the speed selected by the fan switch.

The compressor will operate in the DE-ICE position if the ambient temperature is above approximately 32°F. to close the ambient switch.

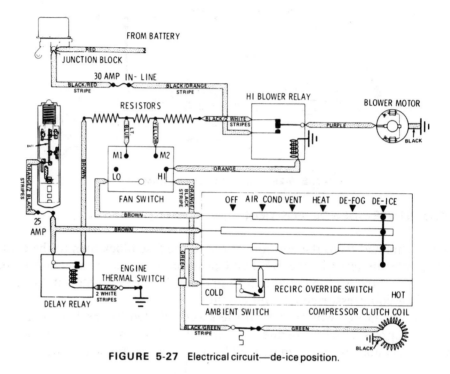

FIGURE 5-27 Electrical circuit—de-ice position.

# Chapter 6

# Air Distribution Controls

This chapter will relate to some of the systems that are used for air distribution, electrical and vacuum. However, there are several variations in the vacuum and electrical operating circuits in different makes and year of production. These variables would be difficult to cover in detail. The diagnostician should understand the normal position of all air doors and the resulting air flow for each of the various positions of the dash control.

An operational check of the air distribution components can be made by operating the air-conditioning system in each of the different selector and temperature lever positions. Should the desired result not be obtained, it will be necessary to determine whether a problem exists in the electrical or vacuum circuits. This check should always be made before diagnosing problems in the refrigeration portion.

## CHRYSLER CONTROLS

The evaporator–heater housing assembly is installed in the passenger compartment beneath the instrument panel. The air-conditioner controls and the air outlet assembly are integral with the instrument panel. In this unit air is pulled through the evaporator coil and pushed toward the heater core by the blower. A blend air door proportions the amount of air through or around the heater core to control the temperature of the outlet air. This door position is controlled by the temperature lever through a flexible cable. The shutoff water valve is also controlled by this lever, through a vacuum switch mounted on the control. When the temperature lever is in the full cool (extreme left) position and the mode lever is on

OFF, MAX A/C, A/C, or VENT, the coolant flow through the heater core will be shut off.

The doors in the unit, except for the blend air door, control the source of the incoming air and the outlet through which it will be discharged. These doors are moved into proper position, as determined by the position of the mode selector lever, by vacuum actuators.

### Mode Lever

The mode lever operates a six-position vacuum-electric switch to select the operating mode of the system as follows:

OFF: shuts off entire system.

MAX A/C: maximum air conditioning using inside air.

A/C: air conditioning with outside air.

VENT: ventilation with outside air. Compressor off.

HEAT: heating.

DEF: windshield defrosting.

### Temperature Lever

The temperature lever controls the temperature of the discharge air in all mode lever positions. Moving the lever to the left provides cooler air and moving it to the right provides warmer air.

### Blower Switch

The blower switch can be operated at three speeds, from low to medium to high. The blower will be on and operating at the fan speed selected in all mode lever positions except OFF.

### Air-Conditioning Outlets

Three air outlets are contained in one unit secured to the lower edge of the instrument panel. Each outlet can be adjusted independently to direct the air up, down, or to either side. Fixed openings in the distribution duct direct cool air to the floor. Each outlet can be shut off independently by moving the vanes completely left.

### Vacuum and Electrical Circuits (Figs. 6-1 and 6-2)

The electrical feed for the air-conditioning circuit is from two fuses in the fuse block (Fig. 6-2). One 20-ampere fuse, cavity 2, protects the compressor clutch circuit, and one 20-ampere fuse, cavity 4, protects the blower motor circuit.

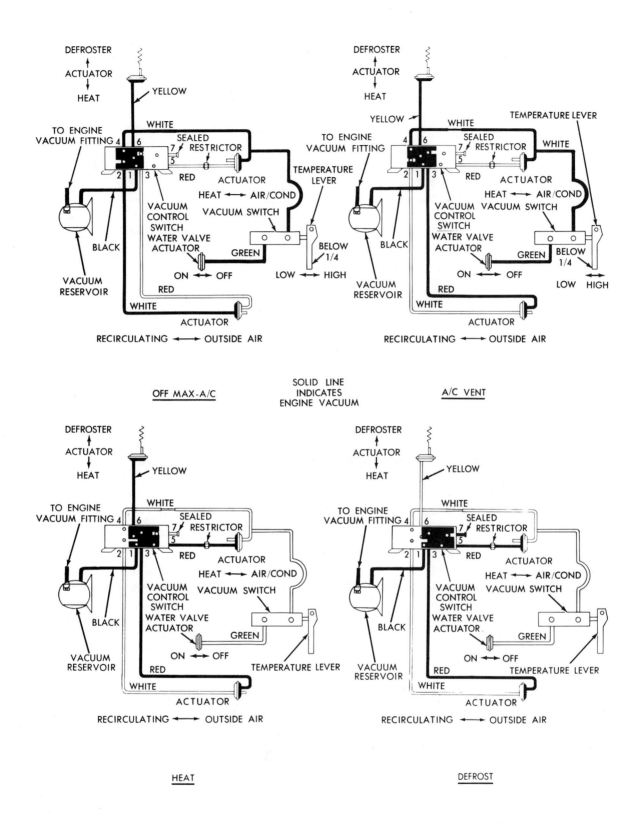

OFF MAX-A/C

SOLID LINE
INDICATES
ENGINE VACUUM

A/C VENT

HEAT

DEFROST

**FIGURE 6-1** Vacuum circuits—heaters and air conditioning. (Courtesy of the Chrysler Corporation.)

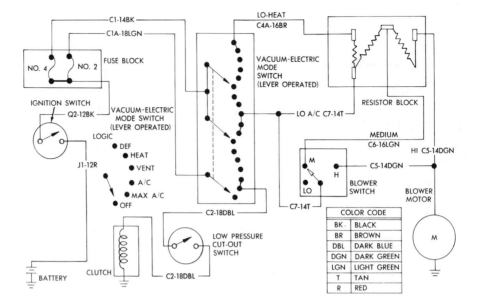

**FIGURE 6-2** Electrical circuit—air conditioning. (Courtesy of the Chrysler Corporation.)

## MODES

The combination vacuum and electrical switch is operated by the mode lever. The vacuum portion of the switch controls the shutoff water valve and positions all doors in the unit except the blend air door. The electrical portion of the switch controls the compressor and blower options. The following is a breakdown of the vacuum and electrical logic for each mode.

### OFF

Vacuum application is Fig. 6-1. The inlet air door is closed to the outside, open to recirculating air. The mode door is in the A/C position. The heat/defrost door is in the HEAT position. The heater core coolant flow is shut off. No air flows through the unit and the compressor is shut off because the blower and compressor clutch circuits are open.

### MAX A/C

All of the doors are in the same position as they are in OFF. The MAX A/C mode merely closes the electrical circuits to the blower motor and the compressor clutch. This mode is recommended for initial cool down, extreme outside humidity, or high ambient temperature.

### A/C

This mode is recommended for use after the car has been cooled to the desired temperature. The vacuum application at the outside-recirculating air door actuator is transferred to the rod side. This moves the door away from the outside-air inlet and closes the recirculating inlet. All other vacuum applications and door positions are the same for the MAX A/C position. The blower motor and compressor is on.

### VENT

The vacuum circuit remains the same as in the A/C position, but the compressor clutch electrical circuit is open, preventing the compressor from operating. The blower motor is used to force outside air into the passenger compartment through the A/C outlets in the instrument panel.

### HEAT

In the HEAT mode the outside air door is open the same as the A/C mode. Vacuum is applied to the rod side of the air-conditioning door actuator, closing off the passage to the air-conditioning distribution duct and opening the passage to the heater–defroster duct. Since the heater–defroster door is raised, the full flow of heated air goes through the heater outlets, except for a small amount that bleeds off through the defroster outlets. The water valve is opened and the blower switch is activated; the compressor is off.

### DEFROST

When the defrost mode is selected, all the conditions are the same as for the heater operation, except that no vacuum is applied to the defroster door actuator, which is spring-loaded to defrost position. The door moves away from the defroster outlets and partially closes off the heater outlets. The heater outlets are left open far enough to direct about 30% of the air to the floor. The other 70% is directed to the windshield area.

#### Temperature Control (Reheat)

A blend air system is used to control the temperature of the outside air flow in all modes. When the temperature lever is on full warm (extreme right), the blend air door directs all the air through the heater core. When the temperature lever is on full cool (extreme left), the blend air door directs all the air around the heater core. When the lever is between the full cool and warm position, the blend air door divides the amount of air going through or around the heater core, depending on the amount of heat called for by the setting of the temperature lever. The heated and unheated air are blended back together to form the final discharge air temperature.

When referring to the temperature control for this unit on A/C or MAX A/C mode, it is known as a reheat system. We call it a reheat system because the heater core and blend air door are positioned after the evaporator, so the air that has been cooled by refrigeration can be reheated by the blend air system. The air-conditioning refrigerant system operates continuously because the compressor is engaged at all times in MAX A/C and A/C modes.

### Water Valve Operation

A vacuum switch mounted on the air-conditioning control controls the operation of a spring-loaded, vacuum-operated water valve. Applying vacuum to the water valve shuts off engine coolant flow to the heater core. The vacuum transfer switch is open when the temperature control lever is in the full cool (extreme left) position. The feed for the switch is taken from the A/C mode door vacuum line so that the coolant shut off system is activated only when the mode door is in the A/C position. Therefore, coolant flow shut off can only be obtained when the temperature lever is in the cool position and the mode lever is in OFF, MAX A/C, A/C, or VENT positions.

#### TESTING WATER VALVE

To test the valve, start the engine, and remove the radiator cap to minimize pressure in the vehicle's cooling system. With the MAX A/C mode selected and the temperature lever in full cool position, test the water valve by momentarily disconnecting the heater outlet hose. A slight spillage of water when the hose is removed is normal. A continuous flow of water indicates that the valve is not closing properly or the vacuum hose is not properly connected or the vacuum switch is not positioned correctly on the instrument panel control. If the shut off valve does not close completely, replace the valve.

### FORD CONTROLS

The Ford and Mercury Heater and Power Ventilation System is a split case design, integral blower system and will control the flow of air inside the car (Figs. 6-3 and 6-4). Two control levers are provided to adjust the desired temperature and system functions. The system will deliver heated or ambient (surrounding) temperature

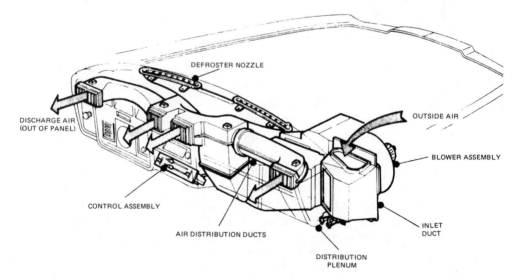

**FIGURE 6-3**   Power ventilation. (Courtesy of the Ford Motor Company.)

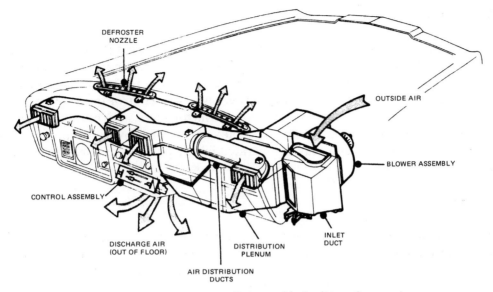

**FIGURE 6-4** Heater system. (Courtesy of the Ford Motor Company.)

outside air as directed by the operator. Blower speeds can be adjusted for more or less air, as desired.

Manual control of the passenger-compartment temperature may be maintained in all function control settings (Fig. 6-5), except when the system is turned off. In hot weather, it will ventilate the car to the outside air temperature. In cold weather, the system may be turned to the OFF position of the function lever to delay the operation of the system until engine coolant has warmed enough to minimize the discharge of cold air. When turned on, the system will then heat the car to the desired temperature. During system operation, outside air is drawn from the cowl vent just below the windshield at all times.

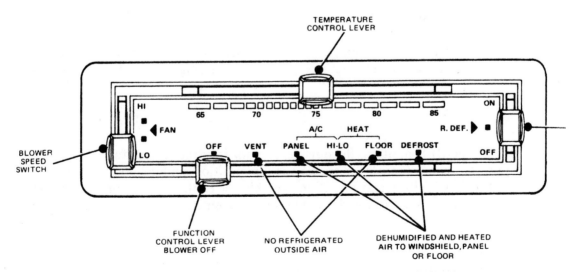

**FIGURE 6-5** Temperature control panel. (Courtesy of the Ford Motor Company.)

**Control Lever Operation**

The Heater and Power Ventilation Control includes a function control lever for OFF, VENT, HI-LO or FLOOR, and DEFROST that determines the manner in which the system will operate, a temperature control lever for manually setting the desired comfort temperature, and a blower switch to control the volume of air movement. Each position of the function control lever and blower switch is detented for positive engagement. The blower switch provides four manually selected blower speeds and may be operated in any position to select the desired amount of air flow.

**Temperature Control**

Temperature control of the heater and power ventilation system is determined by the position of the temperature control lever (between COOL and WARM) of the control assembly (Fig. 6-5) and is accomplished by means of a control cable between the control assembly and the temperature blend door. System air flow is manually controlled by the control assembly. A vacuum selector valve, controlled by the function control lever, distributes vacuum to the various door vacuum motors, which in turn direct the air flow through the system.

The system utilizes what is called a "temperature blend" method to provide controlled temperature to the car interior. With this method all outside air flow from the blower passes through the heater case to the plenum assembly. Temperature is then regulated by heating a portion of the outside air and blending it with the remaining cooler outside air to the desired temperature. Temperature blending is varied by the temperature blend door, which controls the amount of air that flows through or around the heater core, where it is mixed and directed into the distribution plenum. The air is finally directed to the heater ducts, the defroster nozzles, or the instrument panel registers according to the selected function lever position.

**System Air Flow**

Figures 6-6 and 6-7 contain system vacuum schematics and vacuum motor charts which illustrate vacuum routings and air flow during the various system conditions.

*OFF*

In the OFF position, the outside air door is in the closed (full-vacuum) position. The panel doors are in the no-vacuum position, and the floor-defrost door is in the floor (full-vacuum) position. The blower is off and the temperature blend door maintains a position depending on the temperature control lever position.

*VENT*

When the function lever is in the VENT position, the outside air door is open to admit outside air into the system (no vacuum). Both the partial and full panel

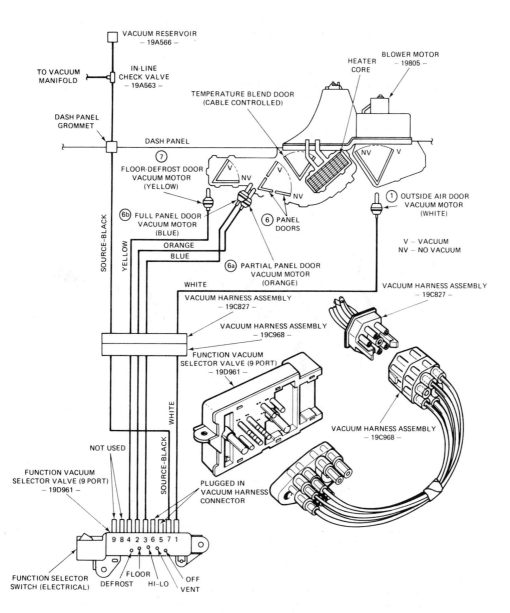

| PORT | FUNCTION | FUNCTION SELECTOR LEVER POSITIONS | | | | | HOSE COLOR |
|------|----------|-----|------|-------|-------|---------|------------|
| | | OFF | VENT | HI-LO | FLOOR | DEFROST | |
| 1 | OUTSIDE AIR | V | | | | | WHITE 1 |
| 2 | PARTIAL PANEL | | V | V | | | ORANGE 6a |
| 3 | FULL PANEL | | V | | | | BLUE 6b |
| 4 | FLOOR-DEFROST | V | V | V | V | | YELLOW 7 |
| 5 | NONE | | TO 6 | TO 6 | TO 6 | TO 6 | PLUGGED |
| 6 | NONE | SEALED | TO 5 | TO 5 | TO 5 | TO 5 | PLUGGED |
| 7 | SOURCE | V. | V | V | V | V | BLACK |
| 8 | NONE | | | | | | OPEN |
| 9 | NONE | | | | | | OPEN |

V = VACUUM    BLANK ATMOSPHERE

P1733-247

**FIGURE 6-6** Heater system air flow schematic and vacuum control chart. (Courtesy of the Ford Motor Company.)

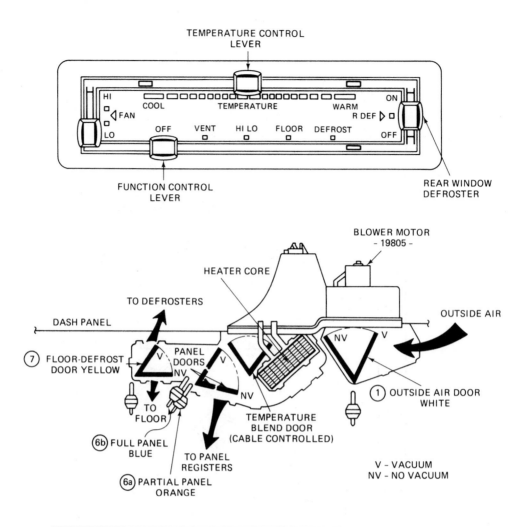

FIGURE 6-7 Heater system vacuum diagram and selector test. (Courtesy of the Ford Motor Company.)

| FORD AND MERCURY HEATER SYSTEM VACUUM MOTOR TEST CHART | | | | |
|---|---|---|---|---|
| FUNCTION CONTROL LEVER POSITION | VACUUM MOTORS APPLIED WITH VACUUM | | | |
| | OUTSIDE | PANEL | | FLOOR-DEFROST |
| | | PARTIAL | FULL | |
| OFF | 1 | 6a | 6b | 7 |
| VENT | – | 6a | – | 7 |
| HI-LO | – | – | – | 7 |
| FLOOR | – | – | – | 7 |
| DEFROST | – | – | – | – |
| VACUUM LINE COLOR CODE | WHITE | ORANGE | BLUE | YELLOW |

– NO VACUUM

doors are in the panel position (vacuum) and the air is distributed out of the instrument panel registers. The floor-defrost door is also applied with vacuum, directing a small amount of air to the floor area. The outside air can be heated to a higher desired temperature by moving the temperature lever toward WARM.

*HI-LO*

HI-LO operation is similar to that described in the VENT position, except that the air flow is divided between the panel registers and the floor ducts. The partial panel door is in the panel position (vacuum), while the full-panel door (no vacuum) routes some of the air flow toward the floor area. A small quantity of this air flow will be directed, through the defroster nozzles, onto the windshield.

### FLOOR

With the function lever in the FLOOR position, the air flow is directed to the floor outlets with a slight amount directed to the windshield through the defroster ducts. The same door positioning exists as in HI-LO except that the partial panel door does not have vacuum applied and panel airflow is stopped.

### DEFROST

When the function lever is in DEFROST position, the panel doors and the floor-defrost door are in the full-defrost (no-vacuum) positions, so that all incoming air is directed to the defroster nozzles with a slight bleed to the floor. Maximum heat is obtained by moving the temperature lever to the highest temperature (warm) position.

## AMERICAN MOTORS CONTROLS

In the air-conditioning mode, a blend of fresh and recirculated cool air may be obtained for the range of travel of the temperature control lever from warm to cold. Total recirculated air may be obtained at the MAX cold position of the temperature control lever. The MAX COLD setting also reduces evaporator temperature approximately 6°F below freezing and is intended for use in extreme conditions until the car interior is cooled. Extended use, particularly in humid conditions, will cause blockage of air due to icing of the evaporator core. Air flow in the A/C mode is shown in Fig. 6-8. Air is drawn into the recirculation door and from outside through the heater core. The air is then directed into the blower housing. The blower forces the air into the evaporator housing, where it is directed through the evaporator core and cooled. The cool air is directed to the panel door and then into the car through the panel registers.

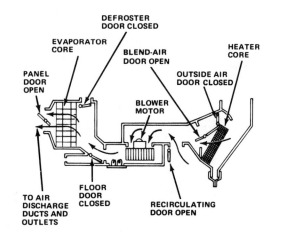

**FIGURE 6-8** View C air conditioning airflow.

## Heater Operation

Move the temperature control lever to the right and press the HEAT or HI-LO pushbuttons. Pressing the heat button will direct heated air to the floor only. Pressing the HI-LO pushbutton will direct heated air to enter through the floor door, the panel register, and defroster door (Fig. 6-9).

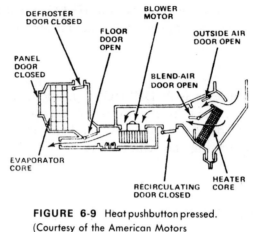

**FIGURE 6-9** Heat pushbutton pressed. (Courtesy of the American Motors Corporation.)

## Fresh Air Ventilation

Fresh air ventilation is accomplished by moving the temperature control lever to the extreme left MAX position, press the HI-LO pushbutton to direct air to the floor, instrument panel registers, and windshield. Move the fan control lever to the speed desired (Fig. 6-10).

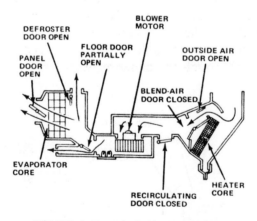

**FIGURE 6-10** Hi-lo pushbutton pressed.

## Defroster Operation

For windshield defrosting, move the temperature control lever to the right and press the DEF pushbutton to direct air through defroster door and onto the windshield (Fig. 6-11).

124

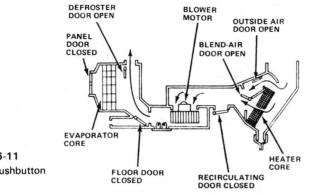

DEFROSTER DOOR OPEN

PANEL DOOR CLOSED

BLOWER MOTOR

OUTSIDE AIR DOOR OPEN

BLEND-AIR DOOR OPEN

EVAPORATOR CORE

HEATER CORE

FLOOR DOOR CLOSED

RECIRCULATING DOOR CLOSED

**FIGURE 6-11**
Defroster pushbutton pressed.

### Heater Water Valve

The heater water valve regulates coolant flow to the heater core. It is vacuum operated by the temperature control lever assembly or pushbutton vacuum-control switch and requires vacuum to shut off flow to the heater core. Vacuum is applied to the valve when the OFF or A/C pushbutton is pressed regardless of temperature control lever position. Vacuum is also applied when the temperature control lever is at the extreme left and the HEAT, HI-LO, or DEF pushbutton is pressed. The water valve is installed in the inlet heater hose.

#### WATER VALVE TEST

A vacuum gauge and tee are required for this test.

1. Disconnect the vacuum hose from the heater water valve.

2. Connect the tee between the vacuum hose and the water valve nipple.

3. Start the engine.

4. Move the temperature control lever to the right and push the HEAT pushbutton. No vacuum should be indicated on the gauge.

5. Observe the water valve while pressing the OFF or A/C pushbutton. Water valve should close and the manifold vacuum should be indicated on the gauge.

6. Observe the water valve while pressing the HEAT pushbutton. The water valve should open and no vacuum should be indicated.

7. Observe the water valve while moving the temperature control lever to the MAX COLD position. The water valve should close and the manifold vacuum should be indicated on the gauge.

### GENERAL MOTORS CONTROLS

The air distribution portion of the air-conditioning system operates essentially the same on all current-model cars. However, there are several variations in the vacuum and electrical operating circuits for different makes and year of production. These variables would be most difficult to cover in detail.

For practical purposes the diagnostician should understand the normal position of all air doors and the resulting air flow distribution that should be anticipated for each of the various positions of the dash control selector and temperature lever. These conditions are shown and described in Figures 6-12 through 6-20.

An operational check of the air distribution components can be made by operating the air-conditioning system in each of the different selector and temperature lever positions. Should the desired results not be obtained, it will be necessary to determine whether a problem exists in the electrical or vacuum circuits. It is essential to make this operational check and correct any difficulties before diagnosing for troubles in the refrigeration portion of the air-conditioning system.

It should be noted that in most 1971 and later model cars, the blower motor is operating when the ignition switch is in the run position even if the select lever is in the off position. Some installations also have a provision that prevents the blower motor from operating until the engine coolant temperature reaches approximately 120°F. (49.0°C).

**Air Flow**

*SELECTOR LEVER—HEAT POSITION*

With the selector lever in the HEAT position, the vacuum-operated doors are positioned as follows:

1. Outside air—fully open to the outside air.

2. Upper mode—open to heat; closed to A/C mode.

3. Lower mode—open to heat mode; closed to A/C mode.

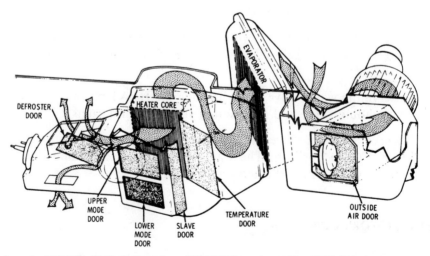

**FIGURE 6-12** Selector lever HEATER Temp. Lever Max. HOT. (Courtesy of AC-Delco.)

4. Slave—in air flow stream (actuated by lower mode door).

5. Defroster—partially open.

Air is being directed out of the heater outlets with a small amount of air being directed on the windshield from the defrost outlets.

### TEMPERATURE LEVER—MAXIMUM HEAT POSITION SHOWN

With the temperature lever in the MAXIMUM HEAT position, all air from the evaporator is directed through the heater core for maximum heating.

Airflow through the heater core may be regulated by moving the temperature lever which regulates the discharge air temperature.

### SELECTOR LEVER—VENT POSITION

With the selector lever in the VENT position, the vacuum-operated doors are positioned as follows:

1. Outside air—fully open to outside air.

2. Upper mode—open to heat mode; closed to A/C mode.

3. Lower mode—closed to heat mode; open to A/C mode.

4. Slave—out of air flow stream (actuated by lower mode door)

5. Defroster—closed to defroster outlets; fully open to heater outlet.

Air is being directed out of both the A/C and heater outlets to provide bilevel ventilation.

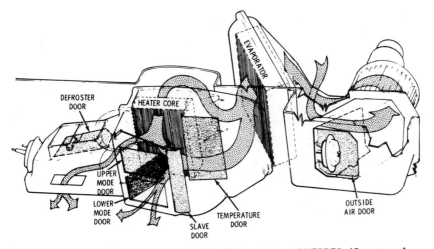

FIGURE 6-13 Selector lever VENT—Temp. Lever CENTERED. (Courtesy of AC-Delco.)

### TEMPERATURE LEVER—CENTERED POSITION

With the temperature lever positioned near the center of the control, the temperature door is positioned so some of the air from the evaporator is directed through the heater core as shown. This air then mixes with the air that bypasses the heater core.

Air flow through the heater core may be regulated by moving the temperature lever which regulates the discharge air temperature.

### SELECTOR LEVER—AIR-CONDITIONING POSITION

With the selector lever in the AIR-CONDITIONING position, the speed of the blower motor is controlled by the fan speed switch unless the temperature lever is in the MAXIMUM COLD position and the vacuum operated doors are positioned as follows:

1. Outside air—see Temperature Lever.

2. Upper mode—closed to heat mode; open to A/C mode.

3. Lower mode—closed to heat mode; open to A/C mode.

4. Slave—out of air flow stream (actuated by lower mode door).

5. Defroster—closed to defroster outlets.

### TEMPERATURE LEVER—MAXIMUM COLD POSITION SHOWN

With the temperature lever at the extreme left, MAXIMUM COLD position, the outside air door opens to recirculate air position and the blower motor operates at high speed. Air discharged from the air-conditioning outlets is approximately 80% air from inside the car (recirculated air) and 20% outside air. The outside air door never fully seals to outside air.

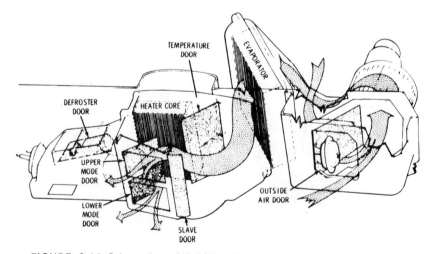

**FIGURE 6-14** Selector lever AIR COND. Temp. Lever Max. COLD. (Courtesy of AC-Delco.)

The temperature door is positioned so that conditioned air from the evaporator core bypasses the heater core, allowing maximum cold air to be discharged from the air-conditioning outlets. By moving the selector lever to the right approximately 1/2 in., to the detent position, the speed of the blower motor is controlled by the fan speed switch and the outside air door returns to the outside air position, completely sealing to recirculate air. Continuing to move the temperature lever from this position to the right will move the temperature door so some or all the air from the evaporator will be directed through the heater core for passenger comfort.

### SELECTOR LEVER—HEAT POSITION

Current is directed from the ignition switch to the fuse block, then to the control. With the selector lever in the HEAT position, the only electrical connection through the control is to the fan switch to operate the blower motor.

Current is directed through the control to the fan switch.

LO blower speed is obtained the same as low speed with the selector lever in the OFF position. Engine coolant temperature must be at least 120°F to close the engine thermo switch in order to energize the delay relay coil.

M1 and M2 blower speeds are obtained in the same manner, as shown with the selector lever in the air-condition position.

HI blower speed is obtained by energizing the HI blower relay, which directs current from the junction block, through the closed set of points, and directly to the blower motor.

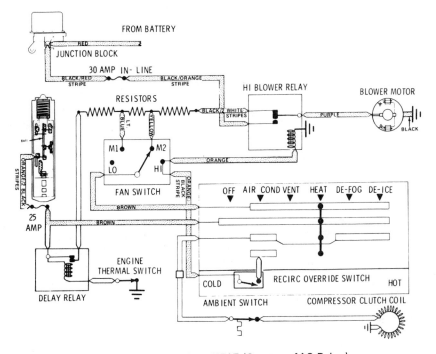

**FIGURE 6-15** Selector lever HEAT. (Courtesy of AC-Delco.)

### SELECTOR LEVER—VENT POSITION

Current is directed from the ignition switch to the fuse block, then to the control. With the selector lever in the VENT position, the only electrical connection through the control is to the fan switch to operate the blower motor.

Current is directed through the control to the fan switch.

LO blower speed is obtained the same as low speed with the selector lever in the OFF position. Engine coolant temperature must be at least 120°F to close the engine thermo switch in order to energize the delay relay coil.

M1 and M2 blower speeds are obtained in the same manner as shown with the selector lever in the AIR–CONDITIONING position.

HI blower speed is obtained by energizing the HI blower relay, which directs current from the junction block, through the closed set of points, and directly to the blower motor.

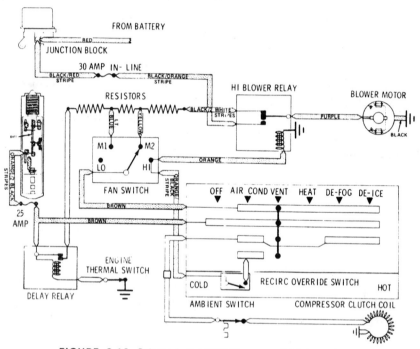

**FIGURE 6-16** Selector lever VENT. (Courtesy of AC-Delco.)

### SELECTOR LEVER—AIR-CONDITIONING POSITION

Current is directed from the ignition switch to the fuse block then to the control. With the selector lever in the AIR–CONDITIONING position, current is then directed through the contacts in the switch to the other three contact bars.

From the upper contact bar, current is directed to the fan switch. With the fan switch in the M2 position, as shown, current is directed through the resistor on the right, through the normally closed HI blower relay points to the blower motor. The blower motor is operating at medium two speed. Medium one (M1) is obtained by adding another resistor in series with the blower motor.

With fan speed switch in the LO position, the feed circuit from the control is opened at the switch. Low speed is then obtained in the same manner as when the selector lever is in the OFF position.

With the fan speed switch in the HI position, current from the control is directed through the fan speed switch to the HI blower relay, energizing the coil. With the coil energized, the lower set of points in the relay close and current from the junction block is directed through a 30-ampere in-line fuse to the lower points in the HI blower relay. Current is then directed through the closed relay points to operate the blower motor at high speed.

From the control, current is directed to the ambient switch. If ambient temperature is above approximately 32°F, the ambient switch is closed and the compressor clutch coil is energized.

Also from the control, current is directed to the Recirc override switch. With the temperature lever in the MAXIMUM COLD position, the Recirc override switch is closed and current is directed to the HI terminal at the fan speed switch. Current is then directed to the HI blower relay coil and the blower motor will operate at high speed.

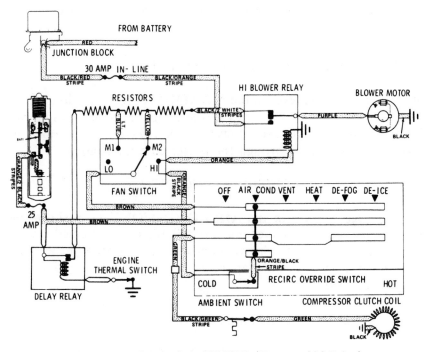

**FIGURE 6-17** Selector lever AIR COND. (Courtesy of AC-Delco.)

### SELECTOR LEVER—HEAT POSITION

With the selector lever in the HEAT position, engine vacuum is directed to port 1 of the selector valve. Vacuum is then directed from port 1 to port 2 which applies vacuum to the lower port of the defroster door diaphragm to partially open the defroster door. All other ports are vented or sealed.

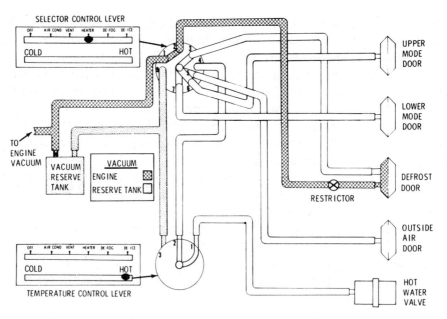

**FIGURE 6-18** Selector lever HEAT Temp. Lever Max. HOT. (Courtesy of AC-Delco.)

### TEMPERATURE LEVER—MAXIMUM HOT POSITION

With the temperature lever in the MAXIMUM HOT position, vacuum from the reserve tank is directed to port 3 of the temperature lever valve, where it is sealed. Ports 1 and 2 are vented, allowing the hot water valve to open, providing engine coolant to circulate through the heater core for heating.

### SELECTOR LEVER—AIR–CONDITIONING POSITION

With the selector lever in the AIR-CONDITIONING position, vacuum is directed from the vacuum reserve tank to port 9, where it is directed to ports 7 and 6 on the selector lever valve. Engine vacuum is sealed at port 1 of the valve. Ports 2 and 3 are vented at the valve. All diaphragms, except the defroster door diaphragm, have vacuum applied.

### TEMPERATURE LEVER—MAXIMUM COLD POSITION SHOWN

With the temperature lever in MAXIMUM COLD position vacuum from the reserve tank is directed from port 3 to ports 2 and 1 of the temperature lever valve. Port 2 directs vacuum to port 4 of the selector lever valve. With the selector lever in the AIR-CONDITIONING position, port 4 is connected to port 5, which moves the outside air door to the recirculate position.

Vacuum is applied to the hot water valve from port 1, which shuts off engine coolant circulation through the heater core.

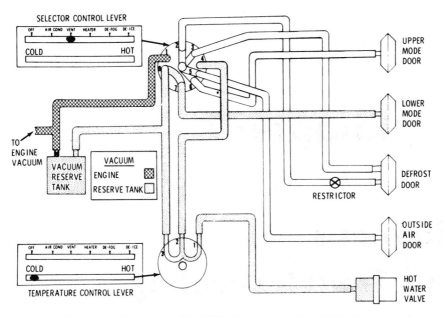

**FIGURE 6-19** Selector level AIR COND. Temp. Lever Max. COLD. (Courtesy of AC-Delco).

As the temperature lever is moved to the right approximately 1/2 in (to detent), port 2 is vented, which vents port 5 to port 4 at the selector lever valve. This allows the outside air door to move to the outside air position closing to recirculate air.

When the temperature lever is moved approximately ¾ in from the MAXIMUM COLD position, toward MAXIMUM HOT, port 1 is also vented, which allows the hot water valve to open.

## REVIEW QUESTIONS

1.  The two fuses in Figure 6-2 protect 2 circuits. What are they?

2.  The water valve operation is controlled by vacuum. If vacuum is applied to the water valve, it will _____ engine coolant flow.

3.  Temperature control of the heater is determined by the position of the _____ .

4.  The A.M.C. water valve is vacuum operated. If no vacuum was applied to the valve, the valve would be in the _____ position.

5.  The G.M. water valve is vacuum operated. To open the water valve vacuum must be _____ .

# Chapter 7

# Diagnosis and Troubleshooting

Because of the many construction and operational variations that exist, there is no uniform or standard diagnosis procedure applicable to all air-conditioning systems. Here are three basic prerequisites to total diagnosis:

1. Be sure that the system has an adequate, but not excessive refrigerant charge.

2. Determine how the system is controlled:

    a. Cycling clutch compressor.

    b. Evaporator pressure control valve.

3. Check the operation of the

    a. Air distribution system.

    b. Blower motor.

    c. Vacuum lines.

    d. Switches.

    e. Hoses.

    f. Air ducts.

These checks will ensure proper operation before diagnosing for faulty units in the refrigeration system.

Following is a brief description of the symptoms that will be in evidence if a malfunction occurs.

## COMPRESSOR

Compressor problems will appear in one of four ways:

1. Noise.

2. Seizure.

3. Leakage—internal and external.

4. Low discharge pressure.

Vibration noises (resonant) are not a cause for alarm; however, irregular noise or rattles are likely to indicate broken parts.

To check for seizure, deenergize the magnetic clutch and check to see if the drive plate can be rotated. If it cannot be rotated, the compressor is seized.

If the compressor has internal leaks, the symptoms would be:

1. Low-side pressure too high.

2. High-side pressure too low.

3. Sight glass clear.

4. Discharge air not sufficiently cool.

Low discharge pressure may be due to:

1. Faulty internal seal of the compressor.

2. Restriction in the compressor.

3. Low refrigerant charge.

## CONDENSER

A condenser may malfunction in two ways:

1. It may leak.

2. It may be restricted.

A condenser restriction will result in excessive compressor discharge pressure. If a small restriction is present, ice or frost will form after the restriction. If air flow through the condenser or radiator is blocked, high discharge pressure will result. During normal condenser operation, the outlet pipe will be slightly cooler than the inlet pipe.

Improper condenser operation would have the following symptoms.

1. Low-side pressure very high.

2. High-side pressure very high.

3. Bubbles may appear in sight glass.

4. Liquid line very hot.

5. Discharge air warm.

## THERMOSTATIC EXPANSION VALVE

Expansion valve failures usually will be indicated by low suction and discharge pressures and inadequate cooling. The failure is generally due to malfunction of the sensing bulb and the closing of the valve. Another cause of the symptom is a clogged inlet screen. Starving the evaporator of refrigerant is the result of too little refrigerant being metered by the expansion valve. This condition will usually be accompanied by frosting at the inlet valve. Another problem the thermostatic expansion valve can cause is flooding of the evaporator. This condition can cause severe damage to the compressor by allowing liquid refrigerant to be drawn into the compressor. A good indication that the evaporator is flooded is a high low-side gauge reading and a low high-side gauge reading. This condition can be caused by:

1. Moisture in the system.

2. Sensing bulb misplaced or defective.

3. Superheat spring defective.

4. Valve stuck open due to dirt.

If dirt is found in the valve, a new screen should be installed and the receiver-dehydrator replaced.

## RECEIVER-DEHYDRATOR

A receiver-dehydrator may fail due to a restriction inside the unit. A restriction at the inlet to the receiver-dehydrator will cause high head pressures. Outlet tube restrictions will be indicated by low head pressure and little or no cooling. The low-pressure side will have a low-pressure reading because the liquid refrigerant will not be getting to the expansion valve. The low-pressure side may go into a vacuum because of a starved evaporator. The liquid line will be cool to the touch, or sweating. The receiver-dehydrator may show heavy sweating.

## EVAPORATOR

When the evaporator is defective, the trouble will show up as an inadequate supply of cool air.

1. Partially plugged core due to dirt.

2. Cracked case.

3. Leaking seal.

## POA OR SUCTION THROTTLING VALVE

If the POA valve is defective, it may cause evaporator pressure to be either too high or too low, depending on the type of failure. No adjustment is possible on POA valves. If the POA valve has failed, it should be replaced. If the POA valve is stuck open, frost may appear all the way to the compressor. If the POA valve is stuck closed, frost may appear up to the valve.

### NOTE:

MOISTURE IN THE SYSTEM CAN CAUSE EITHER THE TXV OR POA VALVE TO FREEZE UP AND MALFUNCTION. BEFORE REPLACING A VALVE, DEFROST THE SYSTEM BY SHUTTING IT DOWN MOMENTARILY AND REPEAT THE PERFORMANCE TEST.

## REFRIGERANT-LINE RESTRICTION

A restriction in the refrigerant line will indicate:

1. Suction line: will cause low suction pressure at the compressor, low discharge pressure, and little or no cooling.

2. Discharge line: will cause the pressure relief valve to open.

3. Liquid line: will cause low discharge and suction pressure, and little cooling.

The sight-glass quick check (Fig. 7-1) can be used to determine if the air-conditioning system has the proper charge.

## SIGHT-GLASS DIAGNOSIS (Fig. 7-1)

At temperatures higher than 70°F (21.1°C) the sight glass may indicate whether the refrigerant charge is suffiicient. A shortage of liquid refrigerant is indicated after 5 minutes of compressor operation by the appearance of slow-moving bubbles or a broken column of refrigerant under the glass. Continuous bubbles may appear in a properly charged system on a cool day. This is a normal condition. If the sight glass is generally clear and the performance is satisfactory, occasional bubbles do not indicate refrigerant shortage. If the sight glass shows foaming or a broken liquid column, partially block the air to the condenser. The high pressure

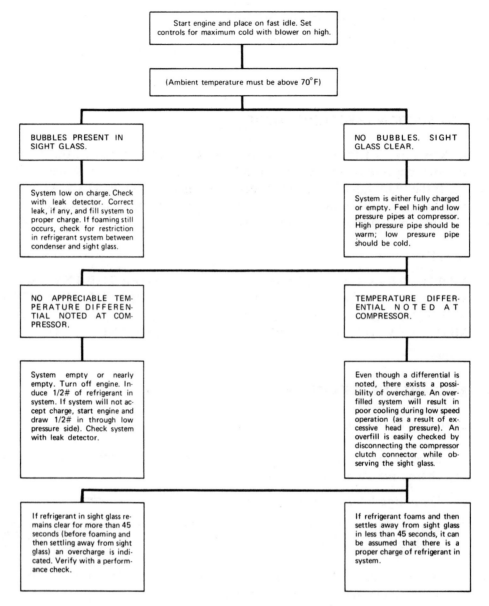

Start engine and place on fast idle. Set
controls for maximum cold with blower on high.

(Ambient temperature must be above 70°F)

BUBBLES PRESENT IN
SIGHT GLASS.

NO BUBBLES. SIGHT
GLASS CLEAR.

System low on charge. Check
with leak detector. Correct
leak, if any, and fill system to
proper charge. If foaming still
occurs, check for restriction
in refrigerant system between
condenser and sight glass.

System is either fully charged
or empty. Feel high and low
pressure pipes at compressor.
High pressure pipe should be
warm; low pressure pipe
should be cold.

NO APPRECIABLE TEM-
PERATURE DIFFEREN-
TIAL NOTED AT COM-
PRESSOR.

TEMPERATURE DIFFER-
ENTIAL NOTED AT
COMPRESSOR.

System empty or nearly
empty. Turn off engine. Induce 1/2# of refrigerant in
system. If system will not ac-
cept charge, start engine and
draw 1/2# in through low
pressure side). Check system
with leak detector.

Even though a differential is
noted, there exists a possibility of overcharge. An overfilled system will result in
poor cooling during low speed
operation (as a result of excessive head pressure). An
overfill is easily checked by
disconnecting the compressor
clutch connector while observing the sight glass.

If refrigerant in sight glass remains clear for more than 45
seconds (before foaming and
then settling away from sight
glass) an overcharge is indicated. Verify with a performance check.

If refrigerant foams and then
settles away from sight glass
in less than 45 seconds, it can
be assumed that there is a
proper charge of refrigerant in
system.

**FIGURE 7-1**   Sight glass quick check procedure. (Courtesy of AC-Delco.)

should go up to at least 250 psi (1723.75 kPa). If the sight glass is clear, the charge is sufficient.

In all instances where the indications of refrigerant shortage continues, additional refrigerant should be added in ¼-lb increments until the sight glass is clear. An additional charge of ½ to 1 lb should be added as a reserve. In no case should the system be overcharged. This procedure can be used to quickly determine whether or not an air-conditioning system has a proper charge of refrigerant. This check can be made in a matter of minutes and help system diagnosis by pinpointing the problem to the amount or charge in the system.

## SYSTEM DIAGNOSIS PROCEDURES

Before making a full performance-diagnosis test, the following should be checked:

1. Proper belt tension and alignment: 140 lb for new belt, 110 lb for used belt.

2. Proper clutch coil terminal connection.

3. Proper clutch engagement.

4. Loose or broken fitting and hoses.

5. Blocked condenser due to foreign material.

6. Proper air duct hose connections.

After making these checks, install pressure gauges and thermometers and conduct a diagnosis test according to the type of system being worked on.

### Cycling Clutch Compressor with Thermostatic Expansion Valve

Follow the steps in Fig. 7-2.

### System Equipped with POA Valve, VIR, or EEVIR

Follow the steps in Fig. 7-3.

> **WARNING:**
>
> DO NOT CONNECT AN R-12 CONTAINER TO THE HIGH-PRESSURE SIDE OF THE SYSTEM OR ANY SYSTEM OF HIGHER PRESSURE. THIS MAY CAUSE EXCESSIVE PRESSURE AND RESULT IN VIOLENT BURSTING OF THE CONTAINER, CAUSING SERIOUS INJURY.

### Cycling Clutch Orifice Tube

Follow the steps in Fig. 7-4.

> **CAUTION:**
>
> ALWAYS REMEMBER TO:

1. Wear goggles.

2. Avoid contact of R-12.

3. Work in a well-ventilated area.

4. Avoid exposure of R-12 to an open flame (phosgene gas).

5. Keep hands, clothing, and equipment away from moving parts.

6. Store R-12 in a cool area and out of the sunlight.

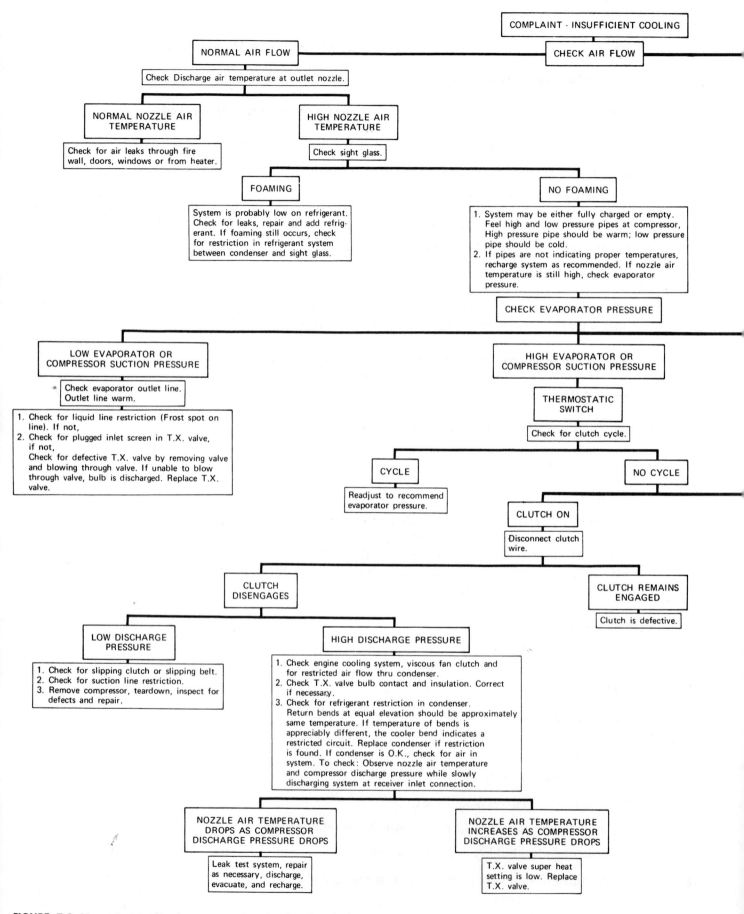

**FIGURE 7-2** Diagnosis procedure for system equipped with cycling clutch compressor and thermostatic expansion valve. (Courtesy of AC-Delco.)

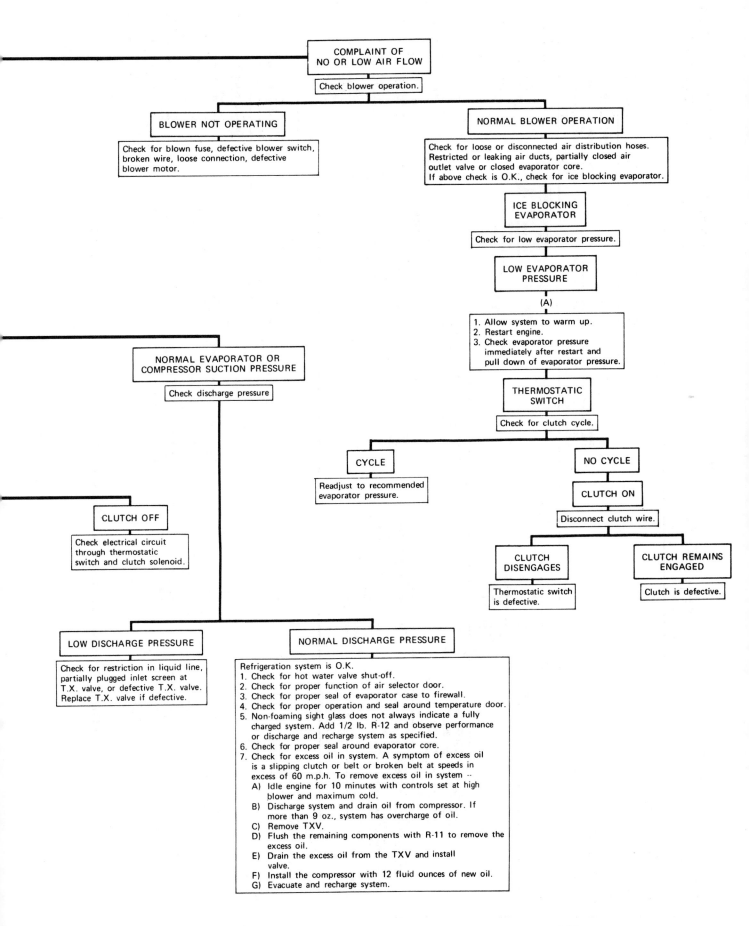

**COMPLAINT OF NO OR LOW AIR FLOW**

Check blower operation.

**BLOWER NOT OPERATING**

Check for blown fuse, defective blower switch, broken wire, loose connection, defective blower motor.

**NORMAL BLOWER OPERATION**

Check for loose or disconnected air distribution hoses.
Restricted or leaking air ducts, partially closed air outlet valve or closed evaporator core.
If above check is O.K., check for ice blocking evaporator.

**ICE BLOCKING EVAPORATOR**

Check for low evaporator pressure.

**LOW EVAPORATOR PRESSURE**

(A)

1. Allow system to warm up.
2. Restart engine.
3. Check evaporator pressure immediately after restart and pull down of evaporator pressure.

**THERMOSTATIC SWITCH**

Check for clutch cycle.

**CYCLE**

Readjust to recommended evaporator pressure.

**NO CYCLE**

**CLUTCH ON**

Disconnect clutch wire.

**CLUTCH DISENGAGES**

Thermostatic switch is defective.

**CLUTCH REMAINS ENGAGED**

Clutch is defective.

**NORMAL EVAPORATOR OR COMPRESSOR SUCTION PRESSURE**

Check discharge pressure

**CLUTCH OFF**

Check electrical circuit through thermostatic switch and clutch solenoid.

**LOW DISCHARGE PRESSURE**

Check for restriction in liquid line, partially plugged inlet screen at T.X. valve, or defective T.X. valve. Replace T.X. valve if defective.

**NORMAL DISCHARGE PRESSURE**

Refrigeration system is O.K.
1. Check for hot water valve shut-off.
2. Check for proper function of air selector door.
3. Check for proper seal of evaporator case to firewall.
4. Check for proper operation and seal around temperature door.
5. Non-foaming sight glass does not always indicate a fully charged system. Add 1/2 lb. R-12 and observe performance or discharge and recharge system as specified.
6. Check for proper seal around evaporator core.
7. Check for excess oil in system. A symptom of excess oil is a slipping clutch or belt or broken belt at speeds in excess of 60 m.p.h. To remove excess oil in system --
   A) Idle engine for 10 minutes with controls set at high blower and maximum cold.
   B) Discharge system and drain oil from compressor. If more than 9 oz., system has overcharge of oil.
   C) Remove TXV.
   D) Flush the remaining components with R-11 to remove the excess oil.
   E) Drain the excess oil from the TXV and install valve.
   F) Install the compressor with 12 fluid ounces of new oil.
   G) Evacuate and recharge system.

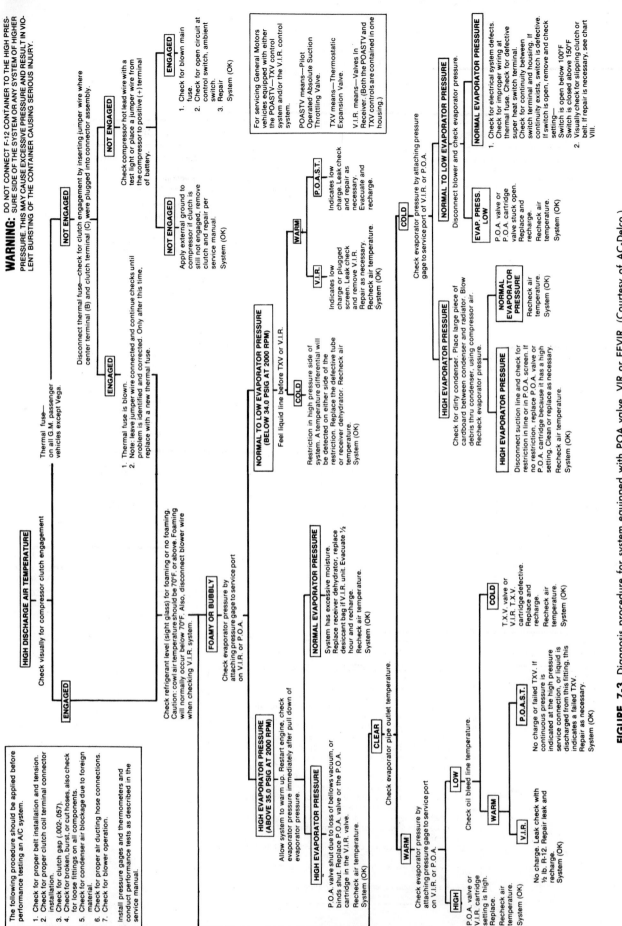

**FIGURE 7-3** Diagnosis procedure for system equipped with POA valve, VIR or EEVIR. (Courtesy of AC-Delco.)

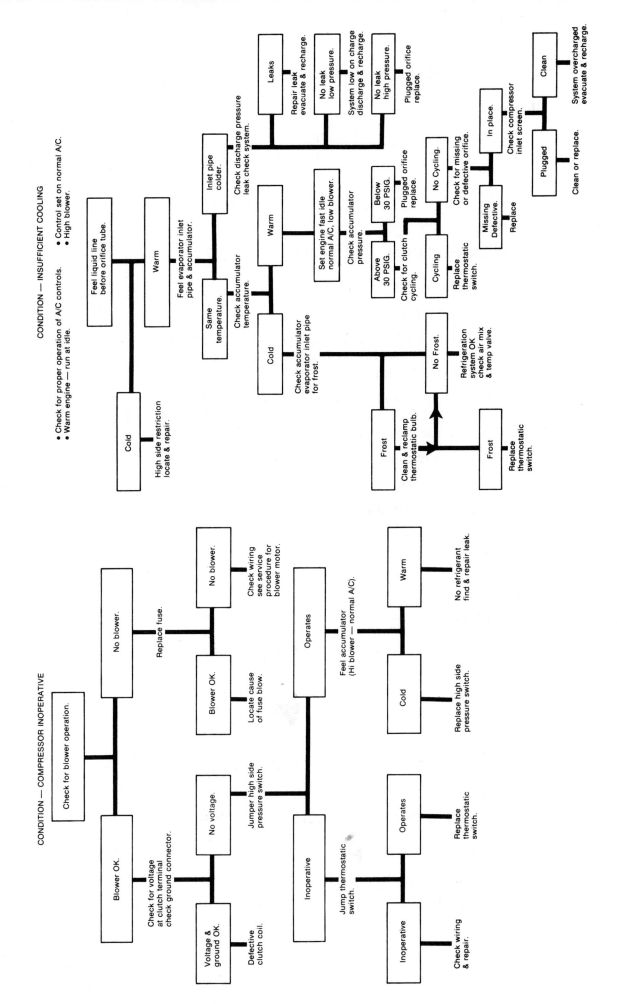

**FIGURE 7-4** Diagnosis procedure for system equipped with cycling clutch compressor, expansion tube (orifice) and accumulator (CCOT). (Courtesy of AC-Delco.)

**Low on Refrigerant**

| Gauge readings | Low side | Low. |
| | High side | Low. |
| Evidence | | Bubbles in sight glass. |
| | | Low gauge readings. |

**NOTE:**

CHECK PERFORMANCE TABLES 7-1 AND 7-2.

1. Add 1 lb of R-12 into the system.

2. Leak-test the system:

   a. To test for leaks on the high-pressure side, operate the air conditioner until the high pressure reaches maximum pressure. Shut the engine off and test for leaks.

   b. To test for leaks on the low-pressure side, leave the engine off and test for leaks. The pressure should be higher than normal at this time because the system pressure is trying to equalize.

3. Discharge refrigerant from the system.

4. Repair the leak.

5. Check the compressor oil

6. Evacuate the system.

7. Charge the system with refrigerant.

8. Check the performance.

**Air in System**

| Gauge readings | Low side | Remains the same. |
| | | Should drop or show |
| | | modulation. |
| | High side | Slightly high. |
| | | Slightly lower if |
| | | large fan is used in |
| | | front of radiator. |
| Evidence | | Discharge air only slightly cool. |

**NOTE:**

CHECK PERFORMANCE TABLES 7-1 AND 7-2.

1. Leak-test the system.

2. Discharge the refrigerant from the system.

3. Repair the leak.

**TABLE 7-1** Performance.

| IN FRONT OF CONDENSER | | | | | | | | |
|---|---|---|---|---|---|---|---|---|
| Relative Humidity (%) | Air Temp. °F | Air Temp. °C | Evaporator Pressure | Engine Speed (rpm) | Discharge Air Temperature °F | Discharge Air Temperature °C | High Pressure psi | High Pressure kPa |
| 20 | 70 | 21 | 29.5 | 2000 | 40 | 4 | 150 | 1034.25 |
|  | 80 | 27 | 29.5 |  | 44 | 7 | 190 | 1310.05 |
|  | 90 | 32 | 30.0 |  | 48 | 9 | 245 | 1689.27 |
|  | 100 | 38 | 31.0 |  | 57 | 14 | 305 | 2102.97 |
| 30 | 70 | 21 | 29.5 | 2000 | 42 | 6 | 150 | 1034.25 |
|  | 80 | 27 | 30.0 |  | 47 | 8 | 205 | 1413.47 |
|  | 90 | 32 | 31.0 |  | 51 | 11 | 265 | 1827.17 |
|  | 100 | 38 | 32.0 |  | 61 | 16 | 325 | 2240.87 |
| 40 | 70 | 21 | 29.5 | 2000 | 45 | 7 | 165 | 1137.67 |
|  | 80 | 27 | 30.0 |  | 49 | 9 | 215 | 1482.42 |
|  | 90 | 32 | 32.0 |  | 55 | 13 | 280 | 1930.60 |
|  | 100 | 38 | 39.0 |  | 65 | 18 | 345 | 2378.77 |
| 50 | 70 | 21 | 30.0 | 2000 | 47 | 8 | 180 | 1241.10 |
|  | 80 | 27 | 32.0 |  | 53 | 12 | 235 | 1620.32 |
|  | 90 | 32 | 34.0 |  | 59 | 15 | 295 | 2034.02 |
|  | 100 | 38 | 40.0 |  | 69 | 21 | 350 | 2413.25 |
| 60 | 70 | 21 | 30.0 | 2000 | 48 | 9 | 180 | 1241.10 |
|  | 80 | 27 | 33.0 |  | 56 | 13 | 240 | 1654.80 |
|  | 90 | 32 | 36.0 |  | 63 | 17 | 300 | 2068.50 |
|  | 100 | 38 | 43.0 |  | 73 | 23 | 360 | 2482.20 |
| 70 | 70 | 21 | 30.0 | 2000 | 50 | 10 | 185 | 1275.57 |
|  | 80 | 27 | 34.0 |  | 58 | 14 | 245 | 1689.27 |
|  | 90 | 32 | 38.0 |  | 65 | 18 | 305 | 2102.97 |
|  | 100 | 38 | 44.0 |  | 75 | 24 | 365 | 2516.67 |
| 80 | 70 | 21 | 30.0 | 2000 | 50 | 10 | 190 | 1310.05 |
|  | 80 | 27 | 34.0 |  | 59 | 15 | 250 | 1723.75 |
|  | 90 | 32 | 39.0 |  | 67 | 19 | 310 | 2137.45 |
| 90 | 70 | 21 | 30.0 | 2000 | 50 | 10 | 200 | 1379.00 |
|  | 80 | 27 | 36.0 |  | 62 | 17 | 265 | 1827.17 |
|  | 90 | 32 | 42.0 |  | 71 | 22 | 330 | 2275.35 |

4. Replace the receiver-dehydrator or desiccant bag.

5. Evacuate the system using a vacuum pump (30 minutes).

6. Charge the system with new R-12.

7. Check the performance.

**NOTE:**

WITH A LEAK IN THE SYSTEM, AIR AND MOISTURE CAN BE DRAWN INTO THE SYSTEM. AFTER THE LEAK HAS BEEN

REPAIRED, EVACUATE THE SYSTEM LONG ENOUGH TO BE
CERTAIN THAT ALL THE MOISTURE HAS BEEN REMOVED.

### Moisture in System

Gauge readings Low side    Normal (may drop into a vacuum).
            High side  Normal (will drop when low side goes into a vacuum).

Evidence  Discharge air is cold but becomes warm when the
low side goes into a vacuum.
The moisture is freezing at the expansion valve,
closing the valve and causing the low-pressure
side to drop into a vacuum.

**TABLE 7-2**  AMC performance.

| Relative Humidity (%) | Air Temp. °F | °C | Engine Speed (rpm) | Discharge Air Temp. °F | °C | Suction Pressure psi | kPa | High Pressure psi | kPa |
|---|---|---|---|---|---|---|---|---|---|
| 20 | 70 | 21 | 1500 | 40 | 4 | 11 | 75.84 | 177 | 1220.41 |
|  | 80 | 27 |  | 41 | 5 | 15 | 103.42 | 208 | 1434.16 |
|  | 90 | 32 |  | 42 | 5.6 | 20 | 137.90 | 226 | 1558.27 |
|  | 100 | 37 |  | 43 | 6.1 | 23 | 158.58 | 255 | 1758.22 |
| 30 | 70 | 21 | 1500 | 40 | 4 | 12 | 82.74 | 181 | 1247.99 |
|  | 80 | 27 |  | 41 | 5 | 16 | 110.32 | 214 | 1475.53 |
|  | 90 | 32 |  | 42 | 5.6 | 22 | 151.69 | 234 | 1613.43 |
|  | 100 | 37 |  | 44 | 6.7 | 26 | 179.27 | 267 | 1840.96 |
| 40 | 70 | 21 | 1500 | 40 | 4 | 13 | 89.63 | 185 | 1275.57 |
|  | 80 | 27 |  | 42 | 5.6 | 18 | 124.11 | 220 | 1516.90 |
|  | 90 | 32 |  | 43 | 6.1 | 23 | 158.58 | 243 | 1675.48 |
|  | 100 | 37 |  | 44 | 6.7 | 26 | 179.27 | 278 | 1916.81 |
| 50 | 70 | 21 | 1500 | 40 | 4 | 14 | 96.53 | 189 | 1303.15 |
|  | 80 | 27 |  | 43 | 5.6 | 19 | 131.00 | 226 | 1558.27 |
|  | 90 | 32 |  | 44 | 6.7 | 25 | 172.37 | 251 | 1730.64 |
|  | 100 | 37 |  | 46 | 7.8 | 27 | 186.16 | 289 | 1992.65 |
| 60 | 70 | 21 | 1500 | 41 | 5 | 15 | 103.42 | 193 | 1330.73 |
|  | 80 | 27 |  | 43 | 6.1 | 21 | 144.79 | 233 | 1606.53 |
|  | 90 | 32 |  | 45 | 7.2 | 25 | 172.37 | 259 | 1785.80 |
|  | 100 | 37 |  | 46 | 7.8 | 28 | 193.06 | 300 | 2068.50 |
| 70 | 70 | 21 | 1500 | 41 | 5 | 16 | 110.32 | 198 | 1365.21 |
|  | 80 | 27 |  | 43 | 6.1 | 22 | 151.69 | 238 | 1641.01 |
|  | 90 | 32 |  | 45 | 7.2 | 26 | 179.27 | 267 | 1840.96 |
|  | 100 | 37 |  | 46 | 7.8 | 29 | 199.95 | 312 | 2151.24 |
| 80 | 70 | 21 | 1500 | 42 | 5.6 | 18 | 124.11 | 202 | 1392.79 |
|  | 80 | 27 |  | 44 | 6.7 | 23 | 158.58 | 244 | 1682.38 |
|  | 90 | 32 |  | 47 | 8.3 | 27 | 186.16 | 277 | 1909.91 |
|  | 100 | 37 |  | — | — | — | — | — | — |
| 90 | 70 | 21 | 1500 | 42 | 5.6 | 19 | 131.00 | 206 | 1420.37 |
|  | 80 | 27 |  | 47 | 8.3 | 24 | 165.48 | 250 | 1723.75 |
|  | 90 | 32 |  | 48 | 8.9 | 28 | 193.06 | 284 | 1958.18 |
|  | 100 | 37 |  | — | — | — | — | — | — |

1. Discharge refrigerant from the system.

2. Replace the receiver-dehydrator or desiccant bag.

3. Evacuate the system with a vacuum pump (30 minutes).

4. Charge the system with R-12.

5. Check the performance.

**NOTE:**

CHECK PERFORMANCE TABLES 7-1 AND 7-2.

### Defective POA Valve

| Gauge readings | Low side | High |
|---|---|---|
| | High side | High. |
| | TXV valve can have the same symptoms. | |

| Evidence | Discharge air only slightly cool. |
|---|---|

If the POA valve is defective, it may cause the evaporator pressure to be either too high or too low, depending on the type of failure. No adjustment is possible on the POA valve. If the POA valve is stuck open, frost may appear all the way to the compressor.

If the POA valve is stuck closed, frost may appear up to the valve and on the oil bleed line. If the POA valve is stuck shut, it will restrict the Freon flow to the compressor, causing the high-side pressure to be lower than normal.

### Replacement

1. Discharge refrigerant from the system.

2. Replace the POA valve with the same type of valve.

3. Evacuate the system using a vacuum pump.

4. Charge the system with R-12.

5. Check the performance of the system.

**NOTE:**

CHECK PERFORMANCE TABLES 7-1 and 7-2.

### System Overcharged or Improper Condenser Operation

| Gauge readings | Low side | Very high. |
|---|---|---|
| | High side | Very high. |

| Evidence | Discharge air warm. |
|---|---|
| | Liquid line very hot. |

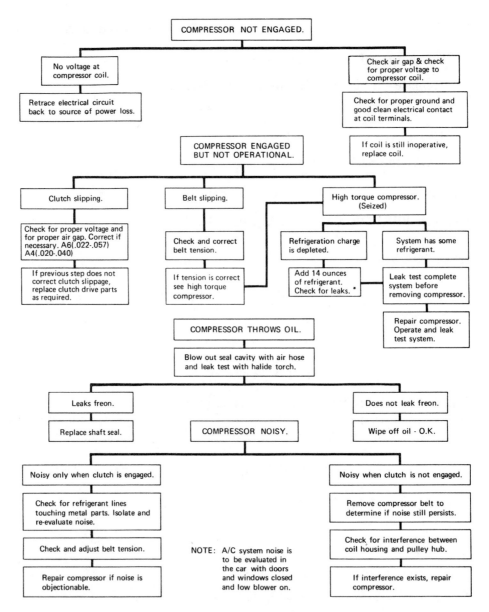

**FIGURE 7-5** Diagnosis GM compressor. (Courtesy of AC-Delco.)

1. Check the drive belts. Loose or worn.

2. Check the condenser for obstructions preventing air flow.

3. Check for a slipping fan clutch.

4. Check the radiator pressure cap and radiator for proper operation.

## OVERCHARGED

1. Discharge the refrigerant until bubbles appear in the sight glass.

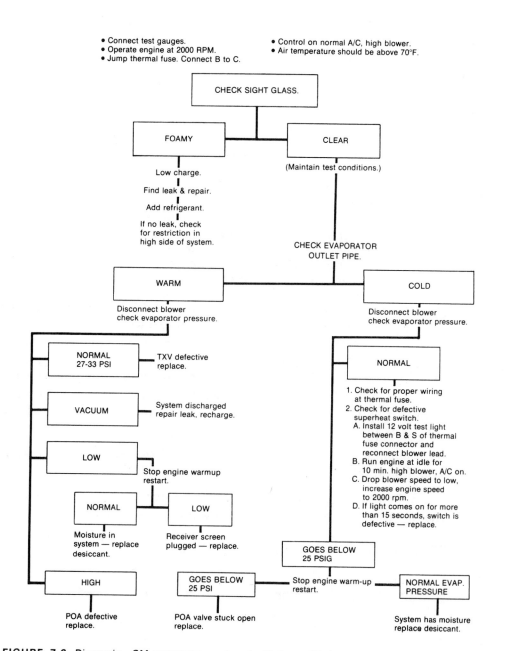

- Connect test gauges.
- Operate engine at 2000 RPM.
- Jump thermal fuse. Connect B to C.

- Control on normal A/C, high blower.
- Air temperature should be above 70°F.

CHECK SIGHT GLASS.

FOAMY

Low charge.

Find leak & repair.

Add refrigerant.

If no leak, check
for restriction in
high side of system.

CLEAR

(Maintain test conditions.)

CHECK EVAPORATOR
OUTLET PIPE.

WARM

Disconnect blower
check evaporator pressure.

COLD

Disconnect blower
check evaporator pressure.

NORMAL
27-33 PSI

TXV defective
replace.

VACUUM

System discharged
repair leak, recharge.

LOW

Stop engine warmup
restart.

NORMAL

Moisture in
system — replace
desiccant.

LOW

Receiver screen
plugged — replace.

HIGH

POA defective
replace.

GOES BELOW
25 PSI

POA valve stuck open
replace.

NORMAL

1. Check for proper wiring
   at thermal fuse.
2. Check for defective
   superheat switch.
   A. Install 12 volt test light
      between B & S of thermal
      fuse connector and
      reconnect blower lead.
   B. Run engine at idle for
      10 min. high blower, A/C on.
   C. Drop blower speed to low,
      increase engine speed
      to 2000 rpm.
   D. If light comes on for more
      than 15 seconds, switch is
      defective — replace.

GOES BELOW
25 PSIG

Stop engine warm-up
restart.

NORMAL EVAP.
PRESSURE

System has moisture
replace desiccant.

FIGURE 7-6 Diagnosis—GM compressor equipped with thermal limiter and super heat switch. (Courtesy of AC-Delco.)

2. High and low gauge readings should drop below normal.

3. Add R-12 until bubbles disappear and pressures return to normal.

4. Add ½ lb more refrigerant.

5. Check the performance.

**NOTE:**

CHECK PERFORMANCE TABLES 7-1 AND 7-2.

### Thermostatic Expansion Valve Stuck

*OPEN*

| | | |
|---|---|---|
| Gauge readings | Low side | High. |
| | High side | Normal to lower than normal. |

Evidence          Discharge air warm.
Suction hose shows heavy sweating.

Expansion valve stuck open will allow excessive refrigerant to flow into the evaporator. This condition can cause *severe* damage to the compressor by allowing liquid refrigerant to be drawn into the compressor.

1. Check for improper mounting of the sensing bulb. Evaporator performance depends largely upon good thermostatic expansion valve control, and good valve control depends upon response to a temperature change in the refrigerant gas leaving the evaporator. Care must be given to remote bulb location. It should be clamped to the suction line near the evaporator outlet. The sensing bulb should be protected from the effect of an air stream. Use material that will not absorb water, to prevent ice from forming at the sensing bulb.

2. Spray liquid R-12 on the sensing bulb and watch the low-pressure gauge. It should drop into a vacuum.

3. Warm the sensing bulb with your hand and watch the low-pressure gauge. The low pressure should start to climb to a normal reading.

### TO REPLACE THE EXPANSION VALVE

1. Discharge the system.

2. Replace the expansion valve.

3. Evacuate the system with a vacuum pump.

4. Charge the system.

5. Check the performance.

*CLOSED*

| | | |
|---|---|---|
| Gauge readings | Low side | Very low (0 to vacuum). |
| | High side | Low |

Evidence          Discharge air slightly cool.
Sweating or frost on expansion valve.

The expansion valve is restricting the flow of refrigerant into the evaporator, causing a starved condition. The cause may be due to

1. Stuck valve.

2. Clogged screen.

3. Sensing bulb lost its charge or broken.

**NOTE:**

THE SIGHT GLASS SHOULD BE CLEAR. IF BUBBLES APPEAR, THE SYSTEM COULD BE VERY LOW ON REFRIGERANT. ADD ½ LB OF R-12 AND CHECK THE PRESSURES.

**CHECKING**

If the expansion valve is cool to the touch, proceed as follows:

1. Adjust the air conditioning for maximum cooling.

2. Spray liquid R-12 over the sensing bulb and the expansion valve.

3. Note the low-side gauge reading. Should drop into a vacuum.

4. Warm the expansion valve with your hand and repeat step 3.

5. If the tests indicate that the valve operation is O.K., clean the contact surface of the evaporator outlet pipe and sensing bulb.

6. Clamp the sensing bulb securely to the evaporator outlet pipe and check the gauge readings again.

**REPLACING**

1. Discharge the system.

2. Disconnect the expansion valve.

3. Inspect the inlet screen. (If clear, replace the valve.)

4. Replace the expansion valve.

5. Evacuate the system.

6. Charge the system.

7. Check the performance.

### Restriction in High Side

| Gauge Readings | Low side | Low. |
| --- | --- | --- |
| | High side | Low. |
| | | |
| Evidence | Discharge air slightly cool. | |
| | Receiver-dehydrator may show frost | |
| | or sweating. | |
| | Liquid line will be cool. | |

The restriction may be in the receiver-dehydrator or the liquid line, causing the compressor to remove refrigerant from the evaporator faster than it can be replaced. Examine the condenser tubes for damage and look for temperature changes, which will indicate a restriction.

1. Discharge the system.

2. Remove the defective part.

3. Evacuate the system with a vacuum pump.

4. Charge the system.

5. Check the performance.

### Chrysler Evaporator Pressure Regulator Valve

Testing the EPR valve requires three gauges: the regular manifold gauge set plus an auxiliary low-pressure compound gauge. Connect the gauges as seen in Fig. 7-7.

1. The regular manifold low-pressure gauge is connected to a service fitting at a point where the low-pressure line enters the compressor. It will read evaporator outlet pressure *before* the EPR valve.

2. The auxiliary low-pressure gauge is connected to a service fitting on the compressor head. It will read the compressor inlet pressure *after* the EPR valve.

3. The regular manifold high-pressure gauge is connected to a service fitting usually found on the muffler. It will read the compressor outlet pressure.

**FIGURE 7-7** Diagnosis Chrysler EPR and ETR. (Courtesy of AC-Delco.)

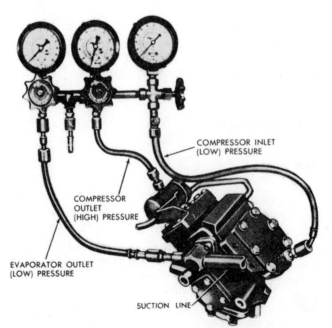

Operate the engine at 1300 rpm for 15 to 20 minutes with A/C controls at maximum cooling, hood and windows open to stabilize the system. At normal operation at 75°F (23.9°C) ambient temperature, the high-pressure gauge reading should be in the range 185 to 205 psi (1275.57 to 1413.47 kPa) and the low-pressure gauge reading should be in the range 22 to 30 psi (151.69 to 206.85 kPa).

The auxiliary gauge should read 15 psi (103.42 kPa) or less. If pressure will not drop to 15 psi (103.42 kPa), increase the engine speed to 2000 rpm.

At higher temperatures (85 to 90°F) (29.4 to 32.2°C) the evaporator pressure may be 35 to 37 psi (241.32 to 255.15 kPa) and the compressor inlet pressure only 1 to 4 psi (6.899 to 27.58 kPa) lower.

### EPR VALVE STUCK CLOSED

| | |
|---|---|
| Gauge readings | Low side (evaporator) High.<br>Low side (comp. inlet) Low.<br>High side Low. |
| Evidence | Evaporator freezes.<br>No cooling. |

Operate the system for 5 minutes to stablize the system. The high side should be about 140 to 210 psi (965.30 to 1447.95 kPa). If the pressure drop between evaporator suction and compressor inlet is not greater than 6 psi (41.37 kPa), the system is operating normal. If the pressure drop is greater than 6 psi (41.37 kPa), there is a low-side restriction or the EPR valve is stuck *closed*. Check for low-side restrictions and if none is found, replace the EPR valve.

### NOTE:

1.  There should be 2 to 5 psi (13.79 to 34.47 kPa) difference between evaporator suction and compressor inlet when the EPR is open.

2.  There should be 10 to 20 psi (68.95 to 137.90 kPa) difference when the EPR valve is regulating.

3.  The evaporator suction should never be below 22 psi (151.69 kPa).

4.  The EPR valve should be fully open when the evaporator suction is above 28 to 30 psi (193.06 to 206.85 kPa), and the compressor inlet should be 2 to 5 psi less than evaporator suction.

If the EPR valve is defective, it must be replaced.

1.  Discharge the system.

2.  Remove the EPR valve from the compressor suction passage. Use the special tool (Chrysler C-3822) to rotate the EPR valve counterclockwise and then withdraw the valve and O-ring.

3.  Install a new O-ring on the new EPR valve and lubricate the seal with refrigerant oil. Insert the valve in the compressor suction passage and rotate the valve clockwise to lock it in place. Use the special tool (C-3822).

Be careful when handling the EPR valve and always wipe it clean with a lint-free cloth before installing.

4. Evacuate the system using vacuum pump.

5. Charge the system.

6. Check the performance.

7. Refer to Fig. 7-8 if thermal sensing tube expansion valve is used.

8. Refer to Fig. 7-9 if "H" type expansion valve is used.

**FIGURE 7-8** Diagnosis with thermo sensing tube expansion valve. (Courtesy of the Chrysler Corporation.)

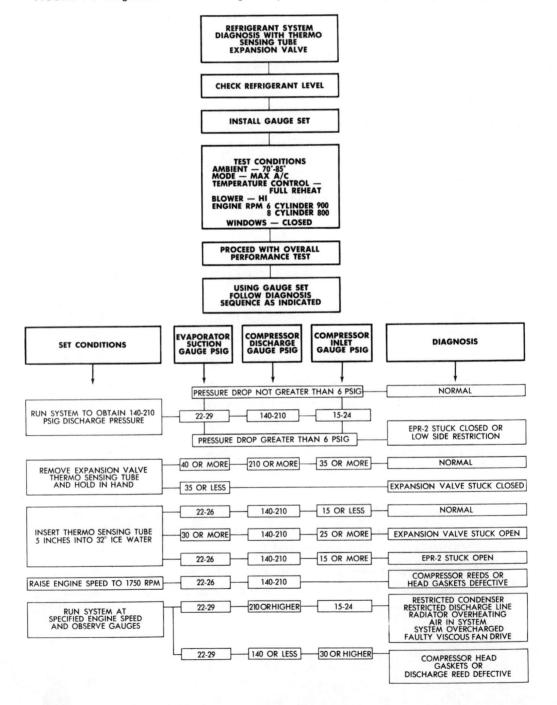

*EPR VALVE STUCK OPEN*

Gauge readings       Low side (evaporator) Low.
                               Low side (compressor inlet) High.
                               High side High.

Evidence              Little cooling.

The EPR valve is defective and must be replaced.

1. Discharge refrigerant from the system.

**FIGURE 7-9** Diagnosis with "H" type expansion valve. (Courtesy of the Chrysler Corporation.)

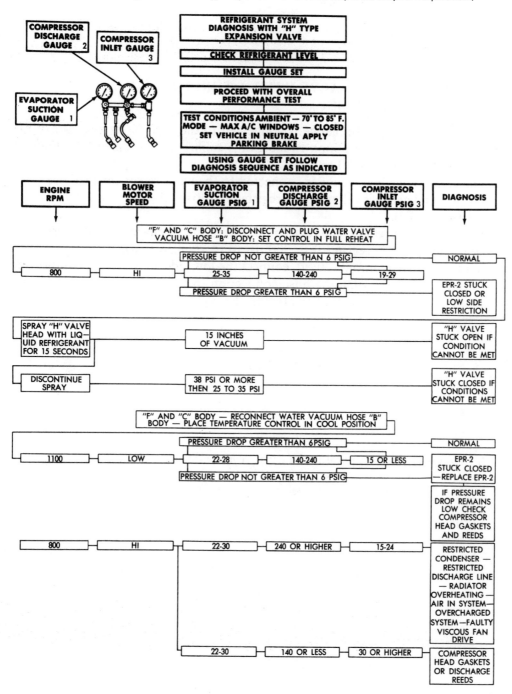

2. Remove the EPR valve from the compressor suction passage. Use the special tool (Chrysler C-3822) to rotate the EPR valve counterclockwise and then withdraw the valve and O-ring.

3. Install a new O-ring on the new EPR valve and lubricate the seal with refrigerant oil. Insert the valve in the compressor suction passage and rotate the valve clockwise to lock it in place. Use the special tool (C-3822). Be careful when handling the EPR valve and always wipe it clean with a lint-free cloth before installing.

4. Evacuate the system using a vacuum pump.

5. Charge the system.

6. Check the performance.

7. Refer to Fig. 7-8 if thermal sensing tube expansion valve is used.

8. Refer to Fig. 7-9 if "H" type expansion valve is used.

### TESTING THE EPR VALVE WITH A THREE-GAUGE MANIFOLD GAUGE SET

The evaporator suction gauge is connected to the suction service port of the compressor. This is a compound gauge and is calibrated to register 0 to 30 in. of vacuum and 0 to 150 psi (0 to 1034.25 kPa).

The compressor inlet gauge is connected to the compressor inlet service port. This compound gauge is calibrated to register 0 to 30 in. of vacuum and 0 to 150 psi (0 to 1034.25 kPa).

The discharge pressure gauge is connected to the discharge service port. This gauge is calibrated to register 0 to 300 psi (0 to 2068.50 kPa).

If a two-gauge manifold is used, connect the low-side gauge to the compressor inlet fitting and then switch the hose connection to the evaporator outlet fitting. Purge air from the hose before tightening the connection.

### REVIEW QUESTIONS

1. Starving the evaporator is the result of too little refrigerant being metered by the _____.

2. Flooding of the evaporator can cause severe damage to the _____.

3. The POA Valve can be adjusted for better pressure. T or F.

4. If the EPR valve is defective, the system must be discharged before the valve can be replaced. T or F.

5. A 2-gauge manifold set cannot be used to check the EPR valve. T. or F.

# Chapter 8

# Compressor—Minor Repairs

## GM SIX-CYLINDER COMPRESSOR (A-6)

The following operations to the compressor clutch plate and hub, pulley and bearing, and coil housing are covered as minor repairs because they may be performed without first discharging the system or removing the compressor from the car.

The compressor shaft seal, pressure relief valve, and superheat switch may also be serviced without removing the compressor from the car, but these operations require the system to be completely discharged.

The procedures used in describing these operations will be with the compressor removed from the car. When servicing the compressor, remove only the necessary parts that need to be serviced.

## Clutch Plate and Hub Assembly (Fig. 8-1)

### REMOVAL

1. Place the holding fixture (J-9396) in a vise and clamp the compressor in the holding fixture.

2. Keep the clutch hub from turning with the clutch hub holder (J-9403) and remove the lock nut from the end of the shaft using a 9/16" thin-wall socket.

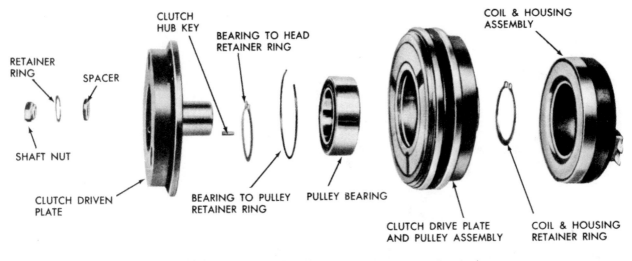

FIGURE 8-1  Clutch plate and hub assembly. (Courtesy of AC-Delco.)

## NOTE:

TO AVOID INTERNAL DAMAGE TO THE COMPRESSOR, DO NOT DRIVE OR POUND ON THE CLUTCH PLATE AND HUB ASSEMBLY OR THE END OF THE SHAFT. IT IS POSSIBLE TO DISTURB THE POSITION OF THE AXIAL PLATE, RESULTING IN COMPRESSOR DAMAGE AND SEAL LEAKAGE DUE TO SHIFTING OF THE CRANKSHAFT.

3. Thread clutch plate and hub assembly remover J-9401 into hub. Hold the body of the remover with a wrench and tighten the center screw to remove the clutch plate and hub assembly.

4. Remove the square drive key from the shaft or drive plate hub.

5. Remove the hub spacer retainer ring using snap-ring pliers J-5403, and then remove the hub spacer (Fig. 8-2).

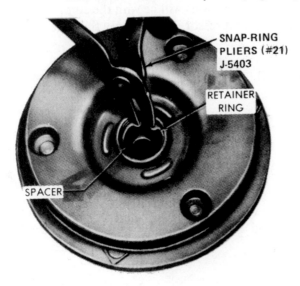

FIGURE 8-2 Remove retainer ring and spacer. (Courtesy of Oldsmobile Division of General Motors Corp.)

6. Inspect the drive plate for cracks or stress in the drive surface. Do not replace the drive plate for just a scoring condition. If the frictional surface shows signs of damage due to excessive heat, the clutch plate and hub and pulley and bearing should be replaced. Check for:

   a.  Low coil voltage. Should be 3.2 amperes at 12 volts.

   b.  Internal compressor parts binding.

   c.  Clutch air gap too wide.

   d.  Broken drive plate to hub assembly springs.

## INSTALLATION

1.  Insert the square drive key into the hub of the driven plate; allow it to project about 3/16 in. out of the keyway.

2.  Line up the key in the hub with the keyway in the shaft.

3.  Position the drive plate installer J-9480-1 on the threaded end of the shaft. The spacer J-9480-2 should be in place under the hex nut on the tool. This tool has a left-hand thread on the body.

4.  Press the driven plate onto the shaft until there is about 3/32 in. of space between the frictional faces of the clutch drive plate and pulley.

5.  Install the hub spacer and, using snap-ring pliers J-5403, install the retainer ring with the convex side of ring facing spacer.

6.  Use a thin wall socket and a clutch hub holder to install a new shaft locknut with the shoulder or circular projection on the locknut facing toward the retainer ring. Tighten the nut to 14 to 26 ft-lb torque. Air gap between the frictional faces should now be 0.022 to 0.057 in. If not, check for a mispositioned key or shaft (Fig. 8-3).

**FIGURE 8-3** Checking air gap. (Courtesy of Oldsmobile Division of General Motors Corp.)

7. The pulley should now rotate freely.

8. Install the compressor on the car and adjust the belts.

9. Operate the system under maximum-load conditions and engine speed at 2000 rpm. Rapidly engage and disengage the clutch at least 15 times to burnish the mating parts of the clutch.

### Pulley and Bearing Assembly

#### REMOVAL

1. Remove the clutch plate and the hub assembly.

2. Remove the pulley and bearing assembly.

3. Remove the pulley bearing retainer ring (Fig. 8-4)

4. Place the pulley and bearing assembly on J-21352 and, using the pulley bearing remover J-9398 with a handle or a brass drift, drive the bearing out of the pulley (Fig. 8-5).

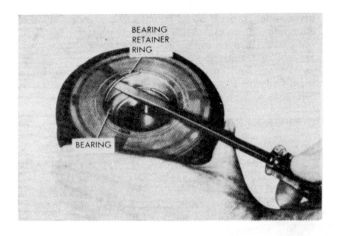

FIGURE 8-4 Remove pulley bearing retainer. (Courtesy of Oldsmobile Division of General Motors Corp.)

FIGURE 8-5 Remove pulley bearing. (Courtesy of Oldsmobile Division of General Motors Corp.)

**NOTE:**

DO NOT CLEAN THE NEW BEARING WITH ANY TYPE OF SOLVENT.

#### INSTALLATION

1. Install the new bearing in the pulley using the pulley and bearing installer J-9481 and handle J-8092. The installer will apply force to the outer race of the bearing (Fig. 8-6).

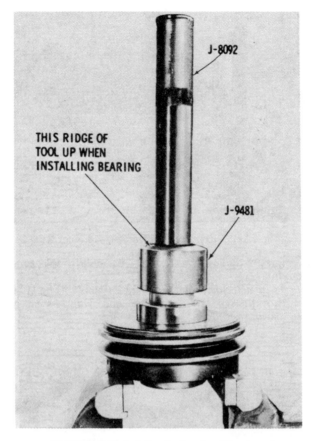

J-8092

THIS RIDGE OF
TOOL UP WHEN
INSTALLING BEARING

J-9481

**FIGURE 8-6** Install pulley bearing. (Courtesy of
Oldsmobile Division of General Motors Corp.)

2. Install the bearing retainer ring. Make sure that it is properly seated in the ring groove.

3. Install the pulley and bearing assembly.

4. Install the clutch plate and hub assembly.

## Clutch Coil and Housing Assembly

### REMOVAL

1. Remove the clutch plate and hub assembly.

2. Remove the pulley and bearing assembly.

3. Note the position of the terminals on the coil housing and scribe the location on the front of the compressor head casting.

4. Remove the coil housing retaining ring using snap-ring pliers J-6435.

5. Lift off the coil and housing.

*INSTALLATION*

1.  Position the coil and housing assembly on the compressor so that the electrical terminals line up with the marks previously scribed.

2.  Align the locating tabs on the coil housing with the holes in the front head casting.

3.  Install the coil housing retainer ring with the flat side of the ring facing the coil.

4.  Install the pulley and bearing assembly.

5.  Install the clutch plate and hub assembly.

**NOTE:**

IT WILL BE NECESSARY TO DISCHARGE THE REFRIGERANT FROM THE SYSTEM BEFORE PROCEEDING WITH THE NEXT OPERATION.

### Shaft Seal

The shaft seal should not be replaced because of an oil line on the hood insulator. The seal is designed to seep a little oil for lubrication. The shaft seal is only to be replaced if there is a refrigerant leakage as determined by a leak detector.

**NOTE:**

CAST-IRON SEAL SEATS MAY BE FOUND IN GM VEHICLES UP TO AND INCLUDING 1968 MODELS. LATER MODELS AND ALL REPLACEMENT SEAL KITS CONTAIN THE CERAMIC SEAL SEAT.

*REMOVAL*

1.  After discharging the system, remove the clutch plate and hub assembly.

2.  Pry out the sleeve retainer and remove the absorbent sleeve. Remove the shaft seal seat retaining ring, using snap-ring pliers (Fig. 8-7).

3.  Clean the inside of the compressor neck area to prevent dirt or foreign material from getting into the compressor.

4.  Place seal protector J-22974 over the end of the shaft to prevent chipping the ceramic seat. Fully engage the knurled tangs of the seal seat remover-installer J-23128 into the recessed portion of the seal seat by turning the handle clockwise. Lift the seat from the compressor with a twisting motion (Fig. 8-8).

**NOTE:**

DO NOT TIGHTEN THE HANDLE WITH A WRENCH OR PLIERS.

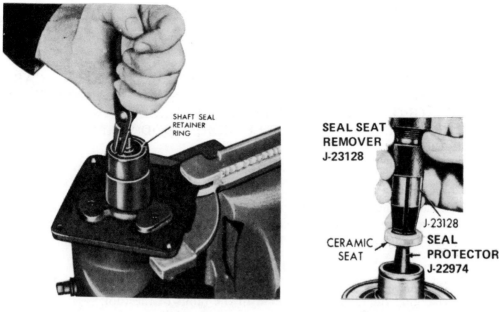

**FIGURE 8-7** Removing and installing shaft seal seat retainer. (Courtesy of AC-Delco.)

**FIGURE 8-8** Remove seal seat. (Courtesy of AC-Delco.)

5. With seal protector J-22974 still over the end of the shaft, engage the tabs on the seal assembly with the tangs on the seal installer J-9392 by twisting the tool clockwise while pressing the tool down. Then lift the seal assembly out (Fig. 8-9).

6. Remove the seal seat O-ring from the compressor neck using the O-ring remover J-9533.

7. Check the inside of the compressor neck for dirt and be sure that this area is clean before installing new parts.

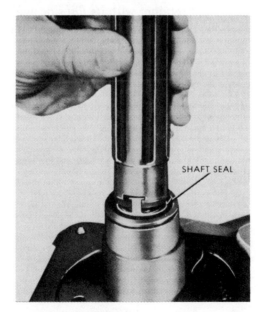

**FIGURE 8-9** Removing and installing shaft seal. (Courtesy of AC-Delco.)

163

**NOTE:**

DO NOT REUSE SEALS, ALWAYS USE A NEW SEAL KIT. BE CARE-
FUL THAT THE FACE OF THE SEAL IS NOT SCRATCHED OR
DAMAGED. MAKE SURE THAT THE SEAL SEAT AND SEAL ARE
FREE OF LINT AND DIRT TO ENSURE GOOD SEALING.

*INSTALLATION*

1.  Coat the new seal seat O-ring with clean refrigerant oil and install in the
    compressor neck, making certain that it is installed in the bottom groove.
    The top groove is for the retainer ring. Use the O-ring installer J-21508.

2.  Coat the O-ring and seal face of the new seal assembly with clean
    refrigerant oil. Mount the seal assembly to the seal installer J-9392 by
    engaging the tabs of the seal with the tangs of the tool.

3.  Place seal protector J-22974 over the end of the shaft and carefully slide the
    new seal onto the shaft. Twist the tool clockwise, while pushing the seal
    assembly down the shaft until the seal assembly engages the flats on the
    shaft and is seated in place. Disengage the tool by pressing downward and
    twisting the tool counterclockwise.

4.  Coat the seal face of the new seal seat with clean refrigerant oil. Mount the
    seal seat on the seal seat remover-installer J-23128 and install it in the com-
    pressor neck. Be careful not to dislodge the seal seat O-ring and be sure that
    the seal seat makes a good seal with the O-ring. Remove the seal protector
    J-22974 from the end of the shaft.

5.  Install the new seal seat retainer with its *flat* side against the seal seat, using
    snap-ring pliers J-5403. Press in on the seal seat retainer ring until it snaps
    into its groove.

6.  Install compressor leak test fixture J-9625 on the rear head of the compres-
    sor and connect the gauge charging lines as shown for the bench test in Fig.
    8-10 or pressurize the suction side of the compressor on the car with R-12

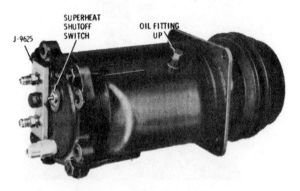

**FIGURE 8-10** Leak test adapter. (Courtesy of Oldsmobile
Division of General Motors Corp.)

vapor to equalize pressure to the drum pressure. Temporarily install the shaft nut and, with the compressor in a horizontal position and the oil sump down, rotate the compressor shaft in the normal direction of rotation several times by hand. Leak-test the seal with a leak detector. Remove and discard the shaft nut.

7.  Remove any excess oil that may be present as a result of installing the new seal parts from the shaft and inside the compressor neck.

8.  Install new absorbent sleeve by rolling the material into a cylinder, overlapping the ends, and then install the sleeve into the compressor neck with the overlap toward the top of the compressor. Spread the sleeve until the ends butt together.

9.  Place the new metal sleeve retainer so that its flange face will be against the front end of the sleeve. Push or tap the retainer and sleeve into place (the retainer should be recessed approximately 1/32 in. from the face of the compressor neck).

10. Install the clutch plate and hub assembly.

11. Evacuate and charge the system.

### Pressure Relief Valve

When it is necessary to replace the pressure relief valve, located in the compressor rear head housing, the valve assembly should be removed after discharging the system of refrigerant and with a new valve and gasket installed. The entire system should be evacuated and then recharged. (Fig. 8-11).

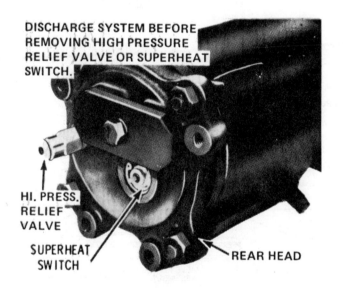

**FIGURE 8-11** Pressure relief valve and superheat switch.
(Courtesy of Oldsmobile Division of General Motors Corp.)

### Superheat Switch

If it becomes necessary to replace the superheat switch, located in the compressor rear head casting, the switch assembly should be removed only after the system has been *discharged of refrigerant*. After the switch has been replaced and a new O-ring seal installed, the system should be evacuated and recharged.

## GM FOUR-CYLINDER COMPRESSOR (R-4) (Fig. 8-12)

### Clutch Plate and Hub Assembly

*REMOVAL*

1. Attach the compressor to the holding fixture, J-25008-1, and clamp the fixture in a vise.

(a)

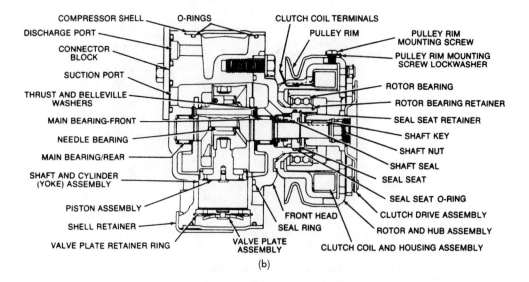

(b)

FIGURE 8-12 (a) GM 4-cylinder compressor—external; (b) GM 4-cylinder compressor—internal. (Courtesy of AC-Delco.)

166

2. Keep the clutch hub from turning with the clutch hub holding tool J-25030, and remove the shaft nut using a thin-wall socket.

3. Thread the clutch plate and hub assembly remover, J-9401, into the hub. Hold the body of the tool with a wrench and turn the center screw into the J-9401 remover body to remove the clutch plate and hub assembly (Fig. 8-13).

4. Remove the shaft key.

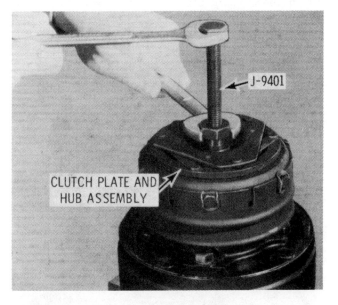

**FIGURE 8-13** Remove clutch plate and hub assembly. (Courtesy of Oldsmobile Division of General Motors Corp.)

## INSTALLATION

1. Install the shaft key into the hub key groove. Allow the key to project about 3/16 in. out of the keyway. The shaft key is curved slightly to provide an interference fit in the shaft key groove, to permit the key projection without falling out.

2. Be sure that the frictional surface of the clutch plate and the clutch rotor are clean before installing the clutch plate and hub assembly on the compressor shaft.

**NOTE:**

TO AVOID INTERNAL DAMAGE TO THE COMPRESSOR, DO NOT DRIVE OR POUND ON THE CLUTCH HUB OR SHAFT.

3. Align the shaft key with the shaft keyway and assemble the clutch plate and hub assembly on the compressor shaft.

4. Place the spacer bearing J-9480-2, on the hub and insert the end of the clutch plate and hub assembly installer J-9480-1, through the J-9480-2 spacer, and thread the tool onto the end of the compressor shaft (Fig. 8-14).

5. Hold the hex portion of the tool body with a wrench and tighten the center screw to press the hub onto the shaft until there is a 0.020 to 0.040 in. air gap between the frictional surfaces of the clutch plate and clutch rotor.

6. Install the new shaft nut with the small-diameter boss of the nut against the crankshaft shoulder using the special thin wall socket. Hold the clutch plate and hub assembly with the clutch hub holding tool, J-25030, and tighten to 12 ft-lb torque.

FIGURE 8-14 Installing clutch plate and hub. (Courtesy of Oldsmobile Division of General Motors Corp.)

**Shaft Seal Replacement**

*REMOVAL*

1. Remove the clutch plate and hub assembly.

2. Remove the shaft seal seat retainer ring using snap ring pliers J-5403 (No. 21).

3. Thoroughly clean the inside of the compressor neck area surrounding the compressor shaft, seal seat, and shaft to remove all dirt and foreign material before removing the seal seat.

4. Insert the seal seat remover and installer tool, J-23128 (Fig. 8-15), over the shaft into the recessed area of the seal seat and tighten tool clockwise to securely engage the knurled tangs of the J-23128 tool with the seal seat. Remove the seal seat with a twisting and pulling motion. Discard the seat.

5. Insert the seal remover and installer, J-9392 (Fig. 8-16), over the shaft and engage the shaft seal by pressing downward on the tool to overcome the shaft seal spring pressure and turn the tool clockwise to engage the seal assembly tabs with the tangs of the J-9392 tool. Remove the seal assembly by pulling straight out from the compressor shaft. Discard the seal.

6. Remove the seal seat O-ring from the compressor neck using tool J-9553. Discard the O-ring.

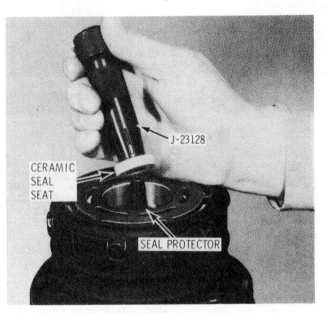

FIGURE 8-15 Removing ceramic seal seat. (Courtesy of Oldsmobile Division of General Motors Corp.)

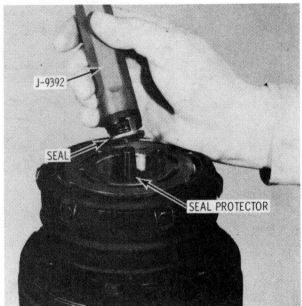

FIGURE 8-16 Removing seal. (Courtesy of Oldsmobile Division of General Motors Corp.)

### INSTALLATION

1. Dip the new seal seat O-ring in clean refrigerant oil and assemble onto O-ring installer J-21508 as shown in Fig. 8-17.

2. Insert the O-ring installer, J-21508, into the compressor neck until the tool bottoms. Lower the movable slide on the O-ring installer to release the O-ring into the seal seat O-ring groove. Rotate the installer tool to seat the O-ring and remove the tool.

3. Dip the new shaft seal O-ring and seal face in clean refrigerant oil and carefully engage the shaft seal assembly with the locking tangs of tool J-9392 seal remover and installer (Fig. 8-18).

FIGURE 8-17 Installing seal seat O-ring. (Courtesy of Oldsmobile Division of General Motors Corp.)

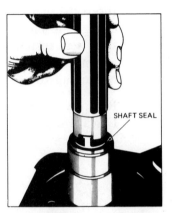

FIGURE 8-18 Installing seal. (Courtesy of Oldsmobile Division of General Motors Corp.)

4. Install the shaft seal protector, J-22974, over the end of the compressor shaft and slide the shaft seal onto the compressor shaft. Slowly turn the tool clockwise while applying light pressure until the seal engages the flats of the compressor shaft and can be seated into place. Rotate the J-9392 tool counterclockwise to disengage the tool from the seal tabs and remove the tool.

5. Attach the ceramic seal seat to the seal seat remover and installer, J-23128, and dip the ceramic seat in clean refrigerant oil to coat the seal face and outer surface. Carefully install the seat over the compressor shaft and J-22974 seal protector and push the seat into place with a turning motion. Remove tools J-23128 and J-22974.

6. Install the new seal seat retainer ring with snap-ring pliers J-5403.

7. Leak-test the compressor and correct any leaks found.

8. Install the clutch plate and hub assembly.

**Clutch Rotor and Bearing Assembly**

1. Remove the clutch plate and hub assembly.

2. Remove the rotor and bearing assembly retaining ring using the snap-ring pliers, J-6083 (No. 24) (Fig. 8-19). Mark the location of the clutch coil terminals. If the clutch rotor and/or rotor bearing only are to be replaced, bend the lockwashers away from the pulley rim mounting screws, and remove the six mounting screws and special lockwashers.

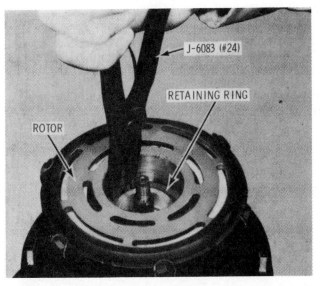

**FIGURE 8-19** Remove rotor and bearing retainer. (Courtesy of Oldsmobile Division of General Motors Corp.)

3. Install the rotor and bearing puller guide, J-25031-1, over the end of the compressor shaft and seat on the front head of the compressor (Fig. 8-20).

4. Install the rotor and bearing puller, J-25031-2, down into the rotor until the puller arms engage the recessed edge of the rotor hub. Hold the puller and arms in place and tighten the puller screw against the puller guide to remove the clutch rotor (Fig. 8-21). If the pulley rim mounting screws and washers were removed in step 2, only the clutch rotor and bearing assembly will be removed for replacement. The clutch coil and housing assembly is pressed on the front head of the compressor with press fit and will not be removed unless the pulley rim mounting screws are left securely in place and the pulley rim pulls the coil and housing assembly off with the total clutch rotor and pulley rim assembly.

**FIGURE 8-20** Rotor and bearing puller guide. (Courtesy of Oldsmobile Division of General Motors Corp.)

**FIGURE 8-21** Rotor and bearing puller. (Courtesy of

*INSTALLATION*

1.  Install the clutch rotor and bearing assembly using tool J-26271 to drive the bearing on the front head (Fig. 8-22).

2.  Install the rotor and bearing assembly retaining ring and reassemble the clutch plate.

**NOTE:**

THE ROTOR AND BEARING ASSEMBLY CAN BE REMOVED AND INSTALLED ON THE CAR WITHOUT DISCHARGING THE SYSTEM.

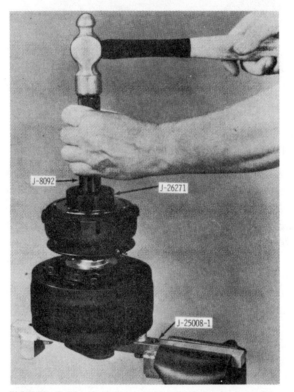

FIGURE 8-22   Installing rotor and bearing assembly.
(Courtesy of Oldsmobile Division of General Motors Corp.)

**Clutch Rotor Bearing Replacement**

*REMOVAL*

1.  Refer to Clutch Rotor and Bearing Assembly, perform steps 1 through 4, and remove the clutch rotor and bearing assembly.

2.  Place the rotor and bearing assembly on blocks (Fig. 8-23) and drive the bearing out of the rotor hub with rotor bearing remover J-25029. It will not be necessary to remove the staking at the rear of the rotor hub to remove the bearing.

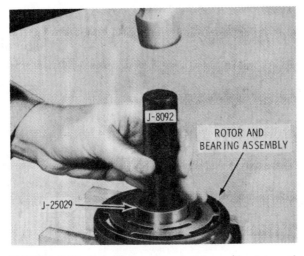

FIGURE 8-23 Removing rotor bearing. (Courtesy of Oldsmobile Division of General Motors Corp.)

## INSTALLATION

1. Place the rotor and hub assembly face down on a clean, flat, and firm surface.

2. Align the new bearing squarely with the hub bore and using pulley bearing installer J-9481 with driver handle J-8092, drive the bearing fully into the hub.

3. Stake the bearing in three places 120 degrees apart. Do not stake too deep and distort the outer race of the bearing.

4. Install the clutch rotor and bearing assembly using tool J-23456 to press bearing on the front head (Fig. 8-24).

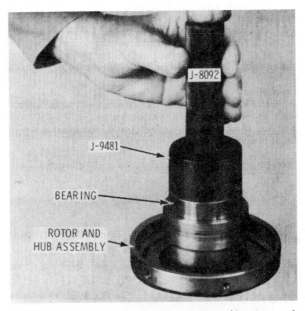

FIGURE 8-24 Installing rotor bearing. (Courtesy of Oldsmobile Division of General Motors Corp.)

5. Install the rotor and bearing assembly retaining ring and reassemble the clutch plate.

### Clutch Coil and Pulley Rim Replacement

*REMOVAL*

1. Refer to Clutch Plate and Hub Assembly and perform steps 1 through 4, but do not loosen or remove the pulley rim mounting screws until the clutch rotor, coil, and pulley rim assembly have been removed from the front head.

2. Remove the pulley rim mounting screws and slide the pulley rim off the rotor hub assembly. The pulley rim and clutch coil are replaceable at this point.

*INSTALLATION*

1. Assemble the clutch coil, pulley rim, and the clutch rotor and bearing assembly (Fig. 8-25). Use R/C No. 75 Loc-tite or equivalent, but do not lock the screw heads in place.

2. Install the clutch rotor and bearing assembly using tool J-23456 to press the bearing on front head. Before fully seating the assembly on the front head, be sure that the clutch coil terminals are in the proper location in relation to the compressor and that the three protrusions on the rear of the clutch coil align with the locator holes in the front head.

3. Install the rotor and bearing assembly retaining ring and reassemble the clutch plate and hub assembly. Check the clutch plate to clutch rotor air gap. It should be 0.020 to 0.040 in.

4. Rotate the pulley rim and rotor to be sure that the pulley rim is rotating "in line" and adjust or replace as required. Tighten the pulley rim mounting screws to 100 in.-lb and lock the screw heads in place.

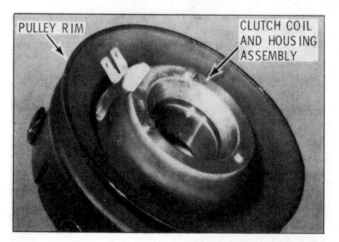

FIGURE 8-25 Clutch rotor and bearing assembly. (Courtesy of Oldsmobile Division of General Motors Corp.)

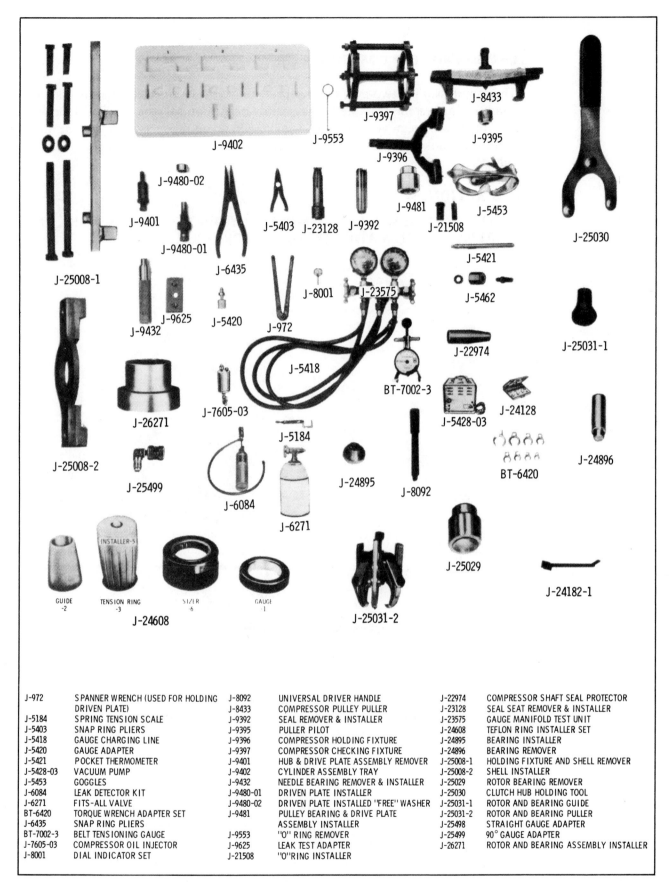

| J-972 | SPANNER WRENCH (USED FOR HOLDING DRIVEN PLATE) | J-8092 | UNIVERSAL DRIVER HANDLE | J-22974 | COMPRESSOR SHAFT SEAL PROTECTOR |
|---|---|---|---|---|---|
| | | J-8433 | COMPRESSOR PULLEY PULLER | J-23128 | SEAL SEAT REMOVER & INSTALLER |
| J-5184 | SPRING TENSION SCALE | J-9392 | SEAL REMOVER & INSTALLER | J-23575 | GAUGE MANIFOLD TEST UNIT |
| J-5403 | SNAP RING PLIERS | J-9395 | PULLER PILOT | J-24608 | TEFLON RING INSTALLER SET |
| J-5418 | GAUGE CHARGING LINE | J-9396 | COMPRESSOR HOLDING FIXTURE | J-24895 | BEARING INSTALLER |
| J-5420 | GAUGE ADAPTER | J-9397 | COMPRESSOR CHECKING FIXTURE | J-24896 | BEARING REMOVER |
| J-5421 | POCKET THERMOMETER | J-9401 | HUB & DRIVE PLATE ASSEMBLY REMOVER | J-25008-1 | HOLDING FIXTURE AND SHELL REMOVER |
| J-5428-03 | VACUUM PUMP | J-9402 | CYLINDER ASSEMBLY TRAY | J-25008-2 | SHELL INSTALLER |
| J-5453 | GOGGLES | J-9432 | NEEDLE BEARING REMOVER & INSTALLER | J-25029 | ROTOR BEARING REMOVER |
| J-6084 | LEAK DETECTOR KIT | J-9480-01 | DRIVEN PLATE INSTALLER | J-25030 | CLUTCH HUB HOLDING TOOL |
| J-6271 | FITS-ALL VALVE | J-9480-02 | DRIVEN PLATE INSTALLED "FREE" WASHER | J-25031-1 | ROTOR AND BEARING GUIDE |
| BT-6420 | TORQUE WRENCH ADAPTER SET | J-9481 | PULLEY BEARING & DRIVE PLATE ASSEMBLY INSTALLER | J-25031-2 | ROTOR AND BEARING PULLER |
| J-6435 | SNAP RING PLIERS | | | J-25498 | STRAIGHT GAUGE ADAPTER |
| BT-7002-3 | BELT TENSIONING GAUGE | J-9553 | "O" RING REMOVER | J-25499 | 90° GAUGE ADAPTER |
| J-7605-03 | COMPRESSOR OIL INJECTOR | J-9625 | LEAK TEST ADAPTER | J-26271 | ROTOR AND BEARING ASSEMBLY INSTALLER |
| J-8001 | DIAL INDICATOR SET | J-21508 | "O"RING INSTALLER | | |

**FIGURE 8-26** Service tools.

## CHRYSLER AIR TEMP COMPRESSOR (Fig. 8-27)

The compressor is a two-cylinder, reciprocating type designed for the Chrysler air-conditioning system. Complete disassembly of the compressor must be done with the compressor removed from the vehicle. On some models, however, the valve plate and crankshaft gas seal can be repaired with the compressor installed on the vehicle.

**CAUTION:**

THE SYSTEM MUST BE COMPLETELY DISCHARGED BEFORE ANY REPAIRS ARE MADE TO THE COMPRESSOR.

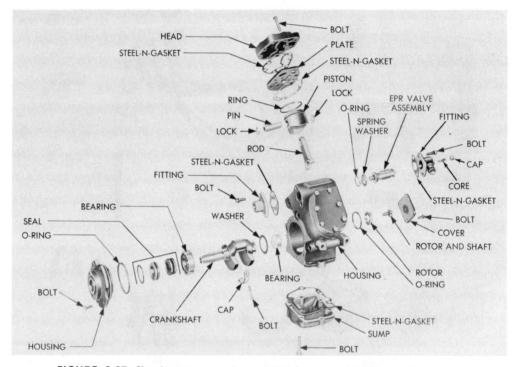

**FIGURE 8-27** Chrysler compressor disassembled. (Courtesy of the Chrysler Corporation.)

### Clutch and Pulley

There are various types of magnetic clutch assemblies used on the Chrysler system, all of which use a stationary electromagnet attached to the compressor. Since the electromagnet does not rotate, collector rings and brushes are eliminated.

*REMOVAL*

1.  Loosen and remove the belts. Disconnect the clutch field lead wire at the connector. Note the location of the coil lead so that the coil can be reinstalled in the same position.

2.   Remove the special locking bolt and the washer from the compressor crankshaft at the front center of the clutch (Fig. 8-28).

3.   Insert a 5/8-11 x 2-1/2 cap screw into the threaded portion of the hub assembly.

4.   Support the clutch with one hand, then tighten the cap screw until the clutch is removed.

5.   Remove the three hexagon-head screws attaching the clutch field assembly to the compressor and lift off the assembly.

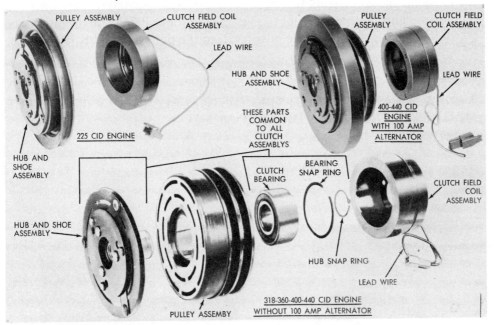

**FIGURE 8-28**   Compressor clutch assemblies. (Courtesy of the Chrysler Corporation.)

### INSTALLATION

1.   Install the clutch field coil assembly on the base of the compressor bearing housing. Make sure that the coil assembly is positioned so that the lead wire points to the left of the compressor as viewed from the front. Install the three mounting screws and tighten to 17 in.-lb.

2.   Insert the woodruff key in crankshaft.

3.   Insert the clutch assembly on the crankshaft.

4.   Install the washer and a new self-locking bolt. Hold the clutch from turning with a spanner wrench inserted in the holes of the front bumper plate. Tighten to 20 ft-lb.

5.   Connect field lead wire.

6.   Install the belts and tighten to specified tension.

## Disassembly of Clutch Pulley and Hub

1. Remove the small snap ring from the drive hub.

2. Install the drive hub puller C-4230 aligning the three pins of the tool in the three holes in the hub and shoe assembly. Tighten the hex-head bolt down until the drive hub is removed from the bearing (Fig. 8-29).

3. Remove the bearing snap ring from the pulley.

4. Place the pulley assembly on an arbor press, with the pulley side down and bearing hub centered on tool C-3825. Install tool SP-3496 on the inner race of the bearing and press the bearing from the pulley assembly (Fig. 8-30).

**NOTE:**

A NEW BEARING MUST BE INSTALLED EVERY TIME THE MAGNETIC CLUTCH IS DISASSEMBLED.

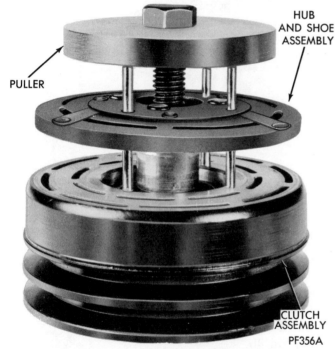

FIGURE 8-29 Remove hub and shoe assembly. (Courtesy of the Chrysler Corporation.)

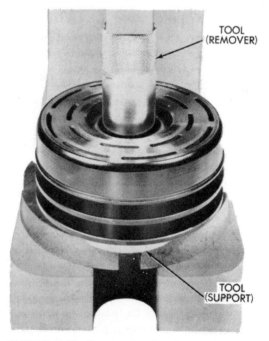

FIGURE 8-30 Remove bearing from the pulley assembly.

*INSTALLATION*

1. Install the pulley assembly with the pulley side up on an arbor press and insert a new bearing into the bore. Install tool C-3807 against the bearing and press into place (Fig. 8-31).

2. Install the pulley assembly with the pulley side facing down on tool C-3807.

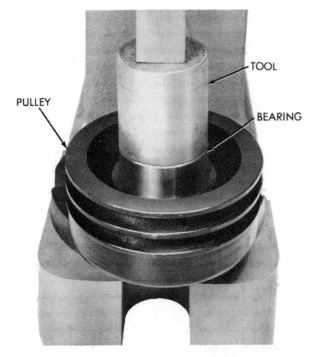

PULLEY

TOOL

BEARING

**FIGURE 8-31** Installing a new bearing in the pulley assembly.

3. Start drive hub into the inner bearing race, and press the hub into position with an arbor press.

4. Install the bearing snap ring and hub snap ring.

**NOTE:**

THE PULLEY ASSEMBLY AND HUB ASSEMBLY ARE MATED PARTS. NO ATTEMPT SHOULD BE MADE TO REPLACE EITHER UNIT SEPARATELY.

**Shaft Seal Replacement**

**NOTE:**

THE SYSTEM MUST BE DISCHARGED FOR THIS REPLACEMENT.

The shaft seal may be replaced with the compressor installed in the vehicle or with the compressor removed and placed on a workbench.

*REMOVAL*

1. Discharge the refrigerant from the system.

2. Loosen the belts and remove the clutch, coil, and drive key.

3. Remove the five crankshaft bearing housing bolts.

4. Remove the bearing housing from the crankshaft, using two screwdrivers inserted into the slots provided, to pry the housing from the case. (Fig. 8-32).

5. Remove the bearing housing oil seal.

6. Remove the gas seal seat plate and O-ring from the bearing housing. This is part of the gas seal replacement package and must be replaced when the gas seal assembly is replaced.

7. Clean the front bearing housing thoroughly with mineral spirits.

**FIGURE 8-32** Removing crankshaft bearing housing. (Courtesy of AC-Delco.)

*INSTALLATION*

1. Immerse the new seal seat assembly in clean refrigerant oil and seat it in the bearing housing with the smooth side up. Use a sleeve with a minimum inside diameter of 1 3/8 in. to avoid damaging the micro-finish sealing service of the face plate. Tap the sleeve lightly until the seal seat is fully seated in the housing (Fig. 8-33).

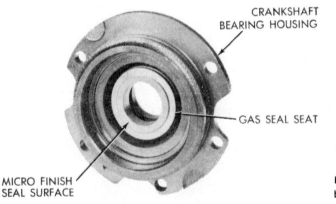

CRANKSHAFT
BEARING HOUSING

GAS SEAL SEAT

MICRO FINISH
SEAL SURFACE

**FIGURE 8-33** Crankshaft bearing housing and gas seal plate.

2. Before installing the cartridge-type assembly, inspect the assembly to make sure that the tangs of the carbon seal, scallops, and the retainer tongs are indexed in the slots of the respective mating, steel part (Fig. 8-34).

3. Immerse the steel assembly in clean refrigerant oil, carbon ring up.

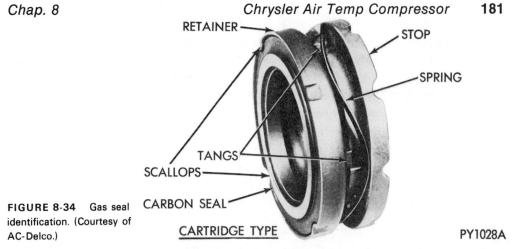

**FIGURE 8-34** Gas seal identification. (Courtesy of AC-Delco.)

4. Hold the seal assembly firmly at the outside edge, at the same time preventing the ring from coming out of position. *Do not touch the polished sealing face of the carbon seal* (Fig. 8-35).

5. When the seal stop bottoms against the crankshaft bearing, inspect the indexing alignment again. The clutch key must be removed for seal installation.

6. Oil the new bearing housing oil seal and install. Make sure that the seal is evenly stretched into position and that the seal is not rolled over.

7. Wipe the seal seat clean with a lint-free cloth, and lubricate with refrigerant oil.

8. Install the bearing housing. Be sure that the nose of the crankshaft does not touch the seal seat in the bearing housing.

9. Insert four 1/4/20 screws and pull the bearing housing into position. This must be done 1/2 turn at a time per screw so that the ball bearing outer race will not be jammed by the bearing housing. Torque the bolts 95 to 135 in.-lb.

10. Replace the drive key in the shaft.

**FIGURE 8-35** Installing seal assembly. (Courtesy of Oldsmobile Division of General Motors Corp.)

11. Assemble the clutch to the compressor and turn the crankshaft by turning the clutch armature. No more than 10 in.-lb of torque should be required to turn the crankshaft. If the shaft is tight, remove the clutch and loosen the bearing housing screws until the shaft turns freely. Then slowly tighten the screws.

12. Check the oil level.

13. Install the clutch package on the compressor, and tighten the clutch center mounting bolt to 20 ft-lb.

14. Install and tighten the belts.

15. Evacuate and recharge the system.

### EPR or ETR Valve Replacement (Fig. 8-36)

FIGURE 8-36 (a) Early model evaporator pressure regulator valve (EPR); (b) late model evaporator pressure regulator valve (EPR). (Courtesy of the Chrysler Corporation.)

1. Discharge the system.

2. Remove the electrical connector on the ETR valve.

3. Remove the two EPR valve suction-line fitting bolts, the fitting that also contains the compressor suction screen, spring, and the gasket.

4. Remove the valve and O-ring from the compressor using the EPR remover and installer tool, by rotating the valve counterclockwise slightly (Fig. 8-37).

**NOTE:**

DO NOT HANDLE THE EPR OR ETR VALVE MORE THAN IS NECESSARY.

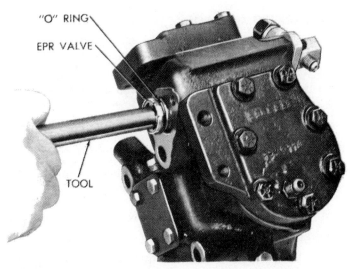

FIGURE 8-37 Removing EPR—2 valve. (Courtesy of the Chrysler Corporation.)

## INSTALLATION

1. Install the new O-ring on the valve.

2. Lubricate the O-ring with refrigerant oil and install the valve in the compressor using the installer tool C-3822A while rotating the valve clockwise until it is locked in place.

3. Install the compressor suction screen in the valve suction line fitting.

4. Install the suction line gasket (beads toward compressor), spring, and fitting, and tighten the attaching bolts to 90 to 130 in.-lb.

5. Install the electrical connector on the ETR valve.

6. Recharge the system.

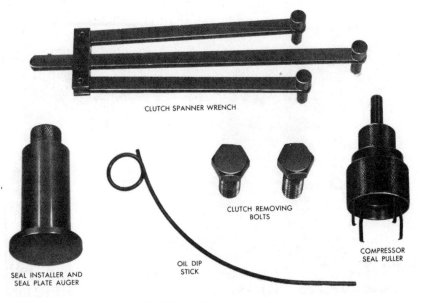

FIGURE 8-38 Service tools.

## TECUMSEH AND YORK COMPRESSORS

If the compressor is equipped with stem-type service valves, it may be isolated from the system for checking oil level, replacing the shaft seal, or complete compressor disassembly. To isolate the compressor, proceed as follows:

1. Back-seat both the high- and low-pressure service valves.

2. Remove the cap from the high-pressure service valve gauge port.

3. Connect the manifold gauge set high-pressure hose to the service gauge port.

4. Make sure that both the high- and low-pressure valves are closed on the manifold gauge set.

5. Front-seat both the high- and low-pressure service valves.

6. Open the high-pressure valve on the manifold gauge set 1/4 turn to allow refrigerant R-12 to escape slowly, to prevent loss of refrigerant oil. Allow R-12 to exhaust until the gauge reading is zero.

**NOTE:**

IF THE COMPRESSOR IS EQUIPPED WITH A SCHRADER VALVE, IT WILL BE NECESSARY TO DISCHARGE THE SYSTEM TO PERFORM THE COMPRESSOR SERVICE.

### Clutch and Pulley

*REMOVAL*

1. Hold the clutch hub stationary using a spanner wrench and remove the retaining bolt from the end of the shaft (Fig. 8-39).

FIGURE 8-39    Removing retaining bolt. (Courtesy of AC-Delco.)

2.  Thread the clutch removing bolt into the outer diameter of the clutch hub. Hold the clutch hub stationary using the spanner wrench. Tighten the bolt until the clutch assembly is removed from the shaft, lift the clutch off, and remove the bolt. (Fig. 8-40).

3.  Take out the two bolts and remove the brush assembly (rotating-coil-type clutch) or take out four bolts and remove the coil assembly (stationary-coil-type clutch).

4.  Remove the woodruff key from the shaft.

**FIGURE 8-40**   Removing clutch & pulley assembly. (Courtesy of AC-Delco.)

*INSTALLATION*

1.  Install the brush assembly (rotating-coil-type clutch) or coil assembly (stationary-coil-type clutch) on the compressor face and tighten the bolts securely.

2.  Install the woodruff key, align the keyway in the clutch assembly, and slide the clutch on the shaft.

**NOTE:**

IF THE CLUTCH IS ROTATING-COIL TYPE, BE CAREFUL NOT TO DAMAGE THE COIL BRUSHES.

3.  Install the bolt and washer in the end of the compressor shaft, use a spanner wrench to hold the clutch assembly stationary, and tighten the bolt to 20 ft-lb.

**Shaft Seal Assembly**

*REMOVAL*

1.  Isolate the compressor or discharge the system.

2.  Remove the clutch and pulley assembly.

3.  On later-model compressors, remove the secondary dust shield from the shaft using care not to mar the shaft. On all compressors, remove the six bolts retaining the seal seat plate assembly.

4.  Remove the seal seat plate and discard.

5.  Remove and discard the O-ring in the groove on the seal plate face of the compressor (Fig. 8-41).

FIGURE 8-41 Removing O-ring. (Courtesy of AC-Delco.)

**NOTE:**

IF A FLAT GASKET IS USED INSTEAD OF AN O-RING, REMOVE ALL TRACES OF THE OLD GASKET. MAKE SURE THAT THE SEAL RECESS, COMPRESSOR SHAFT, AND THE SEAL PLATE FACE ON THE COMPRESSOR ARE COMPLETELY CLEAN.

6.  Position the seal remover tool behind the seal drive ring and attach the sleeve. (Fig. 8-42). Remove the seal assembly by lifting straight up.

FIGURE 8-42 Removing seal. (Courtesy of AC-Delco.)

*INSTALLATION*

1.  Install all new seal parts that are furnished in the seal kit (Figs. 8-43 and 8-44). Lubricate all parts with refrigeration oil before installation.

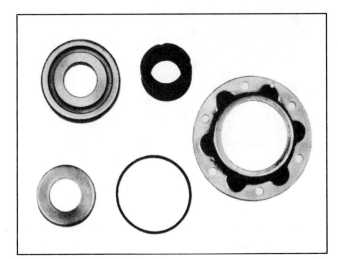

**FIGURE 8-43** Typical Tecumseh shaft seal kit. (Courtesy of AC-Delco.)

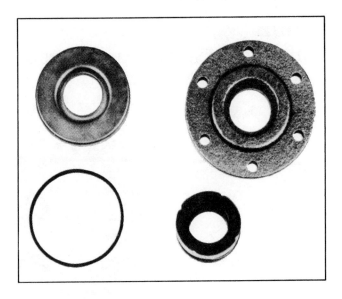

**FIGURE 8-44** Typical York shaft seal kit. (Courtesy of AC-Delco.)

**NOTE:**

AN O-RING AND SEVERAL GASKETS ARE FURNISHED IN THE KIT. SELECT AND USE THE SAME TYPE AS THOSE REMOVED FROM THE COMPRESSOR.

2.  Install an O-ring (or correct type of flat gasket) on the seal plate face of the compressor (Fig. 8-45). Seat the O-ring evenly in the groove.

**FIGURE 8-45** Installing O-ring. (Courtesy of AC-Delco.)

3. Lubricate the exposed surface of the shaft and seal with refrigerant oil. Set the seal on the shaft with the carbon ring and shoulder outward (if the carbon ring is a separate part, place it on the shaft over the seal with the ground face outward; Fig. 8-46).

**NOTE:**

DO NOT TOUCH THE SEALING FACE OF THE CARBON RING WITH YOUR FINGERS.

**FIGURE 8-46** Installing seal. (Courtesy of AC-Delco.)

4.  Lubricate the seal seat plate with refrigerant oil and install the plate on the installer tool with the outer face of the plate against the shoulder on the tool (Fig. 8-47).

**FIGURE 8-47**   Installing seal seat plate. (Courtesy of AC-Delco.)

5.  Position the plate and tool on the shaft, align the bolt holes in the plate and compressor, and press the assembly straight in until the seal plate is seated on the compressor.

6.  Install all the bolts in the seal plate and tighten the bolts finger-tight. Remove the tool.

7.  Tighten all the seal plate bolts evenly in a circular or diagonal pattern to 7 to 13 ft-lb (York), 6 to 10 ft-lb. (Tecumseh).

8.  Rotate the shaft by hand 15 to 20 revolutions to seat the seal parts.

9.  Install the brush assembly (rotating-coil-type clutch) or coil assembly (stationary-coil-type clutch) on the compressor face and tighten the mounting bolts securely.

10. Install the woodruff key in the shaft groove, align the keyway in the clutch assembly, and slide the clutch on the shaft.

**NOTE:**

IF THE CLUTCH IS THE ROTATING–COIL TYPE, USE CARE NOT TO DAMAGE THE COIL BRUSHES.

# Chapter 9

# Automatic Temperature Control

## CHRYSLER AUTO-TEMP II

The Auto-Temp II System automatically controls the heating and air-conditioning operation of the vehicle to maintain a selected comfort level. In cold weather, the system provides heat. In warm weather the system provides cool dehumidified air.

The unit will heat or cool according to the interior temperature, ambient temperature, and control setting without any action on the part of the operator other than selecting a desired temperature setting and setting the system on Lo-Auto, Hi-Auto, Vent, Lo-Def, or Hi-Def.

The automatic temperature control assembly consists of a comfort control potentiometer, a lever, and a pushbutton switch.

### Comfort Control Lever

The comfort control lever operates much like a house thermostat. The front of the pushbutton control assembly has five numbers, 65–70–75–80–85, to allow the operator to select a desired comfort level (Fig. 9-1).

### Pushbutton Positions

*Vent:* Same as Lo-Auto, except that the clutch will be disengaged. The vent position allows greater fuel economy when the outside air does not need to be dehumidified or cooled.

*Lo-Auto:* The blower will automatically remain off and the outside door will remained closed (if heating is required) until the water temperature reaches 125°F

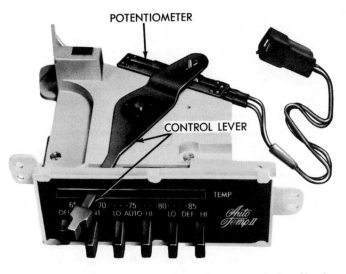

POTENTIOMETER

CONTROL LEVER

TEMP

**FIGURE 9-1** ATC control assembly. (Courtesy of the Chrysler Corporation.)

(51.7°C). Temperature-controlled discharge air will then come out of the heater slots or A/C outlets as required by the system. There are five blower speeds on the A/C mode and the heater mode.

*Hi-Auto:* Same as Lo-Auto except the blower will operate at the higher blower speeds only. There are three blower speeds for the A/C and the heat mode. These speeds are available to allow the operator to select higher blower speeds to

1.  Maintain comfort during city traffic operation.

2.  Satisfy the rear-seat passengers under extreme conditions.

3.  Provide adequate smoke removal.

*Lo-Def:* The blower will come on immediately, air will come out of defroster outlets, and the system will then control the same as Hi-Auto. The blower will operate at higher speeds.

*Hi-Def:* Same as Lo-Def, except the blower speed will be on the highest speed.

Both Lo-Def and Hi-Def positions override a vacuum circuit to start the blower, regardless of the water temperature.

In all positions except Off and Vent, the compressor will operate if the ambient temperature is above 32°F (0°C).

### Major Components

#### IN-CAR SENSOR

This sensor is located behind a grille in the instrument panel. It senses the car's interior temperature and automatically signals the amplifier to compensate for any variation from the comfort setting (Fig. 9-2).

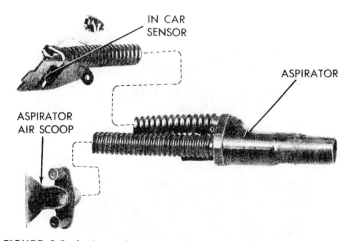

**FIGURE 9-2** Aspirator-air scoop and in-car sensor assemblies. (Courtesy of Cadillac Motor Car Division of General Motors Corp.)

### ASPIRATOR AIR SCOOP

The aspirator is located on the rear of the evaporator assembly. The air scoop is mounted inside the evaporator assembly in such a manner that air flowing through the evaporator is routed to the aspirator. The air creates a slight vacuum in the aspirator, which pulls air over the in-car sensor. The sensor then senses the interior air temperature (Fig. 9-2).

### AMBIENT SENSOR

The ambient sensor is located in the plenum panel above the evaporator assembly. This sensor senses the outside temperature and sends the electrical signal to the amplifier (Fig. 9-3).

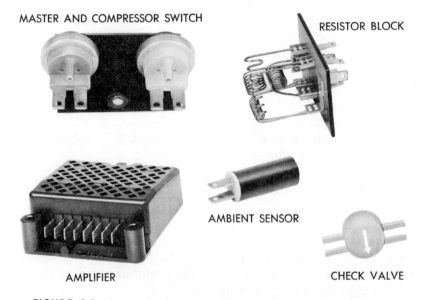

**FIGURE 9-3** Major components group. (Courtesy of the Chrysler Corporation.)

### COMFORT CONTROL POTENTIOMETER

This control allows the operator to select any interior comfort setting from 65 to 85. The potentiometer will create a resistance to signal the amplifier so that it will control at the comfort setting. The potentiometer is replaceable.

### MASTER SWITCH

The master switch is vacuum-operated and turns on the blower when 8 in. or more of vacuum is applied (Fig. 9-3).

### COMPRESSOR SWITCH

The compressor switch is vacuum-operated and actuates the compressor clutch and the amplifier when 2 in. of vacuum is applied (if the low pressure cutoff switch is closed). (Fig. 9-3)

### AMPLIFIER

The amplifier converts the signals from the in-car sensor, ambient sensor, and the temperature-controlled potentiometer into a single signal to the motor in the servo assembly. Signals position to the servo motor and feedback potentiometer, which creates a return signal. This return signal shuts the amplifier off (Fig. 9-3).

### CHECK VALVES

The check valves are located in the vacuum harness near the top of the evaporator (Fig. 9-3).

### RESISTOR BLOCK

The resistor block consists of resistor coils, which provide for different blower motor speeds.

### SERVO ASSEMBLY

The servo-assembly components are positioned by a signal from the amplifier through a small electric motor and gear train assembly. The electric motor rotates a rotary vacuum switch to open and close the vacuum ports, and a wiper arm moves over a printed circuit board to change blower speeds (Fig. 9-4).

### WATER VALVE

The water valve is normally open and is vacuum-operated. It is open in all modes of operation except when the off button is pushed.

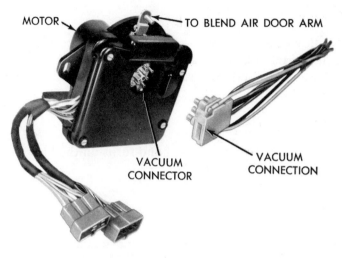

**FIGURE 9-4**   Servo assembly. (Courtesy of the Chrysler Corporation.)

### COLD ENGINE LOCKOUT SWITCH

This switch, mounted on the water valve, prevents the blower motor from starting, when heat is required, until the engine coolant temperature is above 125°F (51.7°C) and the Lo-Auto or Hi-Auto pushbuttons are engaged (Fig. 9-5).

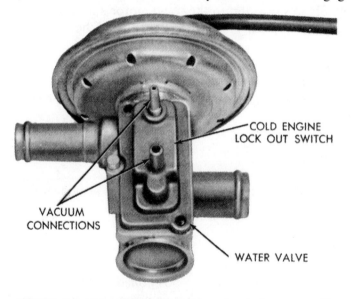

**FIGURE 9-5** Water valve with cold engine lock-out assembly. (Courtesy of Cadillac Motor Car Division of General Motors Corp.)

### VACUUM TRANSFER SWITCH

The vacuum transfer switch positions the door in one of three positions: (1) off, (2) 20% outside air, or (3) 100% outside air. These positions are accomplished by a spring-loaded vacuum actuator and the transfer switch (Fig. 9-6).

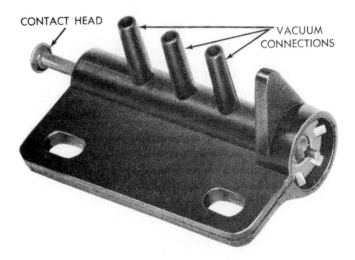

**FIGURE 9-6** Vacuum transfer switch. (Courtesy of Cadillac Motor
Car Division of General Motors Corp.)

## ELECTRICAL SYSTEM

The system is protected by one 30-ampere fuse and two 20-ampere fuses. The
blower motor circuit is protected by the 30-ampere fuse. The clutch circuit is
protected by a 20-ampere fuse and the amplifier is protected by a 20-ampere fuse.

### Component Testing

#### BLOWER MASTER ON–OFF SWITCH

The master switch is vacuum-operated and turns on the blower. A magnet
mounted inside the switch holds the electrical contacts open. When sufficient
vacuum is applied, an internal diaphragm with attached electrical contact is pulled
away from the magnet and the electrical circuit is completed.

This switch can be checked by applying $8 \pm 1$ in. of vacuum to it and checking
for continuity, and by removing the vacuum and checking to see that it opens at
less than 3 in. of vacuum.

#### COMPRESSOR VACUUM SWITCH

This vacuum-operated switch turns on the amplifier and completes the
electrical circuit to the clutch. It is the same as the blower switch except that it
closes at $2 \pm 1$ in. of vacuum.

This switch can be checked by applying $2 \pm 1$ in. of vacuum and checking for
continuity, and by removing the vacuum and checking to see that it opens.

#### COMFORT CONTROL POTENTIOMETER AND LEVER

The control lever allows the operator to select a comfort level from 65 to 85.
Moving the lever controls a resistance potentiometer.

There are three basic problems that may occur with the potentiometer:

1. The potentiometer could have a short circuit. The system would then operate on maximum A/C.

2. The potentiometer could have an open circuit. The system would then operate on maximum heat.

3. The lever and potentiometer could be out of calibration. The lever must be set too high or too low to attain comfort.

To check the potentiometer for an open or short, disconnect the potentiometer leads and connect them to an ohmmeter.

a. If the meter shows infinite resistance, the potentiometer is open and should be replaced.

b. If the meter shows zero resistance, the potentiometer has a short.

c. If the potentiometer is good, there should be a smooth change in resistance from approximately 200 to 1800 ohms as the lever moves from 65 to 85. If not, the potentiometer should be replaced.

d. To check the lever control calibration, set the dial to 75. The meter should read 1000 ohms. If it is out of calibration, it should be replaced.

### IN-CAR SENSOR

This device senses the car's interior temperature.
There are two basic problems that may occur with the sensor:

1. The sensor could be open and the system would operate on maximum heating.

2. The sensor could have a short and the system would operate on maximum A/C.

The calibration can be checked with an ohmmeter:

a. 1850 ohms at 65°F (18.3°C).

b. 1400 ohms at 75°F (23.9°C).

c. 1070 ohms at 85°F (19.4°C).

### AMBIENT SENSOR

These sensors sense the outside ambient temperature.
There are three problems that may occur with these sensors:

1. The sensor could be open and the system would operate in the heat mode at all times.

2. The sensor could have a short and the system would operate in maximum A/C.

3. The sensor could be partially open and the system would operate in the heat mode *most* of the time.

The calibration can be checked with an ohmmeter.

a. 650 ohms at 65°F (18.3°C).

b. 550 ohms at 75°F (23.9°C).

c. 450 ohms at 85°F (29.4°C).

If the resistance is constantly 1500 ohms, the sensor is open. If the resistance is higher than stated above, the shunt resistor is open. In either case the sensor should be replaced.

### ASPIRATOR AND TUBE TEST

The aspirator should pull air into the in-car sensor grill. This can be checked by holding a cigarette next to the grill with the system on HI blower in the heat mode. If smoke is not pulled into the grill, the aspirator is not working properly.

### VACUUM RESERVOIR TANK

The reservoir tank is used for the purpose of maintaining vacuum in the system in cases where vacuum is lost momentarily. The tank has a check valve at the inlet port which closes when the vacuum supply drops off.

### TESTING THE VACUUM TANK

1. Connect a 0 to 29 in. vacuum gauge to the outlet port of the tank.

2. Start the engine and allow it to idle.

3. The vacuum at gauge should build up to 16 in. or above in less than 1 minute.

4. Shut the engine off.

5. If the vacuum does not drop off, the check value and tank are O.K.

6. If the vacuum drops off, there is a leak and the tank assembly should be replaced.

### CHECK VALVES

There are two check valves in the vacuum harness, located near the servo assembly on the passenger side of the evaporator. The valves are referred to as numbers 1 and 2. Number 1 is closest to the servo assembly.

The most probable types of failures with check valves are leakage and incorrect installation.

1. Check valve 1 leaking:

   System will stay on 20% outside air and will not go to 100% outside air. Also, system will shut off when the vacuum supply is lost.

2. Check valve 1 installed backwards:

   The system will act the same as in a leaking valve. Also, with a cold engine the blower will not come on when the Defrost or Hi-Defrost button is pushed.

3. Check valve 2 leaking:

   Blower starts immediately and blows cold air during cold weather.

4. Check valve 2 installed backwards:

   Blower starts immediately and blows cold air during cold weather. When the engine is cold, the blower will not shut off when the Off button is pushed.

## GM AUTOMATIC TEMPERATURE CONTROL

The temperature control system provides automatic regulation of the car interior temperature regardless of outside temperature changes. The control panel consists of a temperature dial with a range of 65 to 85°F (18 to 29°C) and a single sliding lever to permit the driver to choose various modes of operation. The Auto setting is recommended for most situations. There are six additional settings which provide driver control for unusual conditions.

### Control Panel

1. The temperature dial is graduated in 5°F increments between 65 and 85°F (18 to 29°C). The dial varies the resistance of a wire-wound rheostat.

2. The circuit board electrical switch is mounted on the base plate. Attached to and positioned by the control lever are rotary wiper contacts which ride on the circuit board pads to provide the required electrical-circuit connections. The electrical connections from the switch and from the temperature dial rheostat terminate at the circuit board terminals.

3. The in-car turn-on switch is a thermostatic switch which senses the car's interior temperature and will close and turn the system on if that temperature is above 73°F (23°C), even if the engine water is cold and the other turn-on switch, located in the right cylinder head, is cold. This provides immediate cooling in a hot car that has not been run for some time.

4. The control vacuum valve is a nine-port rotary valve which interconnects

or vents the vacuum hoses attached to it to perform various vacuum functions required in the system.

### Sensors

Two sensors are used, one sensing outside air temperature and the other the car's interior temperature. Both are disk-type thermistors. (A thermistor is a special resistor with a resistance valve that changes with temperature change. It differs from an ordinary resistor in that its resistance decreases as it gets hotter.) The changes in resistance of these units form the basic input to the control system (Fig. 9-7).

The ambient sensor is mounted in the programmer. It is exposed to ambient air through a hole in the module wall. The in-car sensor is located behind the slots on the instrument panel top cover. To provide accurate sensing of the car's interior

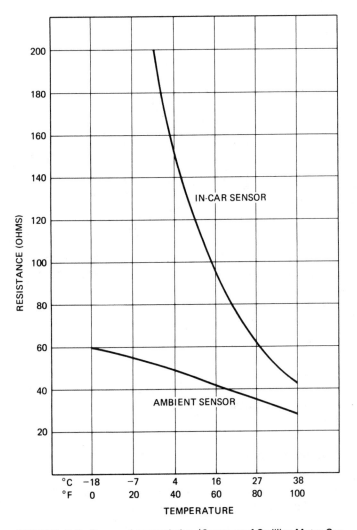

**FIGURE 9-7** Sensor characteristics. (Courtesy of Cadillac Motor Car Division of General Motors Corp.)

temperature, a small amount of in-car air is drawn into the in-car sensor housing and passed over the thermistor. This air movement is accomplished by the aspirator and a rubber hose that connects the in-car sensor housing to the aspirator. The aspirator is a tube within a tube, and air from the module is discharged out of the main outer tube. This air stream causes a suction at the end of the inner tube so that air flows out of it also (Fig. 9-8).

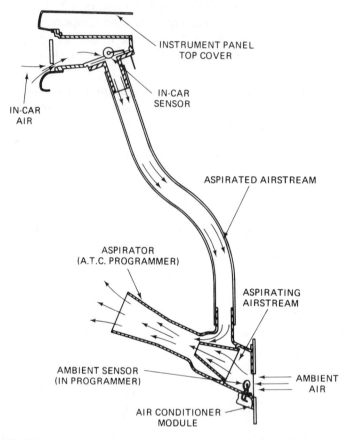

FIGURE 9-8 In-car sensor aspirator. (Courtesy of Cadillac Motor Car Division of General Motors Corp.)

**Programmer**

The programmer contains the bulk of the temperature control components and is located in the passenger compartment on the module. The programmer contains (Figs. 9-9 and 9-10):

1.  The amplifier, mounted to the programmer chassis, is a three-stage dc amplifier that accepts a weak electrical signal from the sensors and the temperature dial and provides a strong output signal proportional to input. The amplifier should be serviced only as an assembly.

2.  The transducer is mounted directly to the amplifier board. This component, in effect, transforms the electrical signal from the amplifier to a vacuum signal that is fed to the vacuum motor.

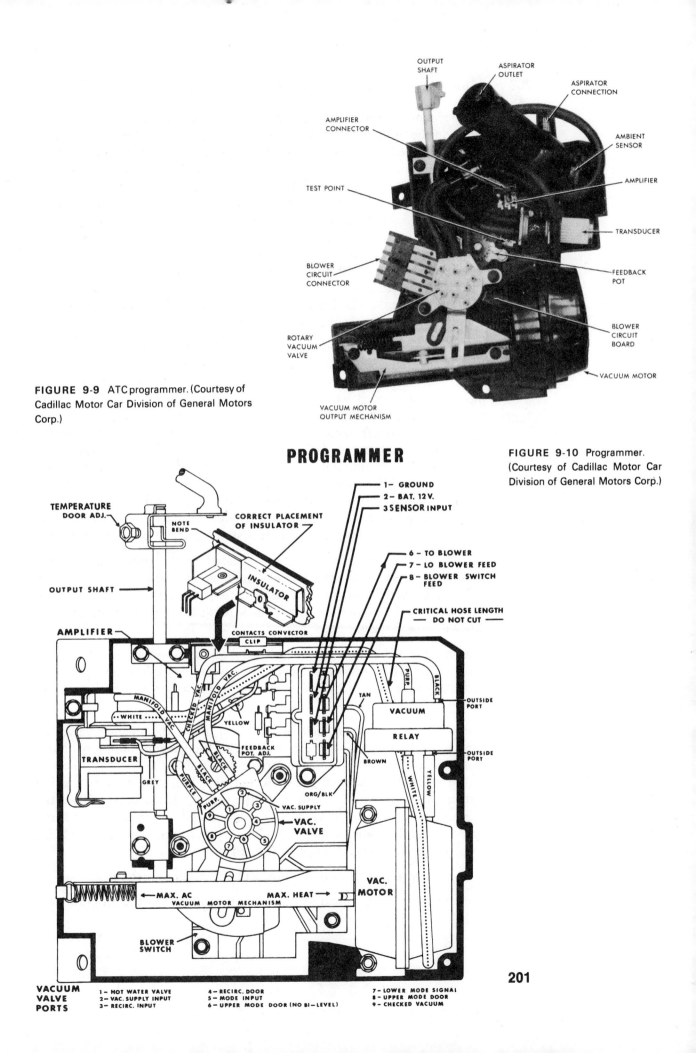

**FIGURE 9-9** ATC programmer. (Courtesy of Cadillac Motor Car Division of General Motors Corp.)

OUTPUT SHAFT

ASPIRATOR OUTLET

ASPIRATOR CONNECTION

AMPLIFIER CONNECTOR

AMBIENT SENSOR

AMPLIFIER

TEST POINT

TRANSDUCER

FEEDBACK POT

BLOWER CIRCUIT CONNECTOR

BLOWER CIRCUIT BOARD

ROTARY VACUUM VALVE

VACUUM MOTOR

VACUUM MOTOR OUTPUT MECHANISM

**FIGURE 9-10** Programmer. (Courtesy of Cadillac Motor Car Division of General Motors Corp.)

# PROGRAMMER

1 — GROUND
2 — BAT. 12 V.
3 SENSOR INPUT

6 — TO BLOWER
7 — LO BLOWER FEED
8 — BLOWER SWITCH FEED

TEMPERATURE DOOR ADJ.

NOTE BEND

CORRECT PLACEMENT OF INSULATOR

INSULATOR

OUTPUT SHAFT

CRITICAL HOSE LENGTH — DO NOT CUT —

AMPLIFIER

CONTACTS CONVECTOR

CLIP

MANIFOLD VAC.

CHECKED VAC.

MANIFOLD VAC.

WHITE

YELLOW

TAN

PURP.

BLACK

VACUUM RELAY

OUTSIDE PORT

TRANSDUCER

GREY

BLACK

BLACK

PURPLE

FEEDBACK POT. ADJ.

BROWN

OUTSIDE PORT

WHITE

YELLOW

PURP.

ORG/BLK

VAC. SUPPLY

VAC. VALVE

VAC. MOTOR

MAX. AC

VACUUM MOTOR MECHANISM

MAX. HEAT

BLOWER SWITCH

**201**

**VACUUM VALVE PORTS**

| | | |
|---|---|---|
| 1 — HOT WATER VALVE | 4 — RECIRC. DOOR | 7 — LOWER MODE SIGNAL |
| 2 — VAC. SUPPLY INPUT | 5 — MODE INPUT | 8 — UPPER MODE DOOR |
| 3 — RECIRC. INPUT | 6 — UPPER MODE DOOR (NO BI—LEVEL) | 9 — CHECKED VACUUM |

3. The vacuum checking relay provides two separate vacuum checking functions. In the upper part of the relay is a conventional rubber check valve which is opened by engine vacuum applied at port 5, allowing port 3, which supplies vacuum to the rotary vacuum valve on the programmer and the control head, to be evacuated. If the engine vacuum drops because of acceleration or steep grades, the check vale closes, maintaining the vacuum level at port 3. In the lower part of the relay is a spring-loaded diaphragm which blocks or passes regulated vacuum from the transducer, which is connected at port 2, to the vacuum motor, which is connected to port 1. When engine vacuum at port 5 is high, the diaphragm is pulled upward, allowing regulated vacuum to pass to the vacuum motor. When engine vacuum drops, the diaphragm moves downward, blocking passage and maintaining vacuum in the vacuum motor.

4. The vacuum motor produces all mechanical motion within the programmer. It positions the vacuum motor mechanism, which actuates the rotary shaft, which drives the air-mix door link. This same mechanism moves the blower circuit board wiper, the vacuum valve operating arm, and the feedback potentiometer. The vacuum motor mechanism is spring-loaded by a spring at its left-hand end so that with no vacuum it is fully extended out of the vacuum motor. This is the MAX A/C position. When vacuum is applied to the vacuum motor, it will start to move into the heat position. About 8 psi (5 kPa) is required to pull mechanism all the way to the MAX HEAT position. In order to prevent the loss of position during stop/restart operations, it is necessary to add a restriction between the vacuum checking relay and the transducer. This is a sintered metal plug in the hose.

5. The blower circuit board switch is located in the center part of the programmer. Spring-loaded contacts move across the board, making the required blower circuit connections. The function of the switch is to place the blower resistors into the circuit at the required point in the program to control blower speed.

6. The vacuum valve, located in the center of the assembly, is a nine-port rotary valve which makes connections between the various ports or vents them, as required, to move air doors, operate the heater water valve, and so on.

7. The feedback potentiometer is located just above the vacuum valve. Its function is to slow down the movement of the vacuum motor so that a small signal from the sensors does not drive the motor all the way, one way or the other. The feedback pot is located, electrically, in the sensor string circuit and operates in opposition to the sensors. If the sensor drives the vacuum motor toward MAX HEAT, for example, when the motor starts to move, it will rotate the potentiometer so that its resistance change tends to offset the resistance change of the sensor.

8. The ambient sensor is also contained in the programmer.

9. The aspirator for the in-car sensor is an integral part of the programmer.

## Temperature Control Circuit

The resistance of the two sensors varies with their temperature. Their resistance, plus that of the temperature dial, form the input to the programmer. This weak electrical signal, which varies with the temperature of the sensor or with temperature dial movements, is amplified by the amplifier to produce a relatively strong current flow through the transducer that varies in accord with input signal changes. The transducer converts this electrical signal to a proportional vacuum signal which is routed through the vacuum relay to the vacuum motor.

The vacuum motor performs the following three output functions:

1. Positions the air-mix door.

2. Positions the wipers on the blower circuit board pads.

3. Positions the vacuum valve.

Input is resistance in ohms; output consists of the three functions listed above. Here are some examples (Fig. 9-11):

1. Assume that the car is stabilized on a sunny 80°F (27°C) day with the in-car sensor being maintained at 75°F (24°C) with a 75°F temperature dial setting. The resistance of the ambient sensor at 80°F (27°C) is 35 ohms, the in-car sensor resistance at 75°F (24°C) is 68 ohms, and the temperature dial resistance at the 75°F (24°C) setting is 36 ohms. These three resistance total 139 ohms. Referring to Fig. 9-11, this resistance will position the programmer to produce M1 blower speed, an intermediate discharge air temperature [approximately 60°F (16°C)], A/C mode, an open water valve, and outside air.

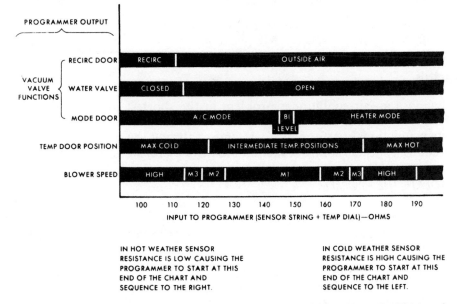

FIGURE 9-11 Programmer input-output chart. (Courtesy of Cadillac Motor Car Division of General Motors Corp.)

2. If the ambient temperature were to increase with ambient sensor resistance decreasing to 22 ohms, this change in resistance would cause the amplifier output current to decrease, which would cause the transducer output vacuum to the vacuum motor to decrease, so that the new point of operation would be at the 126-ohm point, producing M2 blower speed and cooler discharge air. The system would still be in A/C mode, with the water valve open, utilizing outside air. In this way, the in-car temperature is maintained at 75°F (24°C) despite the change in ambient temperature.

3. If the heat load on the car were to be decreased by driving under cloud cover, the in-car sensor temperature would tend to decrease. This would cause its resistance to increase, so that the total resistance to the programmer would increase. This would cause the programmer to move back to the right on the chart, to a warmer position.

**NOTE:**

a. A decrease in amplifier output current causes a decrease in transducer output vacuum.

b. Hot sensors result in low sensor string resistance, which results in low amplifier output current, which results in low transducer output vacuum, which positions the vacuum motor in the cool or cold area of operation.

c. Cold sensors operate at high resistance, which results in high amplifier output, which causes a high transducer vacuum, which positions the vacuum motor in the warm or hot area of operation.

d. An open sensor would represent a high resistance, which would drive the programmer to maximum heat.

e. A shorted sensor would have low resistance, which would drive the system to MAX A/C.

**Diagnosis**

To diagnose an air-conditioner problem in the shortest time and with the least effort, it is essential to follow a logical service procedure. Time spent in conducting a system functional performance test and analyzing the malfunction in order to isolate it to a specific control function area will be repaid in reduced repair time.

*ISOLATE THE PROBLEM*

1. Attempt to get an accurate, detailed description of the owner's complaint in writing on the repair order. "A/C inop." does not provide much information to the repairman.

2. To confirm the system malfunction, make a brief check of system operation by sitting in the car and operating the controls, with the engine warmed up and running at 1000 rpm or higher, in the following sequence:

a. Check to assure that air delivery is not coming from both the A/C and heater outlets when only one mode is indicated. A split air delivery is indicative of a vacuum leak.

b. Note whether program events (air delivery mode change, blower speed change, recirculating air, etc.) occur without a change in the discharge air temperature. This would indicate that the programmer is operating without moving the temperature air door. Check the air mix-door link to the programmer connection.

c. If neither the program events nor the discharge air temperature change, an incorrect vacuum or electrical signal to the programmer or a programmer malfunction is indicated.

d. Malfunction of a specific vacuum-operated door function could indicate a vacuum disconnect of the vacuum diaphragm at that door.

3. Perform the easiest checks first! A simple, visual inspection of the easily accessible underhood and instrument panel electrical and vacuum connections will, in many instances, reveal the problem on the spot.

4. Based on information gained during the functional test performed in step 2, try to relate the problem to one of the following areas:

a. Temperature control problems.

b. Blower control problems.

c. Auxiliary vacuum problems.

d. Refrigeration system problems.

Once a problem has been isolated to one of these areas, refer to the diagnosis section of the service manual.

### TEMPERATURE CONTROL

The primary function of the temperature control circuit is to determine the correct temperature of the air to be discharged into the passenger compartment. Many temperature control problems result from poor electrical or vacuum line connections.

1. A disconnected sensor or temperature dial interrupts the electrical signal and drives the programmer to maximum heating.

2. A poor sensor connection adds resistance to the sensor string, driving the system hotter.

3. An open amplifier power feed eliminates the output signal and drives the programmer to maximum A/C.

4. A disconnected vacuum hose supplying the vacuum checking relay actuating nipple will lock the relay in an intermediate position.

5. A disconnected vacuum hose in the transducer programmer vacuum motor line will drive the system to maximum cooling.

6. A leak in the auxiliary vacuum circuit may reduce the transducer vacuum supply level below control requirements, causing off-calibration or poor heating.

7. A loss of supply vacuum usually results in cold air flow on the floor.

### BLOWER CONTROL CIRCUIT

The components and electrical circuits that make up the blower control circuit are shown in Fig. 9-12. Blower control can be divided into two separate categories, blower turn-on and blower speed control. Blower turn-on is accomplished when a ground path for the relay coil is completed by

1. The heater turn-on switch, which provides a delay for heater water warm-up in winter operation.

2. The in-car switch, which provides immediate turn-on in summer operation.

3. Manual override in the defrost setting. Blower speed control is accomplished by selective use of the blower resistors on the A/C module in the Lo, Economy, Auto, and Bi-Level lever settings, or by high blower override circuit in the Hi and Defrost lever positions.

**FIGURE 9-12** Complete electrical circuit. (Courtesy of Cadillac Motor Car Division of General Motors Corp.)

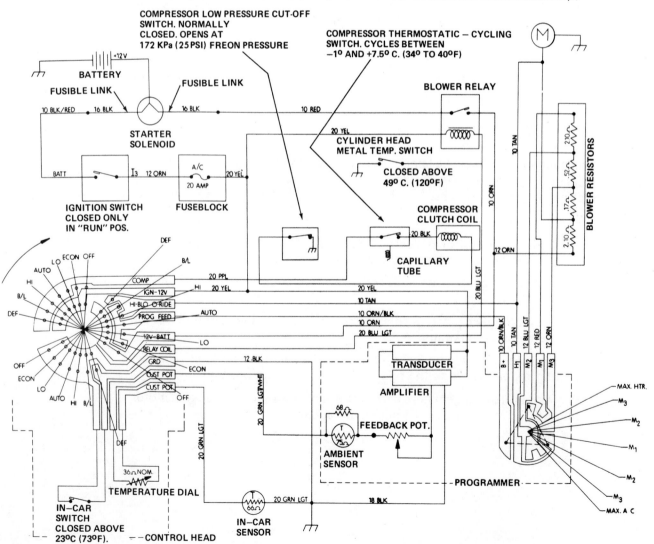

SYSTEM FUNCTIONAL TEST

Always start diagnosis with this test.

**TABLE 9-1**

| Set Control Lever at: | | System should operate as follows (engine running— 70° to 80°F ambient): |
|---|---|---|
| DEF | 85°F | Fixed high blower—most of air delivered from defroster outlets—some air from heater outlet—immediate blower turn-on. |
| BI-LEVEL | 75°F | Lower blower speed—cooler air from both A/C and heater outlets—very small amount of air out of defroster. |
| HI | 65°F | Fixed high blower—cold air from A/C outlets—recirculation should occur (will take approx. 1 minute because of restriction in hose). |
| AUTO | 65°F | Recirculation maintained—blower speed may drop. |
| AUTO | 85°F | Blower speed should drop then increase—air should become warmer—air should change from A/C to bi-level to heater. |
| LO | 85°F | Blower should drop to fixed low speed. |
| ECONOMY | 85°F | Same as auto except no compressor operation. |
| OFF | | Fixed low blower—mild air out heater outlets—no air out A/C or defroster ducts—no compressor operation. |

## FORD AUTOMATIC TEMPERATURE CONTROL

The Ford Automatic Temperature Control System will automatically control the temperature and reduce the relative humidity of air inside the car. The system will deliver heated or cooled air to maintain the car interior temperature and will maintain the set comfort level automatically.

### Components

#### SENSOR ASSEMBLY

A small opening in the instrument panel allows passenger compartment air to enter the sensor. The sensor assembly contains a bimetallic sensor that senses the passenger compartment air temperatures. The bimetallic sensor controls a vacuum modulator, and higher temperatures cause high vacuum gauge readings. A bias to the vacuum output level is accomplished by means of a control arm attached by a cable assembly to the temperature control lever. The modulated vacuum output is the result of the effects of the control bias and the temperature of the air across the bimetallic sensor.

The sensor assembly also includes an aspirator. The aspirator provides a very small vacuum to draw a sampling of the passenger compartment air across the air-temperature-sensing bimetal. Primary air is ducted to the sensor by a tube from the blower stream, providing the power to operate the aspirator for the in-car sensor.

### SERVO ASSEMBLY

The servo assembly is a large calibrated vacuum motor and vacuum diverter valve. The vacuum motor provides specific temperature blend door positions for given vacuum levels. The vacuum diverter valve controls recirculating or outside air operations.

### ELECTRO-VACUUM RELAY (EV RELAY)

The EV relay is a combination, normally closed vacuum solenoid valve and a single-pole single-throw normally closed electrical relay switch, both actuated by one electrical coil. The EV relay is used during cold weather operation, in the floor lever position, to lock out blower operation and to switch the system to a recirculating condition until the engine coolant warms up to above 120°F (49°C).

### ENGINE TEMPERATURE SENDING SWITCH

The engine temperature sender switch senses the engine coolant temperature near the engine thermostat. In the floor position only, a ground circuit from the engine temperature sender switch to the EV relay coil prevents blower operation until the engine coolant temperature reaches 120°F (49°C).

## Control Assembly

The control assembly consists of three main parts:

1. The function selector—a vacuum selector valve combined with three internal electrical switches.

2. The blower switch—four-speed operation.

3. The temperature control lever—connects through a control cable assembly to the sensor assembly.

The vacuum selector valve directs source vacuum to various vacuum motors and connects the vacuum from the electro-vacuum relay to the outside air-recirculation door in the floor. Three single-pole electrical switches are also controlled by the selector. The combination of these electrical switches controls the electrical supply to the A/C clutch and blower switch.

The blower switch is the same as in the manual A/C system.

The temperature control lever is connected to the sensor assembly by a control cable assembly. The movement of the control lever from 65 to 85 causes a corresponding movement on the preload (bias) portion of the sensor assembly and will determine the temperature that the system will maintain.

## REVIEW QUESTIONS

1. In what two positions does the compressor not run?

2. List two reasons why the HI blower speed is needed.

3. What does the aspirator do?

4. Ambient sensors sense_____temperature.

5. What is a thermistor?

6. A shorted in-car sensor will cause the sytem to operate on_____.

7. A shorted ambient sensor will cause the system to operate on_____.

## GLOSSARY

**Air Conditioning:**   Control of the temperature, humidity, cleanness, and movement of air.

**Air Inlet Valve:**   A movable door in the plenum blower assembly that permits the selection of outside air or inside air for both the heating and air-conditioning systems.

**Air Outlet Valve:**   A movable door in the plenum blower assembly that directs air flow either into the heater core or into duct work that leads to the evaporator.

**Ambient:**   Air outside the car.

**Ambient Compressor Switch:**   Energizes the compressor clutch when the outside air temperatures are 32°F or above; similarly, the switch turns off the compressor when air temperatures drop below 32°F.

**Atmosphere:**   Air.

**Atmospheric Pressure:**   Air pressure at a given altitude (14.69 pounds per square inch at sea level). Atmospheric pressure decreases as altitude increases.

**Automatic Control:**   A thermostat on the instrument panel. The dial can be set at a comfortable level and the device will serve the passenger by controlling the air flow and temperature automatically.

**BTU (British Thermal Unit):**   The amount of heat necessary to raise 1 pound of water through 1 degree Fahrenheit.

**Bypass Control Valve:**   Same as "Hot Gas Bypass Valve."

**Center Mount Components:**   Installation of heating and air conditioning which has the evaporator mounted in the center of the firewall on the engine side. The heater is installed directly to the rear, in the passenger compartment.

**Change of State:**   Rearrangement of the molecular structure of matter as it changes between any two of the three physical states (solid, liquid, or vapor).

**Charge:**   A specific amount of refrigerant or refrigerant oil by weight.

**Charging:**   The process of placing a "charge" of refrigerant or refrigerant oil into the system.

**Chemical Instability:** An undesirable condition caused by the presence of contaminants in a refrigeration system. Refrigerant is a stable chemical by itself but in contact with contaminants may break down into harmful chemicals.

**Clutch:** A coupling that transfers torque from a driving to a driven member when desired. The compressor clutch delivers torque transmitted from the engine through a drive belt, causing the compressor drive shaft to rotate.

**Cold:** The absence of heat. An object is considered cold to the touch if it is less than 98.6°F (body temperature).

**Compressor:** Component of a refrigeration system that pumps refrigerant and that increases the pressure and temperature of refrigerant vapor.

**Condensate:** Water taken from air. It forms on the exterior surface of the evaporator.

**Condensation:** Act of changing a vapor to a liquid.

**Condenser:** Component of a refrigeration system in which refrigerant vapor is changed to a liquid by the removal of heat.

**Conditioned Air:** Cook, dry, clean air.

**Conduction:** Transmission of heat through a solid.

**Contaminants:** Anything other than refrigerant and refrigerant oil that is in a refrigeration system, such as rust, dirt, moisture, and air.

**Convection:** The transfer of heat by the circulation of a vapor or liquid.

**Cooling Coil:** *Same as* Evaporator.

**Customer System:** Deluxe air conditioner that uses both outside and inside air. The air distribution ducts and outlets are built into the instrument panel. Air temperature is controlled by a hot gas bypass valve, suction throttling valve or air mixture valve.

**Cycle:** *See* Refrigerant Cycle.

**Cycling Clutch System:** A term referring to air conditioners in which conditioned air temperature is controlled by the engaging and disengaging of the compressor.

**Desiccant:** A drying agent used in the refrigeration system to remove moisture. It is located in the receiver-dehydrator.

**Diagnosis:** The procedure that is followed in locating the cause of a malfunction.

**Dichlorodifluoromethane:** *See* Refrigerant-12.

**Discharge:** To bleed some or all refrigerant from a system by opening a valve or connection and permitting the refrigerant to escape slowly.

**Discharge Air:** Conditioned air as it passes through outlets and enters the passenger compartment.

**Discharge Line:** High pressure upon line.

**Discharge Pressure:** High-side pressure.

**Discharge Side:** That portion of the refrigeration system under high pressure, extending from the compressor outlet to the thermostatic expansion valve.

**Drying Agent:** *Same as* Desiccant.

**Equalizer Line:** Line or connection used specifically for obtaining required operation from certain control valves. Very little if any refrigerant flows through this line.

**Evacuate:** To create a vacuum within a system.

**Evaporation:** Changing from a liquid to a vapor.

**Evaporator:**   Component of an air-conditioning system which conditions the air. Refrigerant liquid is changed into a vapor in this component.

**Expansion Valve:**   *Same as* Thermostatic Expansion Valve.

**Flush:**   To remove solid particles such as metal chips and dirt. Refrigerant passages are purged (flushed) with refrigerant-12. Exterior surfaces of system components are flushed with water or an acceptable solvent.

**Freeze Protection:**   Controlling the evaporator temperature so that moisture on its surface will not change to ice and block air flow.

**Gauge Set:**   One or more instruments attached to a manifold (a pipe fitting with several outlets for connecting pipes) and used for measuring pressure.

**Head Pressure:**   *Same as* Discharge Pressure.

**Heater Core:**   A water–air heat exchange which provides heat for the passenger compartment.

**High-Load Condition:**   Refers to those times when an air-conditioning system must operate continuously at maximum capacity to provide the cool air required, such as at high temperature and high humidity.

**High-Pressure Lines:**   Lines from the compressor outlet to the thermostatic expansion valve inlet that carry high-pressure refrigerant. The two longest high-pressure lines are the "discharge" and "liquid" lines.

**High-Pressure Vapor Line:**   *Same as* Discharge Line.

**High Side:**   *Same as* Discharge Side.

**High-Side Pressure:**   *Same as* Discharge Pressure.

**Humidity:**   *See* Moisture.

**Instability:**   *See* Chemical Instability.

**Latent Heat:**   Amount of heat required for a change of state. Latent heat of vaporization is the amount of heat required to change a liquid to a vapor.

**Liquid Line:**   Connects the receiver-dehydrator outlet and the thermostatic expansion valve inlet. High-pressure liquid refrigerant flows through this line.

**Low-Pressure Line:**   *Same as* Suction Line.

**Low-Pressure Vapor Line:**   *Same as* Suction Line.

**Low Side:**   *Same as* Suction Side.

**Moisture:**   Humidity, dampness, wetness, or very small drops of water in the air.

**Muffler:**   Device to minimize pumping sounds from the compressor.

**Oil Bleed Line:**   Ensures positive oil return to compressor at high compressor speed and under low charge conditions.

**Oil Injection Cylinder:**   A cyclinder containing a measured quantity of refrigerant oil added when servicing the air-conditioning system.

**Operational Test:**   *Same as* Performance Test.

**Performance Test:**   Taking temperature and pressure readings under specified conditions to determine if an air-conditioning system is operating satisfactorily.

**Plenum Blower Assembly:**   Air passes through this assembly on its way to the evaporator. It is located on the engine side of the fire wall and contains air ducts, air valves, and a blower that permits selection of air from the outside or inside of the car and directs it either to the evaporator core or to the heater core.

**Pressure:**   Force per unit of area. The pressure that refrigerant exerts within the system is indicated on gauges in pounds per square inch.

**Pressure Line:** *See* Discharge Line. All refrigerant lines are under pressure.

**Pressure Sensing Line:** Prevents the compressor suction pressure from dropping below a predetermined pressure, by opening the thermostatic expansion valve, allowing liquid refrigerant to flood through the evaporator.

**PSIG:** Pounds per square inch of gauge pressure.

**Purge:** To remove moisture and air from a system or a compound by flushing with a dry gas, such as nitrogen or refrigerant-12.

**Radiation:** One of the processes by which energy is transferred. Heat energy from the sun's rays, for example, raise the temperature of the passenger compartment.

**Receiver-Dehydrator:** A container for storing liquid refrigerant from the condenser. A sack of desiccant in this container removes small traces of moisture that may be left in the system after purging and evacuating.

**Refrigerant:** The chemical compound used in a refrigerant system to produce the desired cooling.

**Refrigerant Cycle:** Complete course of operation of refrigeration back to a starting point, evidenced by temperature, pressure, and liquid–vapor changes of the refrigerant as it circulates through the system.

**Refrigerant-12:** The refrigerant used in automative air-conditioning systems. It is sold under such trade names as Freon 12, Genetron 12, Isotron 12, Prestone 12, and Ucon 12.

**Refrigeration:** The removal of heat by mechanical means.

**Relative Humidity:** Actual moisture content of the air in relation to the total moisture that the air can hold at a given temperature. If the air contains three-fourths of the moisture it can hold at its existing temperature, the relative humidity is 75%.

**Room Temperature:** 68 to 72°F.

**Saddlebag:** Air chambers or openings in the left and right front corners of the car body between the kickpads and the exterior of the car. On some customer systems the evaporator is located in the right saddlebag.

**Schrader Valve:** A spring-loaded valve where a connection can be made to the refrigeration system. A gauge set can be used on a Schrader valve only with an adaptor.

**Screens:** Fine mesh metal screens are located in the receiver-dehydrator, thermostatic expansion valve, and compressor. They prevent solid particles from being circulated through the system and carried to vital moving parts, where they might cause damage.

**Side Dash Components:** Installation of heating and air conditioning which has the evaporator mounted on the curb side of the firewall in the engine compartment. The heater is in back of the evaporator in the passenger compartment.

**Sight Glass:** A window, usually in the top of the receiver-dehydrator, used to observe liquid refrigerant flow.

**Specifications:** Information provided by the manufacturer that describes an air-conditioning system, its components, and its proper operation. Service procedures that must be followed in order for the system to operate properly also are called "specifications."

**Suction Line:**   Connects the evaporator outlet and the compressor inlet; low-pressure refrigerant vapor flows through this line.

**Suction Pressure:**   Compressor intake pressure as indicated by a gauge set.

**Suction Side:**   That portion of the refrigerant system under low pressure, extending from the thermostatic expansion valve to the compressor inlet.

**Suction Throttling Valve:**   Prevents evaporator core freeze-up and controls temperature of air that flows from the evaporator.

**Suction Throttling Valve POA:**   Prevents evaporator core freeze-up and compensates for compressor speed changes and evaporator load—is unaffected by elevation above sea level.

**Superheated Vapor:**   Refrigerant vapor at a temperature that is higher than its boiling point for a given pressure.

**System:**   All the components and lines that together make up an automotive air conditioner is a complete system; includes heating and cooling.

**TE Valve:**   *Same as* Thermostatic Expansion Valve.

**Temperature:**   Heat intensity measured in degrees Fahrenheit.

**Thermostatic Expansion Valve:**   Component of a refrigerant system that controls the rate of refrigerant flow to the evaporator. It is commonly called the TE valve or TXV.

**Thermostatic Switch:**   An adjustable component used in a cycling clutch system to engage and disenage the compressor. It prevents water (condensate) from freezing on the evaporator core and controls the temperature of air that flows from the evaporator.

**Torque:**   A turning force such as that required to seal a connection, usually in ft-lb or in.-lb.

**Under Dash Unit:**   The trade name used for the "hang-on" or "under-the-dash" type air-conditioning system that normally uses only recirculated air. All air outlets are in the evaporator case. Discharge air temperature is controlled by a cycling thermostatic expansion switch or suction throttling valve.

**Vacuum Power Unit:**   Device for operating doors and valves using vacuum as a source of power.

**Vacuum Pump:**   A mechanical device to evacuate a system.

**Vapor Lines:**   Lines that carry refrigerant vapor. *See also* Suction Line, and Equalizer Line.

**Viscosity:**   Thickness of a liquid or its resistance to flow. Water has a low viscosity; heavy, sticky oil has a high viscosity.

**Volatile Liquid:**   One that evaporates readily to become a vapor. Refrigerant is volatile at room temperature.


### ANSWERS 1


1. Corrosion and freeze protection.

2. Raise the boiling point of the coolant; for good circulation.

3. Down-flow and cross-flow.

4. Fan belt; crankshaft.

5. Reduce noise and reduce power loss.

6. False.

7. Permanent-magnet and wire-wound.

## ANSWERS 2

1. 103.42.

2. 3.

3. Cold.

4. One pound of water 1 degree warmer (Fahrenheit).

5. One gram of water 1 degree warmer (Celsius).

6. Solid, liquid, and gas.

7. 14.7 psi or 101.35 kPa.

8. True.

9. Make vapor hot; raise refrigerant pressure.

10. Evaporator, condenser, and compressor.

11. Cycle compressor; control the flow of refrigerant.

12. 99.6 psi.

13. 137.90 kPa.

## ANSWERS 3

1. Back-seated.

2. Front-seated.

3. To engage and disengage the compressor.

4.  Vapor; liquid.

5.  Store refrigerant and remove moisture.

6.  Separates the high side from the low side, causes a pressure drop, and controls the flow of refrigerant.

7.  Evaporator outlet.

8.  To cool, dry, and clean the air.

9.  Valve-in-receiver.

10. Evaporator equalized valve-in-receiver.

11. The VIR has an equalizer port between the POA and the TXV.

12. Evaporator pressure regulator.

13. Regulates evaporator pressure.

14. Cycling clutch expansion tube.

15. Liquid and vapor are separated in the accumulator.


### ANSWERS  4

1.  Back-seated, mid-position, and front-seated.

2.  Back-seated—to seal off service gauge port; mid-position—so gauge reading can be taken with the system operating; front-seated—isolate the compressor from the system.

3.  ETR valve is either open or closed.

4.  EPR valve operates in varying degrees of being open or closed.

5.  Flame or electrical.

6.  Fire and poisonous gas.

7.  Running.

8.  Stopped.

9.  To remove air and moisture.

10. Higher.

11. 125°F (51.7°C).

## ANSWERS 6

1. Compressor clutch and blower motor.

2. Stops.

3. Temperature control lever.

4. Open.

5. Vented.

## ANSWERS 7

1. Thermostatic Expansion Valve.

2. Compressor.

3. False.

4. True.

5. False.

## ANSWERS 9

1. Off and Vent.

2. Maintain comfort in city traffic and provide adequate smoke removal.

3. Pulls air over the in-car sensor.

4. Outside.

5. A special resistor which decreases in resistance with heat.

6. Maximum A/C.

7. Maximum A/C.

# Index